JUNG'S TREATMENT OF CHRISTIANITY

The Psychotherapy
of a
Religious Tradition

MURRAY STEIN

CHIRON PUBLICATIONS • WILMETTE, ILLINOIS

First printing 1985
Paperback edition 1986

Printed in the United States of America

Book design by Elaine M. Hill

Library of Congress Cataloging in Publication Data

Stein, Murray, 1943–
Jung's treatment of Christianity.

Includes bibliography and index.
1. Christianity—Psychology—History—20th century.
2. Jung, C. G. (Carl Gustav), 1875–1961.
I. Jung, C. G. (Carl Gustav), 1875–1961. II. Title.
[DNLM: 1. Christianity. 2. Psychotherapy. Religion
and Psychology. WM 460.5.R3 S819j]
BR110.S72 1985   201'.9   85-4739
ISBN 0-933029-00-4
ISBN 0-933029-14-4 [paper]

Cover: Window by Marc Chagall in Fraumunster-Kirche,
Zürich. © 1986 ORELL FÜSSLI VERLAG, Switzerland,
Zürich, A.D.A.G.P. & Cosmopress, Genf. © 1986
A.D.A.G.P., Paris/VAGA, New York.

To

my mother, Jeanette,

and

my father, Walter

CONTENTS

Acknowledgments

Friends, colleagues, students, and others too numerous to name here deserve my gratitude. My teachers, too, have been many, and important, among them Russell Becker, James Hillman, and Peter Homans. To my friend and now my editor, Nathan Schwartz-Salant, I owe a special debt of gratitude for his generous care and acute insights. I also wish to acknowledge the permission of Princeton University Press to quote at length from *The Collected Works of C. G. Jung*, trans. R. F. C. Hull, and to Pantheon Books, a division of Random House, for permission to quote from *Memories, Dreams, Reflections*, by C. G. Jung, recorded and edited by Aniela Jaffé, translated by Richard and Clara Winston.

Most especially I thank my wife, Jan, for faithfully accompanying me on the long march to securing a very old dream.

Chapter 1   **JUNG'S INTERPRETERS**

Religion and religious experience have long been subjects of major concern to modern psychologists. This preoccupation is epitomized by such well-known works as William James's *Varieties of Religious Experience* (1902), Sigmund Freud's *Moses and Monotheism* (1939), and C. G. Jung's *Psychology and Religion* (1938). The volumes produced by these and other figures in psychology and psychiatry fill many shelves, which indicates a remarkable amount of interest devoted by psychological theorists and researchers to religious themes and traditions.

Only in recent years, however, has the question been raised of how to understand this keen interest in religion on the part of the great originative psychologists. Why were they so taken with investigating religion and religious figures? Were they motivated simply by the curiosity of disinterested scientists, or were there other motivations and dynamics at play as well? These questions probe into the relationship between the subjectivities of the researchers and their objects of inquiry.

A number of recent books have begun exploring the psychological and sociological linkages between these psychologists and their religious backgrounds. Perhaps the most novel and arresting of these studies have dealt with Sigmund Freud's relation to Judaism. Bakan's *Sigmund Freud and the Jewish Mystical Tradition* (1958), Cuddihy's *Ordeal of Civility* (1974), and Robert's *From Oedipus to Moses: Freud's Jewish Identity* (1976) are attempts to uncover the indirect and obscure connections between Freud and his religious background. What turns out to be most surprising, because so deftly concealed, are the many subtle personal influences that shaped Freud's psychological thought and his interpretations of religion. What these studies have shown is that Freud's relationship to Judaism was not as detached and vague as he indicated, but rather that it was very important, and indirectly even critical, for his psychological thought. Moreover, his studies of religious figures like Moses and religious doctrines such as monotheism cannot be construed purely as the work of an objectively minded scientist. Freud was personally involved, albeit unconsciously, with his material. What these investigations should teach us is caution about taking these psychologists' published opinions on religion at face value. Often there is a hidden agenda.

Jung's relationship to Christianity has remained largely unexamined to date. No one has ventured a full-scale study of how his life and thought are to be related to Christian tradition or of how his writings on Christianity are to be related to his personal life and psychological thought.

Jung's involvement with Christianity was much more evident than Freud's was with Judaism. Whereas Freud's detachment from all religious claims of the Jewish tradition was a dearly held part of his conscious identity as a scientist and a modern man, Jung's conscious relationship to religious tradition was much less unambigious. His writings about Christianity, moreover, are so numerous, so generally appreciative, and so obviously interested in its future well-being that his secular identity and commitment to modernity have come to look a good deal less crisp than Freud's. Jung and his psychology were generally far less obviously denigrative of religion than were Freud and his psychoanalysis, and certainly his writings on Christianity were anything but hostile.

These works on Christianity, while not voluminous, were considerable, and in the last 20 years of Jung's active intellectual life they occupied the central role. In them Jung constructed an elaborate interpretation of Christian history and doctrine and commented extensively on such major Christian rites as baptism and the Eucharist. He also projected a future form of Christian doctrine that would substantially alter it in its most basic assumptions about the nature of God and man, and in many letters and in some published writings he pressed for deepgoing changes in the way Christianity relates to evil, to nature, to the feminine, and to science. These were not the casual comments of a disinterested person. They were expressions of a deeply felt inner necessity to help Christianity change.

The question becomes, then, how to read these writings. Why was a professional psychologist so engaged in what is usually thought of as a theological task? There have been a large number of interpreters of

Jung's works, and they have used Jung's works to such completely different ends, or have read them in such vastly different ways, that after studying the secondary literature one is tempted to wonder if they are all talking about the same man. While some theologically informed students of Jung have praised his reflections on Christian themes and doctrines and have seen in them a valuable new resource for contemporary Christian theology, others have been extremely critical and a number have vehemently repudiated what they took to be Jung's position.

What was Jung up to in these works? Was he trying to revitalize Christianity or undermine it? Was he a museum-keeper of heretical antiquities and theological oddities? Was he a throwback to Gnostic repudiations of Christian faith? Or was he a modern agnostic trying to invent a psychological substitute for traditional Christianity? A very different view says that he was trying to discover, or to invent, an empirical psychological foundation for the truth and value of Christian claims. Was he in fact a modern-day Christian apologist? Or was he launching a subtle attack on Christian doctrine and disguising his missiles as empirical psychology? These are some of the questions that have been asked and some of the suggestions ventured or implied.

What is most clear after studying the literature is that there has been much focusing on pieces of the relationship between Jung, his thought, and Christianity without any fundamental agreement on a model for conceptualizing the whole of it, and this has produced a thicket of literature that is full of internal contradictions and confusion. While I am not in a position to dismiss the accounts given so far, this stunning variety of opinion does strongly suggest that the fundamental nature of the phenomenon has not yet been grasped.

Within the large body of literature that focuses on Jung's treatment of religion and religious experience, it is remarkable, for starters, that there exists no acknowledged distinction between his writings on religion (and world religions in general) and his works on Christianity in particular. That Christianity must occupy a privileged position in Jung's life and work has not been widely appreciated. As a result, the influence of Jung's emotional and historical relationship to Christianity on his treatment of Christian symbols and history has not received special attention. The importance of this oversight cannot be overestimated when it comes to understanding this body of work.

This is not to deny the accuracy and value of the many descriptive accounts of what Jung wrote and thought about various Christian doctrines and attitudes. Among others, Clift (1982), Cox (1959), Heisig (1973, 1979), Hostie (1957), Moreno (1970), Sanford (1981), and White (1952, 1960) have supplied such descriptions and have analyzed and criticized the content of Jung's positions on Christianity in considerable detail. But none of them has put forward a convincing explanation for why Jung took the positions he did. This lacuna stems from the failure to consider the complex emotional nature of Jung's personal relationship to his subject.

The portraits that Jung's interpreters have painted can, for the most part, be grouped into four basic clusters. Each gives primacy to a particular aspect of Jung's identity. There is Jung the empirical scientist; then Jung the hermeneutical revitalist of Christianity; third, Jung the doctor of souls; and, finally, Jung the post-Christian modern man. Each of these images, as well as the literature based on them, implies a significantly different relationship between Jung and Christianity.

It should be pointed out that specific authors often conflate several images of Jung and mix together several different views on his relationship to Christianity. As will become apparent in the following brief review, much overlapping of this sort exists in the literature, which adds to the confusion in the picture of what Jung was up to in his writings on Christianity.

JUNG THE EMPIRICAL SCIENTIST

The view that Jung's writings on religion, including those on Christian themes, can best be characterized as the work of an empirical scientist has been put forward or presupposed by a number of authors, notably Fordham (1958), Hostie (1957), Kelsey (1968), Meier (1977), and White (1952). This image of Jung originated transparently in a self-image to which he himself was greatly attached (cf. Homans 1979, p. 148). Repeatedly he made the request, most especially of the clergy and the theologians, that he be regarded not as a philosopher or a metaphysician but rather as an empirical scientist.

Starting with this image, the reader of Jung's writings is asked to believe that, on the basis of his discoveries concerning the workings of the human mind, such as the existence and function of archetypes and of the collective unconscious, Jung formulated a psychology of religion which he then applied to Christianity as he applied it to Tibetan Buddhism, primitive religions, Taoism, and all other religions. Jung, in this view, was a disinterested scientist who created a theory based on objective empirical research, which he applied neutrally to the study of Christianity and to other religions. In this case, Jung's findings on the religious function of the human mind, for example, might prove useful to Christian theologians who are attracted to science as a handmaiden to theology.

The high potential for confusion and misunderstanding contained in this misperception was dramatically unleashed in Jung's relationship with Victor White. White, a Dominican priest and theologian, was attracted to Jung's thought because it promised what he hoped would be empirically based, scientific evidence for the existence of psychological structures and dynamics that corresponded in striking ways to Christian teachings about grace, revelation, the *imago Dei*, atonement, and redemption (cf. White 1942). White had carefully studied the works of Jung as they existed in print in the early 1940s and had discussed them in several talks and articles, which he subsequently sent to Jung for his opinion. In return he received a warmly favorable response (Jung 1973, pp. 381–87). "Excuse the irreverential pun," Jung wrote. "You are to me a white raven inasmuch as you are the only theologian I know who has really understood something of what the problem of psychology in our present world means. You have seen its enormous implications" (ibid., p. 383). Since his early psychoanalytic days, Jung had been convinced of the importance of depth psychology's "enormous implications" for culture and religion.

For White, Jung's psychology was much less hostile to Christianity than Freud's and Adler's, and it promised a new way to close the gap between Christian teachings and empirical science (White 1942, p. 15). Ultimately, a correlation between relevant elements of Jung's thought and the doctrines of Christianity could build a foundation for a new and scientifically backed Christian apologetic. It was with Jung's own assurance that White understood his position correctly—"You have rendered justice to my empirical and practical standpoint throughout. . . . I never allow myself to make statements about the divine entity, since that would be a transgression beyond the limit of science" (Jung 1973, p. 384)—that the theologian entered into an intellectual relationship with the psychologist. He must have felt confident that they would enjoy a fruitful intellectual collaboration that would ultimately produce a powerful, modern apologetic for Christian doctrine.

To achieve his goals, however, White discovered, after several tempestuous years, that he had to part company with Jung, as Jung did not share his agenda. From their correspondence (Jung 1973, 1975), it is clear that a variety of personal and intellectual misunderstandings plagued their relationship from the beginning, and these became more and more disruptive as time went on. Toward the end of their attempts at collaboration, White confessed that they had fallen into a "deadlock of assertion and counter-assertion" in spite of good will, and this, he felt, was because "our minds have been formed in different philosophical climates" (Jung 1975, p. 58, n.1). White was baffled by many of Jung's statements regarding Christian teachings on the nature of God, of evil, and of metaphysical claims. Jung, on the other hand, would not accept White's metaphysical and theological commitments but continually interpreted them in psychological terms. While the Dominican theologian held fast to a long-standing metaphysical and theological tradition, the analytical psychologist was subjecting that very tradition to the corrosive effects of psychological interpretation.

Even as early as 1942 White had already commented critically on Jung's views on certain Christian doctrines, such as the Trinity, God, and evil, as well as on his understanding of metaphysics: "Outside his own particular sphere of professional concern, his speculations seem often distinctly amateurish" (White 1942, p. 17). As much as White appreciated Jung as an "intuitive genius of the first order" (ibid.), his own extensive knowledge of the Christian theological tradition gave him a vantage point for seeing Jung's limitations in theological discussion.

> It is curious and characteristic that Jung has been led simply by empirical psychological investigation, to uncover some of the most recondite and intricate problems which have occupied Trinitarian theology such as the a-logical and "non-natural" character of the Second Procession and the impossibility of forming any *nomen proprium* for the Third Person— yet apparently failing to understand at all what the doctrine of the Trinity is all about as the ground of the religious relationship. (Ibid., pp. 18–19)

What White and other theologians objected to in Jung's discussion was his seeming inability to appreciate the religious necessity for maintaining God's absolute transcendence. He, and they as well, felt that Jung's oversight of God's transcendence and his concentration solely on immanence was the cause of his many theological blunders and his evident amateurism. Jung didn't fully understand or appreciate what the theological tradition had to say about God.

Nor did White understand Jung's motives for departing from the empirical observations of psychology and venturing into theological revisionism. By 1958 White was able to articulate his own position on the relation of Jung's thought to Christianity, which he did in *Soul and Psyche* (White 1960), a considerably more sophisticated work than his earlier collection of papers, *God and the Unconscious* (White 1952), which had contained a Foreword by Jung. In the years between the publication of these two volumes, the personal relationship between White and Jung underwent a complete rupture, in large part because White could not understand, much less sympathize with, Jung's attempts at reconstructing Christian theology. In particular, White took exception to the tone and angle of vision expressed by Jung in *Answer to Job* (Jung 1952). In *Soul and Psyche*, White carried out what he had hoped to accomplish with Jung's blessing and collaboration: He built a bridge between Jung's psychological theory and Christian theology that leaves the Christian side unaltered structurally, while at the same time demonstrating that psychology supports Christian doctrine and affirms the soundness of Roman Catholic belief and practice. To structure the relation of psychology to Christianity in this fashion, White had found that he was forced to repudiate Jung's own application of his psychological thought to Christianity.

White's final statement in *Soul and Psyche* is remarkably consistent with his 1942 essay, "The Frontiers of Theology and Psychology." In Jung's psychological theory and observations, White had found many parallels to Christian symbols and doctrines, points of connection between Roman Catholic tradition and modern empirical psychology. All of White's labor in the area of psychology and religion can, in fact, be read as an elaboration of his original perception that "Jung has . . . given a point to Tertullian's '*anima naturaliter christiana*,' such as has never been exhibited with such clearness before" (White 1942, p. 14). Empirical psychological research and analytic practice, as carried out by Jung and Jungian psychotherapists, could establish, he thought, the intimate connections between nature and grace, human experience and divine revelation, knowledge and faith:

> Certain it would seem to be that any deep and successful analysis involves a response to the 'leadership' . . . of manifestations of the unconscious which are closely parallel to, even if not sometimes actually a vehicle of, the redemptive functioning of faith and grace as known to Christian experience and studied in Christian theology. (Ibid.)

White's program was to explore these correlations and parallels with the intention of showing that religion, and especially Christianity, does not contradict, but rather completes, human nature.

By the time White had made his statement concerning a "deadlock of assertion and counter-assertion" (in April 1952), he had concluded that the so-called empirical stance of Jung included an interpretive method that was mortally infected by a neo-Kantian dismissal of metaphysics and by the assumption that the ontological truth of theological assertions could never in principle be demonstrated. Moreover, the person he had taken for an empirical psychologist played—all too often, in his view—the role of an arbitrary and muddle-headed amateur philosopher-theologian. Had Jung been modest enough to stay with his empirical science, cataloguing the contents of the human mind, he might have made a significant contribution to the psychological study of religious thought and experience. As it was, White concluded that Jung was assuming prerogatives beyond his competency.

A major unanswered, and perhaps unanswerable, question for White, and for anyone who starts with the premise that Jung's relationship to Christianity was principally that of an empirical scientist to his object of inquiry, was: What motivated Jung to criticize certain Christian doctrines (e.g., the *privatio boni* doctrine of evil and the Trinity), and why did he go even further and make suggestions for reconstructing Christian theology along quaternitarian lines? If Jung was simply a disinterested empirical scientist, how can these theological initiatives and the great passion behind them be explained?

One explanation is that Jung's identity as empirical scientist was a disguise for another secret identity, that of philosopher-theologian or even prophet. This underlying reality was hidden, and Jung was unwilling to examine his philosophical presuppositions and commitments or to correct his misunderstandings and distortions of Christian doctrine, primarily because he wanted to keep his true intentions in the dark. In this view, a philosophical-theological set of presuppositions controlled Jung's seemingly scientific-empirical method when it came to religious topics (ibid.).

When this interpretation is applied to understanding Jung's relationship to Christianity, his manifest relation to Christianity as empirical psychologist to object of inquiry becomes a mask hiding the more basic identity of critical philosopher or heretical theologian (Buber) or even religious prophet (Stern 1976, Edinger 1979). The proper answer to Jung, therefore, should be one that addresses his hidden agenda and be a theological-philosophical response (Buber 1957, pp. 136–37).

A number of theologians, led by the great Buber, have taken this approach to Jung's thought on religion. Buber warned that Jung's stance as empirical scientist was deceptive, that "the new psychology protests that it is 'no world-view but a science,' [and yet] it no longer contents itself with the rôle of an interpreter of religion. It proclaims the new religion, the only one which can still be true, the religion of pure psychic immanence" (ibid., pp. 83–84). Jung was a modern Gnostic because he emphasized "knowledge" over "faith" and thereby denied the transcendence of the Godhead. Buber's perception that Jung's relation to all religions, including Christianity, was infected by this kind of psychological reductionism persuaded him to criticize Jung's thought on a theological level. This approach to Jung's writings on Christian themes has been taken up, in one form or another, by several other theologians.

Moreno (1970) and Hostie (1957) have subjected Jung's writings on religion, including those on Christianity, to careful analysis and searching theological criticism. Moreno, for example, summarized Jung's psychology in great detail and took issue with Jung point by point wherever his statements on Christian doctrine differed from conventional understandings. He showed where Jung fell into error in his discussion of evil, of God's transcendence, and of the Trinity. This method of approach to Jung's writings on religion and on Christian themes—a careful analysis of the texts followed by theological or philosophical criticism—was essentially repeated by Heisig (1979) in his meticulous examination of Jung's usage of the *imago Dei* concept, and again by Hostie (1957) in his comparisons of Jung's ideas with traditional Christian dogmas. All three of these Roman Catholic theologians have criticized Jung, with great perceptiveness let it be said, for having made fundamental theological or philosophical mistakes. Heisig also vigorously criticizes his "science."

The inadequacy of this approach for understanding the meaning of Jung's writings on Christianity was amply demonstrated in Jung's own lifetime. To this kind of theological argument and rebuttal, Jung routinely responded that he was not a theologian or a philosopher but an empiricist and a psychologist. If one accepted this self-definition, however, one quickly encountered an inexplicable puzzle: Why was he suggesting major changes in Christian theology? But if one attempted to treat this part of his work as philosophical or natural theology and to subject it to the scrutiny proper to those fields, Jung complained that one could not follow a psychological argument. And so the same arguments kept repeating in this circle of misunderstanding, and Jung himself did not assist the task of clarification.

It is clear that these approaches to Jung's writings on Christianity miss the mark. They cannot explain why Jung took precisely the positions he did on certain Christian doctrines, or what motivated him to make his specific suggestions for radically reconstructing Christian theology. The research and analysis piled up by these authors do indeed often describe what Jung said accurately enough, and do analyze many of the philosophical presuppositions behind his statements, but they do not explain why he took the specific positions he did vis-à-vis Christianity.

JUNG THE HERMENEUTICAL REVITALIST

A second group of interpreters has taken the view that Jung's work on Christianity can best be understood by seeing him as a hermeneutical revitalist. These writers have looked upon Jung as an interpreter of Christianity to modern man and have assumed that his intention was to revitalize this moribund religious tradition to show modern man the underlying meaning of ancient Christian symbolism. His writings on Christian themes open the way for modern men and women to return to Christianity and to experience its rich symbolic meanings with new conscious awareness and understanding. "For Jung," Clift writes, "and most of the people who came to him for help the Church had ceased to perform the theological task of translating the truths of the tradition into the thought forms of its day" (Clift 1982, p. ix). It was to address this problem that Jung took up the task of interpreting Christian doctrine and publishing books like *Modern Man in Search of a Soul* (ibid., p. xi).

As different as this image is from Jung the empirical scientist, it is equally based on his own statements about his work. He frequently expressed the opinion that the symbols of Christianity no longer captured the imagination of the modern person. This meant that we had fallen victim to rationalism and needed to be reconnected to the original religious experiences underlying the age-old symbols of Christian faith. It was a task of modern depth psychology to forge the link that would rejoin modern men and women to their ancestral religions. This view of his life's task was indeed profoundly a part of Jung's self-understanding. Miguel Serrano quotes Jung as saying, some five months before his death in June 1961: "What I have tried to do is to show the Christian what the Redeemer really is, and what the resurrection is. Nobody today seems to know, or to remember, but the idea still exists in dreams" (McGuire and Hull 1977, p. 468).

The interpreters of Jung who have drawn primarily on this image of him regard the Zurich doctor's writings on Christian themes in an entirely different light from those who look upon them as either applications of scientific methods or as heretical theology. By them Jung is seen as the committed friend of Christianity, a hermeneut laboring in the service of a program of religious revitalization.

A number of authors (Brown 1981, Burrell 1974, Cox 1959, Hanna 1967, Kelsey 1968, and Sanford 1970) have highlighted this aspect of Jung's work and have themselves gone further by using his hermeneutical methods to reinterpret various Christian doctrines and symbols and, quite self-consciously, to render them more accessible to the modern temperament. In some cases (e.g., Sanford 1970), this has meant the transposition of traditional Christian categories, images, and concepts into Jungian psychological terms; in others (e.g., Cox 1959), it has meant pointing out the significant parallels between a Christian doctrine (justification) and a Jungian psychological concept (individuation). In all cases, these authors share the view that Jung's interpretation of Christian themes can, up to a certain point, help fellow Christians bridge the rift between modern culture and Christian tradition.

The major shortcoming of this image of Jung as hermeneutical revitalist is the same as that of him as empirical scientist: It cannot account for his consistent critique of Christian doctrine or for his suggestions for reconstructing Christian theology. Theologically oriented thinkers who have focused on Jung's hermeneutic of Christian doctrine have generally been forced either to repudiate portions of his substantive work while retaining the method (e.g., White in his own interpretation of the Book of Job in *Soul and Psyche* 1960; Sanford in his book *Evil* 1981), or they have avoided these issues altogether and have simply incorporated aspects of Jung's hermeneutical method into their own theological work (e.g., Burrell 1974, Gelpi 1978). Hanna states the dilemma at the outset of his study of Jung's religious ideas, *The Face of the Deep*:

> The reader must understand that while he will discover in Jung's writings testimonies to the value and importance of the deepest aspects of our Christian faith, he will also find a critique of it that at times quite makes us gasp. What does one do, for instance, with a piece of writing such as *Answer to Job*? (Hanna 1967, p. 13)

Hanna's "gasp" at Jung's audacity in *Answer to Job* echoed Victor White's attack on this book. Jung's controversy with God in *Answer to Job* (1952) was, in White's view, rooted in Jung's own personal religious problems, which had led him to make distorted statements and interpretations. This book, White wrote, "perplexes and disturbs me. It is doubtless meant to do so, but it disturbs me in ways other than those intended. . . . Jung seems to be wrestling with some religious problem that has never been mine: seemingly some memory of a cosy Victorian optimism, masquerading as Christianity . . . " (White 1959, p. 77). Although a careful study of Jung's life contradicts this interpretation that he was wrestling with "cosy Victorian optimism," it is certainly true that in *Answer to Job* Jung was not using his interpretive skills primarily in the service of revitalizing traditional Christianity. *Answer to Job* is an attack on the doctrine of God's absolute transcendence and righteousness.

As many of his writings and letters testify, Jung did indeed recognize the need for the revitalization of Christian tradition. It is equally clear that he was a hermeneut, interpreting Christian symbols and tradition in such works as "A Psychological Approach to the Dogma of the Trinity" (1942a), "Transformation Symbolism in the Mass" (1942b), and *Answer to Job* (1952). But these interpretations of Christian images, rites, and doctrines included an argument that Christianity must transform, and this argument went far beyond what can possibly be understood as simply a hermeneutical effort to recover ancient symbolic meanings for modern men and women.

JUNG THE DOCTOR OF SOULS

Another way of understanding Jung's writings on Christianity has been to view them as derivative of his identity as a psychiatrist, a "doctor of souls." The authors who have adopted this perspective have felt that Jung's main concern was not for Christianity itself but for the individual patients who identified themselves as Christians (or as "post-Christians") and, as a result, had fallen into certain typical psychological conflicts and unhealthy attitudes. For these authors, Jung's primary identity was neither scientist nor theologian nor hermeneut but physician, and the object of his concern was not Christianity but modern men and women who still to one extent or another are bonded to Christian tradition.

Schaer expresses this point of view in his *Religion and the Cure of Souls in Jung's Psychology*:

All Jung's ideas about religion either are very novel or fit in with those of people who have been branded as heretics and cranks by the ortho- dox Church. It is scarcely possible, therefore, for everybody to agree with him. However that may be, one thing above all should be stressed: Jung's ideas are not the result of mere theory or of historical research— they have been wrested from the hard facts of his psychotherapeutic practice. Jung is not one of those psychologists who has a chair in psychology somewhere and gleans his knowledge—with more or less discrimination—in odd nooks and crannies; he is, by profession, a medical *pastor of souls*, and, year in year out, hundreds of people come to him with their psychological difficulties, their troubles and worries, their thoughts and experiences. And not only that: he must, in one way or another, help them. Thus, he not only possesses a very deep insight into the spiritual life of modern man; he has also to look round for what can help these sufferers. (Schaer 1950, p. 201; italics added)

As is true of the other images of Jung, this one is rooted in Jung's own statements. Frequently he claimed that as a physician he was concerned with the psychological effects of the practice of religion. Certain forms of piety could be damaging to the human psyche, and Christianity should consider changing some of its doctrines for the psychological health or growth of its followers.

To a greater extent than the understandings of Jung's writings on Christianity discussed so far, this view can explain Jung's critique of Christian doctrine and theology. A strong case could be made that Jung's recommendations for abandoning the *privatio boni* doctrine of evil and for expanding the Trinitarian into a quaternitarian doctrine of God were put forward because of his concern for the psychological well-being of practicing Christians. Jung's writings on Christianity should be read, then, as a practical theology, stemming from a therapeutic concern for the psychological impact of theological ideas on believers. For Jung the physician, the final criterion of a religious doctrine's value is its psychological impact: The psychological wholeness of the believer is the final arbiter.

While not many authors have pursued this line of thought very far, a much larger number have alluded to the centrality of Jung's identity as physician and to his practical concern for the individual soul's well-being as important factors in his writings on Christian themes. Jung often spoke of religion as a psychotherapeutic system and said that Christianity was no exception. By itself, however, this view of Jung as doctor of Christian souls is insufficient because its focus is too narrowly on Christians and is not broad enough to explain his interest in Christianity per se. While it is true that Jung felt a physician's concern for the individual Christians he treated, his concern for Christian tradition and for Christianity as a whole was far more intense and inclusive than this understanding would make plausible. The view of Jung as a doctor of Christian souls is too limited to explain his studies in the history of Christianity, his complex commentaries on the dynamic relations between Christianity and culture in the development of Western consciousness, and his vital interest in Christianity's future doctrinal evolution.

JUNG THE MODERN MAN

Some of Jung's interpreters, finally, have depicted him as a post-Christian modern man. In this view, which is derived from an essentially sociological perspective, Jung's psychological interpretations of Christian doctrine and tradition were attempts to resolve a conflict between his emotional attachment to tradition and his equally strong intellectual and moral commitment to modernity. According to this image of Jung, his complex relationship to Christianity was the product of a typical dilemma faced by Western intellectuals in the late-nineteenth and early-twentieth centuries. Torn between a commitment to scientific method and to enlightened rationalism on the one hand and an emotional attachment to the traditional religious world-view of parents and cultural ancestors on the other, these modern men and women were caught in a ferocious conflict, and the battleground between science and religion was where they attempted to resolve it. In his psychological theories in general, and in his writings on Christian themes in particular, so this view has it, Jung was negotiating his own resolution of the conflict between modernity and tradition.

One prominent version of this interpretation of Jung's work has been expressed by the sociologist Philip Rieff (1966), who held that Jung created his psychological theory to be a substitute for traditional Christian doctrine. Jung's psychological interpretations of Christianity, then, represented his assimilation of Christian tradition to his own new psychological religion. This new religion for modern man, which was centered on the self and the psyche, has been hailed by some with enthusiasm (Edinger 1979) and denounced by others with quasi-prophetic zeal (Rieff 1966, Stern 1976).

In the most complex and subtle version of this interpretation of Jung's writings on Christianity, Homans has argued that Jung related to

Christianity through a two-fold movement of assimilation and repudiation. This accounts for the combination of hermeneutical and critical
elements in his writings. By assimilating aspects of Christianity, Jung
was able to maintain emotional contact with his traditional Christian
past, and by repudiating the claims of Christianity on his thought and
work, he was able to satisfy the demands of modernity. This interpretation of Jung's work has the great merit of recognizing the unique
position of Christianity in it (Homans 1979, p. 182). It is also able to
explain his hermeneutical interest in retrieving meaning from the Christian tradition while clearly recognizing his distance from it. Moreover,
like the other images of Jung, this one finds ample confirmation in his
own writings. Jung was self-consciously a modern man and admitted it.

From many passages in his writings, it is evident that Jung was
grappling mightily with what may be regarded as a central problem of
modernity, namely, the loss of emotional and intellectual containment
in a tradition of religious belief, symbol, and practice. From early on in
his life, but especially after he had become deeply influenced by Freud
and by modern psychiatry, Jung felt himself to be outside of the Christian *mythos*. After breaking with Freud, he came to the uncomfortable
realization that he was exposed to life without an orienting myth or
religious tradition (Jung 1961a, p. 171). Even psychoanalysis no longer
worked for him. For the remainder of his life, he labored to come to
terms with this absence and to construct a replacement, so this interpretation says, for his lost tradition. And this he achieved by creating a
modern scientific psychological theory that was able to assimilate Christian tradition through psychological interpretation but was also able to
repudiate its central demands for belief and communal identification.

This interpretation of Jung's life and work goes a long way toward
explaining many of the puzzles. On the one hand, since Jung did not
identify himself with the Christian tradition or subscribe to the assigned
meanings of its symbolic universe, he felt free to reinterpret its doctrinal
statements (about the nature of God, about the role of Christ in the
salvation of the human soul, about the meaning of Christian history
and the salvific acts of God, etc.) using his own psychological and
essentially non-theological categories and understandings. This freedom
from the constraints of traditional meanings is characteristic of modern
man. Because of anomie and social-psychological alienation from all
traditional institutions, the modern person does not accept their claims.
This new person is suspicious of them and interprets them in the light
of personal insights and experiences. Thus Jung did not feel obliged to

square his psychological interpretations of Christian doctrine with a theological tradition, nor did he feel constrained to use standard theological arguments to support his views. Because he stood outside the circle of Christian faith and belief, he could freely reinterpret traditional understandings of Scripture and doctrinal symbols, and he could criticize such fundamental premises of Christian faith as the absolute goodness and transcendence of God. Where his own personal views did not correspond to the teachings of tradition, he gave preference to his own. This gives his writings on Christian themes their idiosyncratic (some might say heretical) quality, or what Homans calls "repudiation" (1979, p. 184).

Jung also felt deprived, however, by the loss of attachment to the religious tradition of his forebears. One of the hallmarks of modernity is the acute sense of separation from tradition and from an ancestral religious heritage. Jung responded to this loss, so the argument runs, by using his psychological theory and method of interpretation to assimilate parts of traditional Christianity to his own modern viewpoint, thereby bringing tradition closer. Still, of course, he repudiated its metaphysical and ontological claims and its psychological demands for the subtle intimacies of internalization and identification. In this way, though, he satisfied his personal need, as a modern man, to overcome the radical separation from tradition while still maintaining his intellectually, morally, and psychologically necessary distance from it. The complexity of Jung's writings on Christian themes is created by this rapprochement dynamic: These writings represent his personal achievement in balancing the need for oneness with tradition with the need for separation from it (cf. Homans 1979, pp. 182–92).

The overriding thrust of this ingenious psycho-sociological account is that Jung assimilated parts of Christian tradition for his own special purposes but was fundamentally uninterested in Christianity per se as an objective fact of historical reality, either in the past or the present. Jung's writings on Christianity are much more reflective of his personal struggles for self-coherence (Homans 1979, p. 186) than of any genuine concern for Christianity or for Christians. The relationship is fundamentally narcissistic.

The major weakness of these interpretations based on Jung as a modern man arises from their slanting the angle of focus too sharply in the direction of his personal existential dilemmas and psychological pathology. They underestimate his capacity for object-relatedness and the quality of his concern for Western culture and the Christian reli-

gious tradition. I am persuaded that Jung actually was genuinely concerned with Christianity and Western culture as objective, historical,
and contemporary facts, even if this interest was deeply intertwined
with his own personal psychology. These interpreters tend generally to
be reductionistic, however, and they take his statements as almost
purely personalistic. They fail, therefore, to take seriously his criticisms
of Christian doctrines and his recommendations for restructuring some
of them. Just because he was a modern man obviously does not explain
why he took the specific positions he did on various Christian doctrines
or why he argued for them so strenuously during the last 35 years of
his life.

Beyond repudiating and assimilating Christian tradition and trying
to maintain his own psychological integrity, what was Jung trying to do
with, or for, Christianity? Why did Jung want Christianity to evolve?
And why evolve in the direction of a quaternitarian doctrine of God?
Why did he so strenuously and persistently object to the Christian
doctrine of God's absolute goodness and to the *privatio boni* understanding of evil? The understanding of Jung as modern man and the
interpretations that have followed from this premise have not addressed
these questions, because the assumption is that modern man is basically
uninterested in collective religion and religious tradition and incapable
of showing genuine concern for such objective facts.

TOWARD A NEW INTERPRETATION

Jung himself never completely clarified the nature and full meaning
of his writings on Christianity. While composing them he was in the
grip of a largely unconscious creative spirit and unaware of the overall
pattern his work would take. This could only be seen in retrospect,
looking back over the inner connections, the central obsessions, and
the final outcome of this body of work.

The present study is based on the view that Jung was guided in
these writings by an unseen hand, a largely unconscious *spiritus rector*.
This guidance, as I will try to show, was supplied by his strong urge to
heal Christianity, which led him unerringly to the very heart of the
tradition's ailments and demanded that he offer it his psychotherapeutic
help. As I will demonstrate too, this hidden guide was related to the
memory and image of his father, a Christian pastor whom he perceived
as defeated by his times and his religious commitments. Whether or
not Jung was driven to heal his father, hence also Christianity, out of

guilt and remorse for his astonishing oedipal victory, it is also true that he was responding to a deep need for transformation within Christianity itself. Deeply tuned to a sick Western culture and to an ailing Christian tradition through his personal family background and his individual psychology, he was profoundly drawn to their suffering and their need for transformation. It is this collective and archetypal level of psychic connectedness that Jung discovered in his psychological research, and from this perspective his therapeutic response must be finally judged and measured. Purely reductive interpretations, while valuable for some levels of insight, miss the mark finally because they fail to take the full measure of Jung's considerable achievement. They also trivialize the challenge Jung's writings present to contemporary Christianity.

The present work proposes, then, to interpret Jung's writings on Christianity from the angle of vision that sees his relationship to Christianity as a psychotherapeutic one. My reading of the purpose and the specific detail of his writings on Christian themes follows from this critical insight. Jung's stance toward Christianity was fundamentally that of a psychotherapist, and so the goal of all his efforts with this "patient," Christianity, was its psychotherapeutic transformation. The psychotherapeutic relationship, I will argue, with its central concerns for the patient's psychological health and wholeness and with its highly complex internal psychodynamics, best describes the nature of Jung's relationship to Christianity as expressed in his late writings on Christian themes. This image of Jung as psychotherapist to an ailing religious tradition accounts for what he was trying to do with Christianity and why he made the specific recommendations he did for fundamental changes in Christian doctrine.

For purposes of clarification I need to say that the phrase "Jung's writings on Christian themes" refers to everything he published on Christianity. Altogether these published works make up the object of my study. The central texts that call for special treatment, listed in the order of their original publication, are: "A Psychological Approach to the Dogma of the Trinity" (1942a), "Transformation Symbolism in the Mass" (1942b), "Introduction to the Religious and Psychological Problems of Alchemy" (1944), *Aion* (1951), *Answer to Job* (1952), and *Mysterium Coniunctionis* (1955). In addition to these texts, there are important comments on Christianity in Jung's posthumous autobiography, *Memories, Dreams, Reflections* (1961a), in the two volumes of his *Letters* (1973, 1975), and throughout the *Collected Works*. These latter materials do not belong to his core writings on Christianity, but often they shed light on how to interpret them.

In the next chapter I describe the relevant aspects of Jung's understanding of the therapeutic process and how the Jungian therapist goes about trying to achieve the goal of psychotherapeutic transformation. The importance in analysis of remembering and reconstructing the past, the use of two types of interpretation to bring about psychological change and healing, and the central place of transference/countertransference in psychotherapeutic transformation are the key features of Jung's methods presented in Chapter 2 to prepare for the subsequent analysis of Jung's writings on Christianity as the statements of a psychotherapist.

Chapter 3, "On the Nature of the Relationship between this Doctor and Patient," is largely a biographical, life-and-work study of Jung. There I discuss the evolution of Jung's relationship to Christianity, beginning with his childhood in the home of a Swiss Reformed parson and his wife and extending through his mature years as a world-famous psychiatrist with a special interest in Christianity and Western culture. I try to make clear how, and why, Jung's attitude toward Christianity was critically shaped by a powerful impulse to heal it.

The fourth chapter, "Doctor Jung's Treatment of Christianity," is a detailed analysis and interpretation of Jung's major writings on Christian themes. This chapter should demonstrate conclusively that Jung's writings on Christianity reflect neither a reductionistic nor a revitalistic attitude, as has been claimed by most of his other interpreters, but rather an evolutionary-transformational one. Here, in what is in many ways the heart of my enterprise, I interpret these writings in the perspective of Jung's therapeutic approach and his personal relationship to Christianity.

In the final chapter, "On the Patient's Prospects," I look briefly at contemporary Christianity to see how it squares with Jung's therapeutic recommendations. Does Christianity show any signs of moving in the direction recommended by Doctor Jung? I also ask whether it is possible for Christianity to undergo the kind of fundamental transformation envisioned by Jung and still retain its traditional identity. Perhaps Jung's therapeutic program is too radical for the patient. Or is it possible that a deep transformation is already taking place, which Jung's understanding of the patient can help to identify and guide? What would the doctor say about the patient today?

Chapter 2   **JUNG'S METHODS OF PSYCHOTHERAPEUTIC TREATMENT**

The parallels between Jung's thought on Christianity and on the practice of psychotherapy are so obvious and so important that it is astonishing they have been almost totally neglected by his interpreters. Similarities of analytic method and interpretation, of style and tone, and of theoretical understanding leap from his pages, and yet these have never been seen to provide the key for understanding his approach to Christianity. In the pages that follow, I intend to pursue the leads suggested by these parallels, hoping in this to place Jung's writings on Christianity into a more comprehensible perspective than has been the case.

Until now, one would have been at a loss to explain why Jung bothered so about Christianity. His many comments and works on Christian rites, symbols, and doctrines can be understood adequately only when seen as parts of a large psychotherapeutic design. These parallels also tell us that this therapeutic relationship was what constituted the emotional matrix in which these writings on Christian themes came into existence. When regarded in this context, Jung's numerous works on Christianity can be seen to make up a coherent, internally consistent piece of work that was elaborated, item by item, over a period of about 20 years.

The key points at which it can be shown that these two lines of thought, the one on psychotherapy and the other on Christianity, in Jung's oeuvre overlap, and what this means, will be discussed in detail later, but before launching forth it may be wise to pause for a brief overview of what lies ahead.

The ground before us contains three critical points of similarity, or overlap, between these two aspects of Jung's intellectual lifework. The first point has to do with anamnesis and historical reconstruction; the second pertains to the use of psychological interpretation; and the third focuses on the therapeutic relationship, the transference/counter-transference process. These three focal points will define my interpretation of Jung's writings on Christian themes and tradition.

In analytic psychotherapy, a crucial step of treatment involves uncovering and collecting the pieces of a patient's developmental history and then assembling them into a coherent picture. It is essential to realize that the aim of reconstructing the patient's past is not simply to get a history or to find out "what really happened" in childhood, and afterwards, which has led to the present psychological situation. Anamnesis and reconstruction are meant to serve therapeutic ends. Their object is to lessen the effects of earlier traumas, identifications, repressions, and one-sided developments, as well as to facilitate the patient's present and future healthy functioning and psychological wholeness. Within analytic psychotherapy, a psychological anamnesis and reconstruction of past events facilitates a gradual understanding of the historical relations between the conscious and unconscious portions of the patient's personality and between the patient and his or her human environment. This phase of therapy Jung considered to be reductive, as the analyst often makes genetic interpretations of unhealthy features of the personality, and the present structures of personality and consciousness are interpreted by considering earlier events and developmental outcomes. The creation of this historical awareness serves a practical, therapeutic end, since the patient is meant to benefit therapeutically from these insights.

Jung's assemblage of a history of Christianity runs parallel to this type of therapeutic anamnesis and reconstruction. His history of Christian tradition does not represent an attempt to write an objective history for its own sake. Jung was not an historian by profession, or even by avocation, any more than he was a theologian. His extensive interpretations of Christian history are psychological and aimed at interpreting its *present* conflicts genetically, in order to facilitate the religious and theological equivalent of psychological wholeness. The focus of the therapist is the present and future, not the past. Without an awareness of this therapeutic intent, the meaning of Jung's reconstruction of Christian history is puzzling.

The second major alignment between Jung's psychotherapy and his writings on Christianity relates to his methods of interpretation used in each. In relation to psychotherapy, Jung discusses two basic kinds of interpretation, each having a specific function within the larger strategy of therapy. The first is reductive interpretation, which is personal, psychodynamic, and often genetic. It serves to dismantle or modify pathological and maladaptive attitudes, to create more awareness of the unconscious, and to foster better interpersonal and social relationships. The second type is the prospective, or synthetic, interpretation, which assists in the integration of emerging psychic contents and facilitates a new, more complex and more comprehensive conscious attitude. This type of interpretation relies largely on a method Jung called amplification, which supplements the genetic, reductive type. These two kinds of interpretation are both aimed, however, at improving psychological functioning and at increasing the patient's capacity for understanding, accepting, and living his or her own wholeness.

Corresponding to these two types of interpretation in analytic psychotherapy is an identical two-fold hermeneutic in Jung's writings on Christian themes. Jung interprets many traditional Christian doctrines, rites, and symbols reductively, tracing them back to earlier historical stages of development and showing how they became dominant through a historical process of splitting and repression. The evolution of Christian tradition is analyzed psychologically and seen, finally, as a necessary, but one-sided and only partially adequate, structuring of consciousness. Jung puts forward a genetic interpretation of Christianity's one-sidedness (its "psychopathology") and a psychodynamic understanding of the forces that maintain these pathological features. He does not fail to grant value to this developmental history, but he certainly denies its finality.

These reductive interpretations, however, exist beside others that represent his synthetic, archetypal, prospective approach. Using archetypal amplifications, he makes interpretations designed to anticipate the next stage in Christianity's evolution.

This is clearly a psychotherapeutic hermeneutic: It seeks to ameliorate pathology by interpreting it reductively, and it points ahead toward greater potential approximations of integration and wholeness that are incubating in the collective unconscious.

The third major set of linkages between Jung's views on psychotherapy and his writings on Christianity regards the nature of the psychological relationship between therapist and patient on the one hand and between Jung and Christianity on the other. In the literature of analytical psychology, the therapist's emotional involvement with a patient is discussed under the rubric of countertransference. From Jung's writings and offhand remarks about psychotherapy, it is clear that he believed the relationship between therapist and patient lay at the heart of treatment. Significant structural change in the patient's personality, which he called psychological transformation, depends critically on this transference/countertransference process. Of special importance is Jung's emphasis on the countertransference side. In his view, a profound emotional reaction on the part of the patient toward the therapist (transference) without an equal emotional reaction on the part of the therapist toward the patient (countertransference) holds little transformational potential for the patient. For the patient's transformation to occur, the relationship between therapist and patient must be authentically dialectical, with both persons functioning as emotionally engaged partners, both prepared to undergo change, and both experiencing transformation during the course of therapeutic treatment.

It is apparent from Jung's autobiography, from many of his writings on Christian themes, and from his letters and relationships to various Christian clergy that he related to Christianity viscerally. His relationship to Christianity was not academic. In Chapter 3 I will discuss in detail his emotional involvement with Christianity, but, in brief, it evolved from an early sense of fear, dread, and distrust of Christianity's representative figures during childhood, through a prolonged phase of angry confrontation and bitter repudiation during adolescence and early adulthood, to a stance in later adulthood and old age that can best be characterized as an active struggle for its psychotherapeutic transformation.

Jung's therapeutic designs on Christianity are impossible to envision without understanding his model of treatment and his thinking about the nature of psychotherapeutic transformation. Having described in a capsule fashion the three points of reference that will orient this study as a whole, I turn now to a more detailed explication of the portions of Jung's model of therapy that are relevant to his writings on Christianity. Without this foundation, every dialogue with theologians has invariably degenerated into mutual misunderstandings wrapped up in theological and philosophical charges and counteraccusations, while the dialogue with psychologists has remained imprecise and tentative. Jung's writings on Christianity assumed his own extensive previous work as a psychological theorist and psychotherapist, and his challenge to Christianity can only be understood from this perspective.

THE BEGINNINGS OF JUNG'S THERAPEUTIC METHOD

In the 18 volumes that constitute Jung's *Collected Works*, there are relatively few papers dealing exclusively with the practice of psychotherapy. Only one slim volume, Volume 16, falls specifically into this category. Even though Jung was working actively as a therapist while writing many of these articles and books, his intellectual interests tended more toward psychological theory and cultural hermeneutics than toward the practice of psychotherapy.

His method must be pieced together, therefore, from statements scattered throughout the *Collected Works*, where every volume is interlarded with comments and reflections on therapy, from the autobiographical *Memories, Dreams, Reflections* (Jung 1961a), from letters and lecture notes, from the tradition of Jungian analysis as it has been passed down among practitioners, and from the recorded statements of his students and patients. Assembling these, it becomes evident that Jung's psychotherapeutic method, as it took form over the course of a 50-year career, was a complex amalgam of influence and originality. Jung's formation as a professional therapist began during his psychiatric residency in the Burghölzli Klinik in Zurich; it took a critical turn when he actively joined Freud in the psychoanalytic movement; and it came to its final resting place as a result of his separation from Freud and his own experimentation. While only the final synthesis is relevant to this study—because this was what Jung applied to the Christian tradition when he turned to it seriously in his later years—it is important to understand its origins and early theoretical underpinnings if one is to avoid the glibness that often characterizes the secondary literature on Jung and religion.

In his memoirs, Jung confessed that his "interest in therapy had not awakened" (1961a, p. 113) when he began his psychiatric residency in 1900. His fascination with psychology was largely academic and scientific, and what particularly got his attention were "the pathological variants of so-called normality . . . because they offered . . . the longed-for opportunity to obtain a deeper insight into the psyche in general" (1961a). This curiosity about the human psyche had found an outlet earlier in his philosophical studies during the university years before he chose psychiatry as his medical speciality. He had steeped himself in Kant, Schopenhauer, Leibnitz, Carus, Hartmann, and Nietzsche, and had come away from his studies with a philosophical outlook that included a Kantian epistemology, an empirical methodology, a critique of rationalism and materialism, and a conviction in the existence of an unconscious dimension of the human mind (cf. Henderson 1982, pp. 4–7).

According to Ellenberger, the "germinal cell of Jung's analytic psychology is to be found in his discussions [before] the Zofingia Student Association and in his experiments with his young medium cousin, Helene Preiswerk" (Ellenberger 1970, p. 687). The Zofingiaverein was a Swiss student fraternity with a chapter at the University of Basel where Jung had argued on occasion for the feasibility of studying the human soul empirically, including its mystical and transcendental experiences, through scientific observation of hypnotic and somnambulistic states (Jung 1897). This conviction was what he set out later to operationalize in his doctoral dissertation, a study entitled "On the Psychology and Pathology of So-called Occult Phenomena" (1902).

In the Burghölzli Klinik, Jung plunged into psychiatric studies by immersing himself in the 50 volumes of the *Allgemeine Zeitschrift für Psychiatrie* (1961a, p. 112). He was still pursuing the same questions he had asked of philosophers, only now he approached them scientifically through the study of psychopathological variants. The focus of the dissertation that resulted from these studies was "a case of somnambulism in a girl with poor inheritance," who, it turns out, was Jung's own cousin, Helene Preiswerk, or Helly, the daughter of his mother's brother. In this study, Jung formulated what he later, in 1934, looked back upon as the "idea of the independence of the unconscious which distinguishes my views so radically from those of Freud" (1966a, p. 123). What particularly impressed him in Helly was the sharp and impassable division between her conscious, waking personality and her unconscious, autonomous, split-off personalities that manifested themselves as voices during the somnambulistic states. In the drama of these unconscious splinter personalities, Jung deciphered a deeply disguised version of Helly's own history and of her struggles to become free of the obstacles thrown up by her social and mental limitations (1970a, p. 77). Jung also found a still-unconscious personality that was far superior to the consciously developed one, and he conjectured that psychopathological states like mediumistic somnambulism may actually represent the personality's attempt to overcome inner obstacles and to force contents over into the world of consciousness. In this thought, Ellenberger finds "the germ of what was to become Jung's theory of individuation" (Ellenberger 1970, p. 690).

Understanding how and why psychic splits originate, why there is a lack of memory between the resulting pieces, how states of psychic fragmentation are maintained, and how this pathological condition could be treated were critical issues for Jung from the beginning of his career. They remained fundamental questions throughout his entire life's work.

From the study of Helly, who would have been diagnosed today as an hysteric, Jung learned that the mind's synthesizing activities can be thwarted by psychic splitting and repression (1970a, pp. 77-78), and that these split-off pieces of the psyche can operate relatively autonomously. In Helly's fantasies he was able to identify various complexes that disguised historical persons like her (and his) grandfather. Instead of containing these figures as memory images and experiencing the drama going on among them as simple daydreams, Helly's psyche split into fragments and held these pieces apart from consciousness. Only during trance states did they make an appearance. The mechanism of repression, which Jung had learned about from Freud (ibid., p. 78), was held responsible for maintaining the split, and the reason for splitting was seen to be Helly's unintegrated "budding sexuality" (ibid., p. 70). As Helly's somnambulistic states demonstrated, split-off and repressed psychic contents can occasionally take possession of a person's consciousness and motor functions. From this observation Jung later developed his views on psychosis as a state of psychic possession (cf. Sandner and Beebe 1982, pp. 310ff.).

In the years following his dissertation, Jung penned a number of minor papers on various psychiatric topics. Many of these were quite technical, taking up questions of differential diagnosis and pressing for a more psychodynamic understanding of psychiatric syndromes such as mania (1903), hysteria (1904, 1906), cryptomnesia (1905a), and epilepsy (1905b). A common thread in all of this early work was Jung's interest in psychic splitting and in the dynamics that determine the relations among the resulting pieces ("complexes") of the personality. For this, Freud's theory of repression proved crucial. It is clear that Jung, from these early years onward, recognized a discontinuous sense of history as a symptom of psychological fragmentation, which was maintained by the mechanism of repression.

In 1907 Jung published his second major work, *The Psychology of Dementia Praecox*. Here he applied his insights on psychic splitting and the autonomous complexes to chronic schizophrenia. Here, too, he first introduced the idea that the human personality is essentially affective in nature ("the fundamental basis of our personality is affectivity" [1960,

p. 38]). It was the emotional nature of the psyche, he argued, that accounted for the creation and activity of the complexes: Complexes are formed because of affective reactions to events, and their later stimulation is similarly due to emotional reactivity.

From this work it is obvious that Jung was well acquainted with Freud's writings up to that point. He closely related his own viewpoints and discoveries to Freud's theories about hysteria and parapraxis. But even at this early date, before he had met Freud and begun his discussions with him in person, Jung objected to Freud's generalizations on the importance of childhood trauma and sexuality in the etiology of hysteria.

Apart from developing a number of theoretical viewpoints in this book, Jung applied his concepts to understanding the case of old Babette, a chronic paranoid schizophrenic patient at the Klinik. To analyze her psychic splits and the dynamics of her complexes, he used the word-association experiment and extensive interviews. As a result, he discovered in her often-incoherent ramblings three major complexes and one minor derivative complex at work, which accounted for her various utterances. These complexes he came to see as pieces of split-off consciousness, which from time to time were discharged from her chaotic inner world in a seemingly disorganized fashion. The complex that tended to be dominant most of the time he called a "complex of grandeur" (1960, p. 149). This was made up of a network of fantasies spun around the central idea that she, Babette, was an extremely important and powerful person. The opposite, a "complex of injury," represented her consciousness of inferiority. This complex appeared most frequently in the form of auditory hallucinations and dream images that told her of her reduced status. A third complex was erotic and expressed her unfulfilled sexual feelings and wishes. Finally, a minor splinter complex could be dimly discerned: Of a piece with the "complex of injury" but more realistic, it was a sort of *fonction du réel* that spoke accurately of the actual Babette and her situation. This, too, was expressed primarily in the form of auditory hallucinations, often ironic in tone and spoken through an invisible telephone.

Due to her severe illness, Babette was unable to synthesize these attitudes and feelings about herself. They remained suspended in psychic isolation, and so, kept apart from each other and from reality, they remained untouched by time and experience. The unmodifiability of complexes became for Jung a feature of schizophrenia that differentiated it from other less serious psychopathology: *"if the complex remains*

entirely unchanged" despite all new experience and therapeutic inter-
vention, *"which naturally happens only when there is very severe damage
to the ego-complex and its functions, then we speak of* dementia praecox"
(1960, p. 68).

In schizophrenia, or degenerative hysterical psychosis as it had also
been called, Jung thought that the cause of splitting could be psycho-
genic ("induced by . . . affect," [1960, p. 68]), as it is in hysteria, but that
the chronic maintenance of these splits and the intractability of the
complexes were not due to the mechanism of repression but to a still
unknown mechanism, perhaps a "toxin." Whether the complexes produced the "toxin" (as Jung believed), or the "toxin" produced the
splitting and the complexes (as Jung's superior, the great psychiatrist
Eugen Bleuler believed), their persistence and intransigence were seen
by both psychiatrists as attributable to biochemistry. In schizophrenia,
the psyche's fragmentation is chronic and "the subject can no longer
free himself psychologically from the complex" (ibid., p. 69). This chronic
state of ego possession leads eventually to degeneration of the whole
personality (ibid.).

The intractability of the complex and its unbreakable grip on the
ego would rule out a favorable prognosis for therapy. In schizophrenia,
therefore, a purely psychological course of treatment would not be
indicated.

One of the observations Jung made in his study of Babette, which
could be applied in therapy with more treatable patients, was that there
normally exists an interplay among the complexes that often ends up
striking a degree of psychological balance within the psychic system as
a whole (1960, pp. 147ff.). The more repressed and unconscious complexes act upon the more conscious ones in a compensating fashion,
often canceling out or drastically offsetting their effects. Jung illustrated
this by using cases of "teleological hallucination," and he found this
same dynamic at work in hysteria, somnambulism, and schizophrenia.
Later he would expand it into a general theory of the compensatory
relationship between the unconscious and ego-consciousness.

A goal of therapy with patients whose egos have the capacity to
synthesize complexes once they have become conscious is to raise the
conflicting complexes into consciousness. This creates more conscious
conflict because it increases the awareness of the compensatory action
of the unconscious. The object of strengthening this compensatory
effect is to foster conscious integration and therefore better psychological adaptation and conscious balance in the psyche. Since each complex

is rooted in a person's history, this is actually only a technical way of speaking about the therapeutic value of remembering the past.

ANAMNESIS AND RECONSTRUCTION AS METHODS OF THERAPY

Jung recalled in his autobiography (1961a, pp. 115–17) how an early case taught him that remembering the past and suffering its pain consciously rather than repressing it heals the soul. A young woman with severe melancholia entered the Burghölzli Hospital and was diagnosed as schizophrenic. Jung disagreed with the diagnosis and guessed that the symptoms actually reflected a reactive depression, a much less serious illness. But what had triggered her depression was not clear. Using the word-association test and an analysis of her dreams, he uncovered a story that her anamnesis had not revealed.

Before the woman married, she had been in love with a different man, the son of a wealthy industrialist. All the girls of the neighborhood vied for his attention, and, since the patient was very pretty, her chances of attracting him were good. But apparently he did not care for her, and so eventually she married another man.

Five years later an old friend visited her, and, as they were talking over old times, he said to her, "When you got married it was quite a shock to someone—your Mr. X" (the wealthy industrialist's son). He had been secretly attracted to her after all. Her depression dated from this conversation and several weeks later led to a catastrophe. She was bathing her children, first her four-year-old daughter and then her two-year-old son. She lived in the country where the water supply was not altogether hygienic, for there was pure spring water for drinking, and tainted water from the river for bathing and washing. While she was bathing the little girl, she saw the child sucking at the sponge and did not stop her. She even gave her little son a glass of the impure water to drink. She did this more or less unconsciously, since her mind was already under the shadow of the incipient depression. A short time later, the girl, who had been mother's favorite, came down with typhoid fever and died, although the boy was not infected. At that moment the women's depression became acute, and she was sent to the hospital.

> From the association test I had seen that she was a murderess, and I had learned many of the details of her secret. It was at once apparent that this was a sufficient reason for her depression. Essentially it was a psychogenic disturbance and not a case of schizophrenia. (1961a, p. 116)

This patient's subsequent mental illness, which did not look like depression, was caused by splitting off her painful thoughts and memories and repressing them. She was actually unaware of the links between her unconscious memories, her feelings of loss, her guilt, and her present distracted mental condition. When Jung had put the story together, he wondered if he should tell her what he had found:

> I decided to take a chance on a therapy whose outcome was uncertain. I told her everything I had discovered through the association test. It can easily be imagined how difficult it was for me to do this. To accuse a person point-blank of murder is no small matter. And it was tragic for the patient to have to listen to it and accept it. But the result was that in two weeks it proved possible to discharge her, and she was never again institutionalized. (1961a, p. 116)

From this case Jung learned that recovering the repressed traumatic events of the past can have a strong therapeutic effect. At the time he treated this patient, he could not have given the reasons for this, but, like Freud in Vienna, he had learned the therapeutic value of remembering repressed history and facing up to its pain consciously.

Jung went on in his memoirs to generalize about the need for reconstructing personal history in therapy. The opinion he expressed there was the product of 50 years of psychotherapeutic experience, and it represents an essential feature of his method of analytic psychotherapy:

> In many cases . . . the patient who comes to us has a story that is not told, and which as a rule no one knows of. To my mind, therapy only really begins after the investigation of that wholly personal story. It is the patient's secret, the rock against which he is shattered. If I know his secret story, I have a key to the treatment. The doctor's task is to find out how to gain that knowledge. In most cases exploration of the conscious material is insufficient. Sometimes an association test can open the way; so can the interpretation of dreams, or long and patient human contact with the individual. (1961a, p. 117)

Unearthing the patient's "story," both its conscious and unconscious components, was seen by Jung as the first stage of psychotherapy.

The "story that is not told" is not identical to the conscious anamnesis, or case history, that is typically taken at the beginning of treatment. The story Jung was speaking of is at least partially unconscious and therefore not available to the patient's memory. While Jung noticed this psychological phenomenon on his own, he learned the psychodynamic reason for it from Freud. "Freud's *Interpretation of Dreams*," he acknowledged in his autobiography, "showed me that the repression mechanism was at work here" (1961a, p. 147). So getting the patient's story requires either finding a way to bypass the repression mechanism (by using such techniques as hypnosis, the word-association test, or dream analysis) or working through the repressions analytically until the patient gains access to this unconscious material.

Later developments in Jung's psychological theory and in his views about psychotherapy, which strongly favored a symbolic, archetypal approach to the psyche rather than a personal, developmental one, give reason to emphasize that as far as Jung traveled in his explorations of the collective unconscious and the non-personal levels of the human mind, he never abandoned the practical need for assembling the patient's personal history in therapy. A typical psychotherapeutic analysis by Jung might have been less meticulous than a classical Freudian psychoanalysis about the detailed reconstruction of childhood and later psychological development, but in principle Jung subscribed to the view that this is a necessary step of therapy, and indeed that it is a condition for the deeper therapy and analysis that takes place when archetypal material emerges from the collective unconscious. Even as late as 1944, some 30 years after his break with Freud, he wrote:

> It is of course impossible to free oneself from one's childhood without devoting a great deal of work to it, as Freud's researches have long since shown. Nor can it be achieved through intellectual knowledge only; what is alone effective is a remembering that is also a re-experiencing. The swift passage of the years and the overwhelming inrush of the newly discovered world leave a mass of material behind that is never dealt with. We do not shake this off; we merely remove ourselves from it. So that when, in later years, we return to the memories of childhood we find bits of our personality still alive, which cling round us and suffuse us with the feeling of earlier times. Being still in their childhood state, these fragments are very powerful in their effect. They can lose their infantile aspect and be corrected only when they are reunited with adult consciousness. This "personal unconscious" must always be dealt with first, that is, made conscious, otherwise the gateway to the collective unconscious cannot be opened. The journey with father and mother up and down many ladders represents the making conscious of infantile contents that have not yet been integrated. (1970b, p. 62)

It is essential to note that the reason for remembering the past in psychotherapy is the practical result it brings about, not the construction of an objective psychological history for its own sake. This will become critically important later for understanding Jung's reconstruction of the history of Christianity. Jung's history of Christianity is the story of a religious tradition's psychological development, which includes the dynamics of splitting and repression. The purpose of this reconstruction is to lift repressed—and therefore unconscious—contents into awareness and to bring them into relation with the consciously affirmed values and perspectives of Christian thought and behavior. And the point of this is to provide therapy for this ailing religious tradition.

Assembling and re-experiencing the "story that is not told"—both its conscious and unconscious components—belongs to what Jung, in a small but pivotal paper, called the first two stages of analysis, confession and elucidation (1929). The phase of confession, he says, reveals the part of the story that the patient can tell but often hasn't because of a sense of shame or guilt. In confessing, the patient partially relives the recalled events and re-experiences the affect surrounding them. This phase entails sharing "shadow material" that is conscious to the patient. Elucidation, Jung continues, indicates the phase when the interpretation of unconscious dynamics, such as repression, takes place. This is the Freudian phase, and it brings to light *unconscious* shadow material. It includes interpreting the material and transference dynamics developed in the first phase, and this helps to uncover further unconscious aspects of the patient's personal history and to facilitate the work of historical reconstruction. Here the therapist and patient come upon a part of the story that the patient cannot tell because it is repressed. Both of these first two stages deal with personal history almost exclusively, and the main task during this part of analysis is assembling the patient's psychological history and raising it to consciousness.

While a conscious interest in providing therapy to patients was not a strong motivating force in Jung's original choice of career, it gradually flourished as he worked with patients in the Burghölzli Klinik and in his own practice. In the early years, scientific interest became wedded to practical concerns of patient care and treatment, and these two streams flowed together to turn his scientific discoveries about the psyche toward the practical ends of psychotherapy.

Jung's early theoretical and experimental work created a context for understanding the practical insight that remembering the past has a healing effect. Later he extended this idea to include the need for individuals to integrate aspects of personhood that had been repressed because of familial, social, and cultural pressures. The distorting attitudes and psychological one-sidedness that form the basis for neurosis are not only the result of personal life experience but are also brought about as a result of environmental pressures and influences to which the individual must respond. To achieve wholeness, individuals must often reach beyond purely personal events in life and recover aspects of themselves that were denied because of historical and cultural attitudes. Jung illustrated this informally in an interview with Richard Evans:

> There was a young Jewish girl. Her father was a banker, and she had received an entirely worldly education. She had no idea of tradition, but then I went further into her history and found out that her grandfather had been a saddik in Galicia, and when I knew that I knew the whole story. The girl suffered from a phobia . . . and had already been under psychoanalytic treatment to no effect. She was really badly plagued by that phobia, anxiety states of all sorts. And then I saw that the girl had lost the connection with her past, had lost the fact that her grandfather had been a saddik, that he lived in the myth. And her father had fallen out of it too. So I simply told her, "You will stand up to your fear. You know what you have lost?" She didn't, of course not. I said, "Your fear is the fear of Yahweh." You know, the effect was that within a week she was cured after all those years of bad anxiety states, because that went through her like lightning. But I could say that only because I knew she was absolutely lost. She thought she was in the middle of things, but she was lost, gone. . . .
>
> I have seen plenty of cases of a similar kind, and that, naturally, led me to a profound study of the archetypes. . . . That is an enormous factor, very important for our further development and for our well-being. (McGuire and Hull 1977, pp. 349–50)

This woman had been denied a religious heritage and needed to recover her connection to it.

The therapeutic value of reconstructing and remembering a history that is deeper and broader than the individual's own past accounts for a crucial element in Jung's therapeutic treatment of contemporary Christianity, his placement of its reconstructed history in the context of Western cultural history, and of an archetypal evolutionary pattern underlying both. His perception was that individuals are formed and deformed by their culture and its history far more than they are usually aware. The same is true of religious traditions such as Christianity.

THE ROLE OF INTERPRETATION IN THERAPY

Interpretation plays a central role in Jung's analytic psychotherapy. In reconstructing a patient's developmental history, the analyst's interpretations supplement the patient's conscious anamnesis by helping to uncover the repressed and forgotten aspects of psychological development. But beyond using interpretation in reconstruction, Jung, following Freud, felt that interpretation was needed to understand the products of unconscious processes—dreams, fantasies, parapraxes, symbolic actions—because their meaning is not self-evident to the conscious mind. He believed, too, that these unconscious contents, when interpreted, contain helpful information for the person. Decoded from the symbolic language in which it comes, this information can be extremely therapeutic. Interpretation connects consciousness to its unconscious background, and this results in better conscious functioning and adaptation. So, as with anamnesis and reconstruction of history, the fundamental reason for interpretation in analysis is its therapeutic value.

From 1900 to 1930, Jung worked out his own methods of psychological interpretation, but critically through his conflict with the psychoanalytic approach of Freud. Since this conflict was the mainspring behind the development of his complex method of interpretation, a grasp of the arguments between these two hermeneuts is necessary to understand it.

Jung came to Freud as a novice to a master of psychological interpretation. First from Freud's *Interpretation of Dreams*, then from his other writings, and finally by close personal association with Freud himself, Jung learned a method of interpretation that he employed extensively in his own early psychiatric studies. Like Freud, he showed how fantasies, dreams, and complexes were often disguised forms of sexual wish fulfillment and split-off pieces of personal history. In these early studies, the phrase "nothing but," which he later discarded, was a frequent figure of speech, and Jung was clearly committed to a method of reductionistic interpretation along Freudian lines. From his correspondence with Freud, it is evident that he also applied this same method of interpretation to his patient's dreams and neurotic symptoms as to his own.

By 1912, however, Jung had found what he perceived to be serious flaws in Freud's thinking. The major stumbling block was Freud's understanding of libido as fundamentally sexual and his consequent reductive interpretations of its formations and expressions. Psychological interpretation attempts, among other things, to elucidate the meaning of the libido's many imagistic and symbolic forms; from his experience with schizophrenics, Jung was unconvinced that Freud's sexual interpretations could interpret all fantasies, dreams, and symptoms. Schizophrenia showed a dramatic withdrawal of interest from the object world and an almost exclusive investment of it in the subject, but schizophrenics were withdrawn in more than just a sexual sense. Their fantasy productions, moreover, could not be completely understood in every case as sexual wish fulfillments, as Jung had learned by studying old Babette. So if schizophrenic withdrawal and expressions of libido were more than purely sexual, it followed that libido needed to be understood in more general terms.

The thorny theoretical issue between Jung and Freud became their disagreement on the nature of libido. From this difference followed all their other clashes on the theory of neurosis, the interpretation of incest wishes and castration fears and oedipal fantasies, and the meaning of religious practices and symbols. In Jung's two major works of this period, *Transformations and Symbols of the Libido* (1912a) and *The Theory of Psychoanalysis* (1913a), as well as in such small but seminal papers as "New Paths in Psychology" (1912b) and "A Contribution to the Study of Psychological Types" (1913b), he strongly rejected the view that libido was intrinsically the product of specific drives, such as sexuality or nutrition. He was moving toward a view that libido should be defined more generally, simply as "psychic energy," and he argued that libido can be channeled into any specific activity without being considered a "substitution" or "sublimation" of another more fundamental instinct or drive, any more than electrical energy is considered a sublimation of mechanical energy. This of course completely undermined the rationale for Freud's sexual reductionism.

A stumbling block closely adjacent to the definition of libido was the understanding of psychological development in childhood and youth. If libido is not purely a sexual derivative, then its formations and transformations cannot be construed only as variations on this one theme. Jung found it impossible to accept Freud's view that all infant behavior is essentially sexual and all early psychological development psychosexual. Instead he felt that a nutritive stage of libido expression precedes the sexual stage: The behavior of infants, even the pleasure of nursing at mother's breast, expresses an instinct of nurturance, not sexuality. To explain the libido expressions of childhood, which Freud had referred to as polymorphous perversions (a phrase to which Jung took strong exception anyway, because he felt it was anachronistic and imposed adult standards of normality on childhood), Jung formulated the idea that the transition from one stage of libido consolidation to another (e.g., from the nutritive stage of infancy to the stage of genital sexuality in adolescence) involves a period of "libido dispersion." Here a kind of loosely organized scatter effect sends libido into numerous channels of expression and mental and biological functioning before the next stage of development solidifies. Jung saw the period of childhood between early infancy and adolescence as such a liminality period, and this accounted for the polymorphousness of libido expression in childhood.

Jung did agree with Freud that "fixations" can occur during this transitional period and that libido can become abnormally attached to what is normally a temporary pathway. This could result later in adult perversion, which is a libido canalization that should have been temporary but became permanent. The perversions, Jung argued, indicate a person's unworked-through bond to childhood and a lingering attachment to the original family members and environment (1961b, p. 128). But if a person goes through the transitional phase of childhood without fixating at any points, these temporary formations essentially disappear and leave only faint "traces" in the psyche. During psychological crisis, which forces libido into regression, they can become temporarily reactivated, but they are of themselves not the cause of the regression or the neurosis.

Jung's theories by this point in 1912 could not answer a host of questions about how libido gets organized and channeled. What are the psychic factors that shape libido? What transforms libido from one form to another? Why do these transformations occur? and when? What is the equation between innate psychological factors that shape libido and environmental factors? Jung would not be able to respond to these questions until he had completed his theory of archetypes some 20 years later, but in Transformations and Symbols of the Libido (1912a) and in the Fordham University lectures (1913a) he was beginning to explore avenues that would lead to his later theoretical positions. The theory he ultimately constructed would make a large impact on how he interpreted dreams, fantasies, parapraxes, and pathological symptoms.

In the Fordham lectures (1913a), Jung held that the economic view of mental functioning is purely abstract and hypothetical, as an energic analysis is in physics. The "stuff" of the mind, the material form in which psychic energy presents itself, is *fantasy*. Fantasies are the mind's material, libido is its underlying energy. Psychological interpretation, therefore, deals with conscious and unconscious fantasies, and it takes into account the energic dynamics underlying and controlling them. Jung illustrated this with the case of a young woman who suffered a hysterical conversion reaction after being nearly run down by a team of horses. There was no physical reason for her paralysis, but the interesting question was why the conversion reaction had occurred at precisely this time. Probing the story, Jung found that the young woman was secretly in love with her best friend's husband. She could not consciously face the consequences of this love, and the impossibility of satisfying her desire caused libido to "dam up" in her psyche. This blockage led to regression, and when libido regresses it activates earlier pathways, which appear as memories and fantasy reconstructions of childhood (the "primal scene," oedipal fantasies, transference, etc.) or as symbolic symptoms. The psychological block that begins this whole process is created by the patient's incapacity to suffer the present conflict consciously. The consequent unconsciousness of fantasies and of the conflict as a whole are responsible for symptoms like this one.

Neurotic symptoms, Jung agreed with Freud, represent a compromise (or symbolic) satisfaction, which the paralyzed young woman enjoyed by being taken into her friend's house for the night, where she was put to bed and allowed to remain under the roof of her secret beloved. Jung differed from Freud on the treatment of this type of neurotic problem. Instead of following the patient's fantasies back into childhood and endlessly analyzing, reconstructing, and interpreting the past, Jung would focus on the patient's inability and unwillingness to face the conflict in the present. He would interpret fantasies and transference from the viewpoint of the present emotional stalemate (1961b, p. 167). Thus the weight of interpretation falls on the dynamic factor in the present rather than on meticulous genetic reconstructions, which Jung saw as being primarily seductive elaborations of fantasy under the guise of history.

When Freud pointed out to him (McGuire 1977, p. 507) that his thought showed "a disastrous similarity to a theorem of Adler's," namely that "the incest libido is 'arranged', i.e., the neurotic has no desire at all for his mother," Jung was stung: "The comparison with Adler is a bitter pill," he replied (ibid., p. 509). But his thought was indeed moving along lines similar to Adler's. The fantasy productions of the neurotic do not, he felt, reflect repressed wishes or the actual history of childhood; they are derivative products of a present psychological impasse. Fixations become activated by regression, and the fantasies that occur during a regression reflect, to some extent, earlier formations of libido, but Jung was tending to see regression as a by-product of a person's evasion of psychological tasks in the present. The elaboration of psychic material during regression is a symptom of the patient's unwillingness or inability to separate from childhood and to accept the necessary suffering of a present life situation. To follow these fantasies interminably backward with the patient and to take them as true indicators of where the real psychological problems lie, Jung felt, was to fall into collusion with the patient's wish to avoid the present problems of living.

Yet, up to a point, Jung wanted to affirm the value of following neurotic fantasy formations backward. For treatment, he preferred the psychoanalytic method of attending to the patient's unconscious rather than the Adlerian method of trying to reeducate the will or to insist on a strenuous rational analysis of the psyche's evasiveness (1961b, p. 184). Neurotic symptoms, Jung agreed with Freud, are a compromise between pathogenic causes and normal functioning and can therefore be interpreted as attempts to express normal functioning in a distorted form. So Jung chose to follow the patient's fantasies, not writing them off as mere evasions of duty in the present but interpreting them a) genetically, as reactivations of fixations and libido traces, b) dynamically, as disguised statements of present unconscious conflicts, and c) purposively, as indicators of attempts at normal functioning. It was in tackling the complexity of this interpretive task that Jung developed his two basic types of interpretation.

Jung's Two Types of Interpretation

In 1912, Jung's criticism of psychoanalysis as a method of therapy was not so much that it followed the libido's regression back into the fixations of childhood, but that it stayed there too long. Jung felt that the patient's psyche would indicate when the value of this was turning negative, and that to search for more infantile fantasy material and to continue reconstructing fictive childhood scenes when the therapeutic value of this was questionable and when the patient was ready to use freed libido for new adaptive functioning was bad therapy (1961b, pp. 187ff.). As a therapist, Jung's primary commitment was to the patient's adaptive functioning, and the analyst's interpretations, he felt, should always reflect this attitude.

It was in relation to the topic of transference that Jung began to develop the prospective interpretation of unconscious material, mainly of dreams (ibid., pp. 197ff.). The first phases of analysis, which have to do with uncovering complexes and reconstructing the past, involve a descent into the chaos of the psyche and its regressive fantasy. Often this reactivates the parental imagoes and produces transference. Interpretation during these stages of treatment is predominantly historical-genetic and psychodynamic. In later stages of treatment, however, the therapeutic task becomes focused on resolving the transference that has developed, and at that time dreams can have a "prospective function" (ibid., pp. 200–201): They can point to possible resolutions of the transference impasse, which will lead to better psychological adaptations in the future.

In 1912 Jung expressed rather tentatively his opinion that the psyche has a prospective orientation:

> Without presuming to say that dreams have prophetic foresight, it is nevertheless possible that we might find, in this subliminal material, combinations of future events which are subliminal simply because they have not yet attained the degree of clarity necessary for them to become conscious. Here I am thinking of those dim presentiments we sometimes have of the future, which are nothing but faint, subliminal combinations of events whose objective value we are not yet able to apperceive. (1961b, p. 201)

Jung was not able to make a stronger case at that time because he lacked the experience and the theoretical framework for making prospective interpretations. Later, with his theory of symbols and archetypes in place, he would be able to show that regression leads to a deeper level of the psyche than the personal, infantile one, and that this archetypal level has a healing, transformational function that is directed prospectively forward by the dynamics of the individuation process.

The two types of interpretation, reductive and prospective, were linked to phases of analysis. For the first phase, Jung recommended reductive interpretation, for the later, prospective: "The discovery of its [i.e., the dream's] prospective or final meaning is particularly important when the analysis is so far advanced that the eyes of the patient are turned more readily to the future than to his inner world and the past"

(1961b, p. 238). The two types of interpretation are linked, moreover, to different therapeutic aims. Reductive interpretation is aimed at undoing earlier libido formations and the regressively activated fixations that block adaptive functioning and to clear room for new psychological integrations and structures. Prospective interpretation, on the other hand, is used to weave themes that indicate new lines of development emerging from unconscious fantasy and to point out ways for them to become linked to conscious functioning. The method Jung devised for carrying out this prospective approach was called amplification. The methodological justification for amplification would depend on the theory of archetypes and their relation to the individuation process.

In 1912–13, Jung could not yet give the full elaboration of his method, which would grow out of a pair of distinctions between (1) reductive and prospective interpretations and (2) concrete and symbolic interpretations. These would later come together in a single set of distinctions, but during the time of Jung's break with Freud they ran on parallel tracks without a common set of theoretical ties between them.

Jung's distinction between concrete and symbolic interpretations weighed perhaps more than his distinction between reductive and prospective ones. Jung would agree with Freud that a cigar is sometimes just a cigar, but the question was when. Concrete interpretations take psychic images literally, while symbolic interpretations take them metaphorically. The symbolic approach considers images as statements of the libido's formation and transformation that do not refer literally to wishes or drives but to psychic structures and dynamics whose function and meaning require further interpretation but can never be exhaustively interpreted or explained. In a talk given in England in August 1913 (1913c), Jung suggested a rule of thumb for when to interpret images literally and when symbolically. Again, each type of interpretation is related to a stage of therapy, and the final criterion is therapeutic usefulness.

> If dream-analysis at the beginning of the treatment shows that the dreams have an undoubtedly sexual meaning, this meaning is to be taken realistically; that is, it proves that the sexual problems of the patient need to be subjected to a careful review. For instance, if an incest fantasy is clearly shown to be a latent content of the dream, one must subject the patient's infantile relations with his parents and brothers and sisters, as well as his relations with other persons who are fitted to play the role of father or mother, to a thorough investigation. But if

a dream that comes at a later stage of the analysis has, let us say, an incest fantasy as its essential content—a fantasy that we have reason to consider disposed of—concrete value should not under all circumstances be attached to it; it should be regarded as symbolic. The formula for interpretation is: the unknown meaning of the dream is expressed, by analogy, through a fantasy of incest. In this case symbolic and not real value must be attached to the sexual fantasy. If we did not get beyond the real value we should keep reducing the patient to sexuality, and this would arrest the progress of the development of his personality. The patient's salvation does not lie in thrusting him back again and again into primitive sexuality; this would leave him on a low cultural level whence he could never obtain freedom and complete restoration to health. Retrogression to a state of barbarism is no advantage at all for a civilized human being. (1961b, p. 239)

Interpretation and Archetypal Theory

The next step in integrating these distinctions between reductive and prospective interpretation and concrete and symbolic interpretation and in creating the complex hermeneutic that would become the hallmark of Jungian interpretation depended on a theoretical breakthrough. This was the distinction between the personal unconscious and the archetypal, collective unconscious. The scope of my study does not reach to detailing the development of archetypal theory, but a few comments are in order to show how this became the theoretical underpinning for Jung's hermeneutic.

Already in his earliest period, as evidenced in his doctoral thesis and the work on schizophrenia, Jung was interested in the prospective tendencies shown by fantasy productions. This interest continued in subdued form into and through his Freudian period. But neither in his own theory of complexes and complex formation nor within the Freudian context did Jung have a sufficient theoretical framework on which to mount this observation. For a long time, it remained purely observational and intuitive, and it happened to fall into line with the ideas of Maeder, a close colleague at the time (Jung 1961b, p. 238).

That the psyche could anticipate the future presented a conundrum. If Freud was right, the psyche was formed by a person's past, by the fantasies and events of childhood, by the emotional traumas at various stages of development, by the developmental fixations and arrests of personal history, and by the effect of a few "archaic residues." If this were the whole story, how could the psyche orient itself to the future? What factor could account for a prospective orientation? For Jung the answers to these questions would grow out of his comparative study of fantasy, religion, and mythology.

In the years from 1909 to 1912, Jung became increasingly fascinated by the numerous parallels that were being discovered between mythic patterns and the fantasies of patients (particularly children and psychotics). Many psychoanalytic investigators besides Jung were busy in this field, and their discoveries were extremely provocative and exciting. As Jung's Freudian period was coming to a close, he was working on *Transformations and Symbols of the Libido* (1912a), a study made up largely of mythological parallels to the visions and dreams of an American woman, Miss Miller. This work was published in the psychoanalytic journal of which Jung was then editor, the *Jahrbuch für psychoanalytische und psychopathologische Forschungen*, and it marked his decisive theoretical departure from Freud. Here Jung presented what he felt was convincing evidence for a transformational process that took place within the unconscious, which had the effect of channeling libido out of one set of patterns and attachments into another more mature set. Maturation could be seen, therefore, as a natural process of psychological development, unfolding through time according to an innate plan. It was not primarily the result of interaction with the environment or of threats of punishment from external authorities, which Freud saw as elemental in his castration-fear theory. Jung's new idea implied that the psyche is inherently programmed to develop toward maturation, and, therefore, that the psychological future, and not only the psychological past, is contained latently within it. This maturational program, which Jung later named "individuation," could be thwarted or distorted by experience and environment, but it was not itself the product of influence, education, or nurture but rather an inherent endowment of the human being.

As Jung's theory evolved, the "transformer" of libido within the individuation process became the archetype. Archetypes typically appear in dreams and spontaneous fantasies as numinous images of great fascination and power. These images are symbolic and thus link a person's consciousness to a deeply hidden psychic background, from which structure unfolds over long periods of time. When archetypal images appear, they often indicate deep changes taking place in the structures that organize a person's libidinal investments. Jung saw it as both a theoretical and a therapeutic error to reduce these symbolic statements of the archetypal psyche to the contents of personal history (the complexes) or to a single instinct. The archetype exists on a par with instinct and is as fundamental to psychological life as instinct is. In fact, instincts and archetypes are linked: The archetype is the *form* of the instinct (1969a, p. 157); the archetypal image is the instinct as image.

The distinctions that Jung made between reductive and prospective interpretation and between concrete and symbolic interpretation later became linked to his theoretical distinction between personal and archetypal layers of the psyche. Reductive interpretation focuses on the personal unconscious and on history as a series of past events in an individual's life. This type of psychological interpretation takes unconscious images concretely: The incest motif in a dream, for instance, represents a wish for intimacy with the actual mother or father. Such concrete, reductive interpretation typically takes place in the early phases of analysis, or as otherwise indicated.

The other type of interpretation treats psychic material as symbolic and is oriented by a teleological perspective. It asks not so much whither as whence, and not so much how as why. It works by a comparative method—amplification—and brings nonpersonal associations to bear on the images of the unconscious, in order to penetrate beneath the level of personal associations and individual history. These interpretations elucidate the nonpersonal, collective, archetypal layers of the unconscious. While these layers are nonpersonal, they are not ahistorical. They form the basis for the evolution of psychological patterns over long spans of time and indicate future psychological possibilities and tasks. Interpretation in this mode sees the incest motif in a dream symbolizing the ego's return to the unconscious, an event that may foreshadow a death and rebirth cycle leading to psychological renewal and structural transformation. This type of interpretation is typically practiced in later stages of analysis, with persons in the second half of life, or as otherwise indicated by clinical judgment.

This amplificatory method of interpretation has roots in Jung's Freudian period. In his studies of Miss Miller's fantasies, Jung used a comparative method of interpretation that was later to be refined and deepened but was already a rudimentary form of the method of amplification. The research in *Transformations and Symbols of the Libido* (1912a) consisted in assembling analogies from history, myth, folktale, religious practice, and world literature to Miss Miller's fantasy images. Jung then subjected this set of materials to a (mostly reductive) psychoanalytic interpretation. He surmised that Miss Miller was struggling with debilitating neurotic attachments to her fantasy life and to child-hood, and he saw her unconsciously struggling to free libido from this obstacle to further development and maturation. With this comparative method Jung also found confirmation of his intuition that the uncon-scious is oriented dynamically forward and not only backward. Jung's method suggested how analogous symbolic patterns from myth and literature could be used to show that a specific outcome to Miss Miller's conflicts was being prepared or anticipated by the unconscious. This comparative method created important (and to Freud very disagreeable) modifications in the routine outcomes of psychoanalytic interpretation.

The Method of Amplification

In his Fordham University lectures in 1912, Jung illustrated his comparative method by adverting to Christian baptism as a symbolic action that requires interpretation:

> In order to understand this ceremony, we must gather together from the whole history of ritual, that is, from mankind's memories of the relevant traditions, a body of comparative material culled from the most varied sources. . . .
>
> In this way we build up a comparative study of the act of baptism. We discover the elements out of which the baptismal act is formed; we ascertain, further, its original meaning, and at the same time become acquainted with the rich world of myths that have laid the foundation of religions. . . . The analyst proceeds in the same way with a dream. He collects the historical parallels to every part of the dream, even the remotest, and tries to reconstruct the psychological history of the dream and its underlying meanings. Through this monographic elaboration we obtain, just as in the analysis of baptism, a profound insight into the marvellously delicate and meaningful network of unconscious determi-nation . . . . (1961b, pp. 146–47)

In this same lecture to American psychiatrists and psychologists, Jung went on to explain why a method of interpretation such as this one is needed to understand the meaning of symbols and symbolic acts:

> The dream is one of the clearest examples of psychic contents whose composition eludes direct understanding. When someone knocks in a nail with a hammer in order to hang something up, we can understand every detail of the action; it is immediately evident. It is otherwise with the act of baptism, where every phase is problematic. We call these

actions, whose meaning and purpose are not immediately evident, symbolic actions, or symbols. On the basis of this reasoning we call a dream symbolic, because it is a psychological product whose origin, meaning, and purpose are obscure, and is therefore one of the purest products of unconscious constellation. As Freud aptly says, the dream is the *via regia* to the unconscious. (1961b, p. 148)

At the stage of thought Jung had achieved by 1912, he was still strongly under the influence of Freud, and his interpretation of symbols tended on the whole to remain reductive to biological, regressive, and instinctual processes. By 1916, however, he had changed his thinking considerably and had enlarged his earlier germinal insights. He now had an interpretive method that he called "hermeneutics," as opposed to Freud's "semiotics." In a 1916 lecture entitled "The Structure of the Unconscious," revised in 1928 to become substantially "The Relations between the Ego and the Unconscious," the second of his famous *Two Essays on Analytical Psychology* (1966a), Jung presented a method of interpretation that he would use for the remainder of his intellectual life. In this paper he stated the essence of the method of amplification.

"Whence has fantasy acquired its bad reputation?" he asks rhetorically, preparing to describe his own new method for interpreting psychological materials:

Above all from the circumstance that it cannot be taken literally. *Concretely* understood, it is worthless. If it is understood *semiotically*, as Freud understands it, it is interesting from the scientific point of view; but if it is understood *hermeneutically*, as an authentic symbol, it acts as a signpost, providing the clues we need in order to carry on our lives in harmony with ourselves.

The symbol is not a sign that disguises something generally known. Its meaning resides in the fact that it is an attempt to elucidate, by a more or less apt analogy, something that is still entirely unknown or still in the process of formation. If we reduce this by analysis to something that is generally known, we destroy the true value of the symbol; but to attribute hermeneutic significance to it is consistent with its value and meaning.

The essence of hermeneutics, an art widely practised in former times, consists in adding further analogies to the one already supplied by the symbol: in the first place subjective analogies produced at random by the patient, then objective analogies provided by the analyst out of his general knowledge. This procedure widens and enriches the initial symbol, and the final outcome is an infinitely complex and variegated picture the elements of which can be reduced to their respective *tertia comparationis*. Certain lines of psychological development then stand out that are at once individual and collective. There is no science on earth by which these lines could be proved "right"; on the contrary, rationalism could very easily prove that they are wrong. Their validity is proved by their intense value for life. And that is what matters in practical treatment: that human beings should get a hold on their own lives, not that the principles by which they live should be proved rationally to be "right." (1966a, p. 291) [italics in original]

Besides expressing the essence of amplification, this statement shows the priority of therapy over "rightness" in Jung's deployment of this method. So, to a degree that is exactly parallel to the purpose of historical reconstruction in analysis, the goal of interpretation is therapy. Jung the physician, rather than Jung the empirical scientist or Jung the philosopher, was responsible for and in control of this interpretive method.

In the 40 years following this initial statement, Jung elaborated a great deal on his method of amplification, almost always including a strong argument for its therapeutic advantage over a strictly reductive interpretive approach to the psyche. Of these statements, perhaps the most detailed and carefully considered is contained in "The Psychology of the Child Archetype" (1941). In this paper, published in a collaborative work with the mythologist Karl Kerenyi, Jung wove together his interpretive methodology and his general psychological theory, the pattern revealing the nature of his hermeneutic and the argument for its therapeutic value. In this paper, he also put the method to work, interpreting the archetypal image of the divine child. Jung summarized his position on the nature and function of interpretation as follows:

Not for a moment dare we succumb to the illusion that an archetype can be finally explained or disposed of. Even the best attempts at explanation are only more or less sucessful translations into another metaphorical language. (Indeed, language itself is only an image.) The most we can do is to *dream the myth onwards* and give it a modern dress. And whatever explanation or interpretation does to it, we do to our own souls as well, with corresponding results for our own well-being. The archetype . . . is a psychic organ present in all of us. A bad explanation means a correspondingly bad attitude to this organ, which may thus be injured. But the ultimate sufferer is the bad interpreter himself. Hence the "explanation" should always be such that the functional significance of the archetype remains unimpaired, so that an adequate and meaningful connection between the conscious mind and the archetypes is assured. For the archetype is an element of our psychic structure and thus a vital and necessary component in our psychic economy. (1969b, p. 160)

By the time he wrote this essay, Jung had fully delineated the theory of archetypes and was prepared to argue that universal images like the divine child are symbolic expressions ("self-portraits") of the mind's archetypal strata. Archetypes have a psychological function analogous to the biological function of physical organs. Their healthy functioning is essential to mental and spiritual well-being.

Spontaneous appearances of archetypal images in dreams and fantasies, he argued further in this essay, have developmental import for the person or group to whom they appear, and, because they are symbolic, the conscious appropriation of their meaning requires interpretation. Reductive interpretation alone can be harmful, because it misses the prospective and developmental meanings of the image and can further distort the relationship between an already one-sided ego attitude and the emerging archetypal patterns. So, for therapeutic reasons, these images should be interpreted using the complex hermeneutical method he elaborated.

Many more passages could be cited where Jung emphasized the therapeutic function of interpretation. In this respect, there is no difference between reductive-concrete interpretation and synthetic-symbolic interpretation: Both are meant to serve the further evolution of personality.

The Therapist as Hermeneut

Jung's view on the role and nature of interpretation in his post-Freudian period was considerably different from what it had been in the psychoanalytic days, when a frequent phrase in his writings had been the reductive "nothing but." This change came along with his revision of Freud's view of the unconscious and with the new direction his thinking had taken on psychological development and the etiology of neurosis. As Jung freed himself from Freud's influence, he elaborated the idea that psychological development takes place through a series of psychic fragmentations and integrations. In this process, some psychological potentials become actualized and some psychic contents attach to the conscious ego-attitude; others become repressed, or sink back into the unconscious, where they collect around autonomous complexes and constitute the "shadow." In the second half of life, the repressed and undeveloped aspects of personality (the shadow, the contrasexual opposite, the inferior functions) make strong demands upon a person for attention and integration. If these challenges are accepted and met, wholeness may once again be approached. The polarization of ego-consciousness and the unconscious is both a normal product of developmental dynamics and also the cause of the impasses and conflicts that stand in the way of further development. Jung came to understand neurosis finally as the product of psychological one-sidedness, realizing at the same time that this is inevitable and indeed is even necessary as a developmental outcome that precedes further integration.

The therapist as hermeneut helps to bridge the split between consciousness and the unconscious. This split is the condition for neurosis, when libido no longer flows along a gradient from unconscious to conscious intentionality, but rather becomes blocked and retreats further into the unconscious, producing neurotic symptoms. The function of interpretation, whether reductive or synthetic, is to overcome this stalemate. Life can then move on. Hermeneutics has the therapeutic function of bridging such psychic splits and facilitating new integrations, which will in turn allow for a new progression of libido. The net result of this integrative development, too, is greater conscious appropriation of psychological wholeness.

This hermeneutical effort is essential in therapy, because the "unconscious compensation of a neurotic conscious attitude contains all the elements that could effectively and healthily correct the one-sidedness of the conscious mind if these elements were made conscious, i.e., were understood and integrated into it as realities" (1966a, p. 110). Successful treatment hinges, therefore, largely on effective bridging interpretations that help a person

> to understand and to appreciate, as far as practicable, dreams and all other manifestations of the unconscious, firstly in order to prevent the formation of an unconscious opposition which becomes more dangerous as time goes on, and secondly in order to make the fullest possible use of the healing factor of compensation. (Ibid., p. 110)

When Jung turned seriously to contemporary Christianity in the late 1930s and afterwards, he used the interpretive methods and strategies that he had originally worked out in the context of therapy. As hermeneut, he interpreted Christianity's present conscious attitudes—represented in its doctrines and established rites and practices—both reductively and synthetically: reductively, in the light of history and of the oppositions and splits that have been generated within the tradition; synthetically, through amplification of historic and contemporary religious symbols. He read the history of Christianity as the developmental history of a patient: for splits (between good and evil, masculine and feminine), for repressions (of Gnosticism and alchemy), and for historical developments of one-sidedness (the spiritual perfectionism and antinaturism of Christianity). The contemporary situation of Christianity, read reductively as an outcome of a developmental history, was also interpreted synthetically in the perspective offered by new symbolic developments in the collective unconscious. Christianity's past and present were then placed in an evolutionary perspective in which doctrine and symbol were seen as markers in the tradition's development toward wholeness. Both types of interpretation stand in the service of "transformation," which was Jung's master concept for therapeutic change. As hermeneut, Jung would see himself the bridge builder for this new development within Christianity toward its own inherent *telos*: wholeness.

THE TRANSFERENCE/COUNTERTRANSFERENCE PROCESS

At the heart of what Jung called transformation, the fourth phase of analysis (1929, pp. 69–74) and its ultimate goal—after confession, elucidation, and education—lies the transference/countertransference process.

Typically Jung would relate the goal of therapy to the nature of the patient's suffering, to the degree of psychological development achieved before entering therapy, and to the patient's potential for further development. His wide therapeutic experience, which ranged from treating chronically psychotic patients in the Burghölzli Klinik to consulting with highly gifted individuals in all stages of life, informed all of his discussions of therapy. The four phases of analysis Jung spelled out in 1929 indicate possible stopping points in any specific analytic case as much as they do markers along the road of an extensive long-term analysis.

Occasionally, a patient needs or wants only the relief of confessing a close secret. In other cases, a meticulous elucidation of the unconscious—including the reconstruction of personal history, the uncovering of splitting tendencies and repressions, the examination of dynamics between ego-consciousness and the complexes and archetypes—takes place, and this requires careful reductive and synthetic interpretation. Education, Jung's bow to Adler's approach, includes preparing ego-consciousness for new adaptations to the world and for new integrations of unconscious material. But for the deepest, most complex and extensive analyses, Jung reserved the term "transformation." This he regarded as the ultimate goal of the therapeutic labor, and it was in relation to this phase that he spoke about the transference/countertransference process.

Jung distinguished the therapeutic work taking place within the intimately reciprocal transference/countertransference process from the more common analytic task usually referred to as "interpreting the transference." The latter typically takes place in the elucidation phase of analysis, when the analyst interprets the (typically parental) projections of the patient. The aim of this is to resolve infantile dependency on, regressive attachment to, or hostility toward parent-like figures and thereby extend the ego's freedom and range of operation. For this phase of analysis, the stance of the analyst is ideally neutral, objective, and insight-oriented (1966b, p. 63).

In the fourth phase of analysis, however, psychological chemistry rules. Here the personality of the analyst comes more fully into the picture, and the emotional relationship between analyst and patient becomes primary. The analyst's personhood is now required more than technical know-how, and analysis becomes a drama whose conclusion cannot be scripted beforehand in a treatment plan. As Jung described this process in his major work on the transference, "The Psychology of the Transference" (1946), both patient and analyst must be willing to go to the wall and be tested by one another's personality in the heat of an intensely personal relationship, without reservation and without defensive withdrawal from each other or from the task at hand. Both are required to undergo a transformational process.

The emotional intensity and depth of this relationship and the profound psychological engagement of the two personalities in it are the hallmark of this phase of analysis. It was in this emotional key that he wrote "The Psychology of the Transference," in which he summed up his experience of this type of relationship with patients, illustrating and amplifying it with an alchemical text that demonstrates, in his interpretation, the full reciprocity between analyst and patient within the transference/countertransference process (1946).

Jung on Transference

Looking over the history of Jung's thought on transference, one is quickly convinced that he considered it a key issue in therapy from his earliest psychoanalytic days, long before he had an equal appreciation of the importance of countertransference. His understanding of transference evolved considerably as his thought departed from its Freudian moorings, and his insight into countertransference and into the transformational potential of the transference/countertransference process developed its full depth only long after his Freudian period. In the following discussion, therefore, I will place Jung's thought on transference and countertransference simultaneously within the framework of its historical development and of his later views on transformation. In Chapter 3, I will show that Jung's relationship to Christianity was characterized by the kind of transference/countertransference dynamic described here.

The term transference, softened now by usage into psychological jargon, refers to a type of emotional reaction on the part of patients to their therapists. The pioneers of psychoanalysis found this reaction to occur fairly regularly during therapeutic treatment. Freud, the first to name this reaction, interpreted it as a "carry over" (the literal translation of his *Übertragung*) from childhood. In Freud's original understanding, transference referred to a relationship in the present (typically in adulthood) with a stranger (a professional therapist, in this case), which reflected the emotional climate of childhood and particularly the patient's relationship to parents. Transference creates a sort of illusory relationship between two people, generating assumptions and expectations that are based on the projection of parental figures. Typically transference is characterized by feelings of dependency, awe, anger or hostility, sexual attraction or repulsion, veneration, and ambivalence. To a person experiencing this type of emotional reaction, there is a close resemblance to the childhood relationship to parents. In this emotional nexus a patient repeats the experiences of childhood in the present.

On the importance of working with transference reactions in therapy, Jung saw eye to eye with Freud. "The main problem of medical psychotherapy," Jung wrote in his memoirs, referring to his first meeting with Freud, "is the *transference*. In this matter Freud and I were in complete agreement" (1961a, p. 212). Even in old age he could vividly recall the moment when he first expressed this conviction:

> The enormous importance that Freud attached to the transference phenomenon became clear to me at our first personal meeting in 1907. After a conversation lasting many hours there came a pause. Suddenly he asked me out of the blue, "And what do you think about the transference?" I replied with the deepest conviction that it was the alpha

and omega of the analytical method, whereupon he said, "Then you have grasped the main thing." (1966b, p. 172)

Jung was to hold on to this "main thing" of analytic treatment throughout his lifetime of work as a psychotherapist. Summarizing his position in 1946, he was less dogmatic but still firm on this point:

It is probably no exaggeration to say that almost all cases requiring lengthy treatment gravitate round the phenomenon of transference, and that the success or failure of the treatment appears to be bound up with it in a very fundamental way. . . . It is a critical phenomenon of varying shades of meaning and its absence is as significant as its presence. (Ibid., p. 164)

Even after his break with Freud, Jung agreed that transference was central to therapy and that its appearance could be useful for resolving the lingering infantile components of a patient's personality. In some cases, however, Jung felt that the transference was not a simple reflection of childhood experience but had an archetypal basis, which called for a nonreductive, amplificatory interpretation. Occasionally, too, transference would be met by countertransference, and then a transference/countertransference process would take over the clinical picture. And it was this latter happening that, when well managed, characterized what he called transformation.

How does an emotional relationship of this kind develop in psychotherapy? Generally, Jung felt, it begins with the patient's transference reaction to the analyst, which first emerges as the result of confession. Discussing the role and effect of confession, Jung pointed out in his 1912 lectures at Fordham University that a patient's confession of secrets and of a hidden emotional life may produce dramatic ameliorative effects, but that confession by itself usually has relatively short-lived and superficial therapeutic results. However, it can lead to transference, and this is its most important contribution to a more complete psychotherapeutic experience (1961b, pp. 192–93).

In an interview with Richard Evans in 1957, Jung explained how he saw this happening in practice:

Now, it is a regular observation that when you talk to an individual and he gives you insight into his inner preoccupations, interests, emotions— in other words, hands over his personal complexes—you gradually get into a position of authority whether you like it or not. . . . The things people hand out are not merely indifferent things . . . they hand out themselves. They hand out a big emotional value, as if they were handing over a large sum, as if they were trusting you with the administration of their estate, and they are entirely in your hands. . . . That, you see, creates an emotional relationship to the analyst, and that is what Freud called the transference, which is a central problem in analytical psychology. . . . When they hand out such material its context is associated with all the most important persons in the life of a patient. The most important persons are usually father and mother—that comes up from childhood. . . . In handing over your infantile memories about the father or about the mother, you also hand over the image of father and mother. Then it is just as if the analyst had taken the place of the father, or even of the mother. . . . So the patients hand themselves over in the hope that I can swallow that stuff and digest it for them. I am *in loco parentis* and have a high authority. Naturally I am also persecuted by the corresponding resistances, by all the manifold emotional reactions they have had against their parents. (McGuire and Hull 1977, pp. 343–45)

In the transference, patients typically color the analyst the emotional tones of their parents. These figures now appear disguised in fantasies and dreams about the analyst, and, Jung observed, this transferential material may consist of "incestuous sexuality" (1966b, p. 178). When one is drawn into this "peculiar atmosphere of family incest," there enters a feeling of "unreal intimacy which is highly distressing to both doctor and patient and arouses resistances and doubts on both sides" (ibid.).

The object of working through the transference, Jung felt, is to free the patient's ego from the domination of the inner parental figures and from infantile wishes and fears related to them. Through careful analysis of the transference, a person gains greater personal autonomy and maturity and broader freedom of libidinal expression (1961b, p. 284). The resolution of transference also had cultural and historical meaning for Jung. The dissolution of parental authority increased the individual's authority, and this was in line, Jung argued, with "one of the predominating trends of our stage of civilization—the urge towards individualization" (ibid.). Jung was from the beginning of his association with Freud and psychoanalysis keenly aware of the cultural task that psychoanalysis was performing in freeing modern men and women from a traditional (and, to analysts, an infantile) relation to authority.

Even in 1913, however, Jung was pursuing another avenue of thought regarding transference, which departed from Freud's views and would eventually lead to his own very different understanding of the transference/countertransference process and its central role in the transformational phase of therapy. In an exchange of letters with the Swiss physician Dr. R. Löy during the first three months of 1913 (Jung 1961b, pp. 252–89), Jung speculated that transference in therapy is useful not only because it eventually may lead to greater moral autonomy, but also because it created a psychological milieu in which the patient's conscious attitudes can be restructured. In the transference, he pointed out, the patient's psyche follows the rule of analogy and unconsciously reaches back to a time when a similar psychological relationship existed—typically in childhood. Jung called this parallel form of relating, "empathy." Whereas transference typically creates gross distortions in perception and expectation, it also creates an emotional sensitivity to the analyst that is often acutely accurate. By adapting to the analyst through this combination of transference distortion and sensitivity, the patient gradually acquires new inner structures that are modeled on those of the analyst, as the earlier structures were modeled on the parent. Transference, therefore, creates an opportunity for the patient to repeat earlier phases of development. The therapeutic usefulness of transference lies not only in its conscious dissolution, then, but also in the fact that its constellation can be used for restructuring the patient's psyche along more adaptive lines (ibid., p. 286). This is very closely related to what would later, in psychoanalytic circles, be discussed as "the corrective emotional experience" of therapy. The new structures developed by patients during therapy would be more useful for life than the former attitudes were, Jung supposed, because the analyst had, through a lengthy personal analysis of his or her own, achieved a better adaptation to reality than the patient's original parents had.

In his correspondence with Dr. Löy, Jung expressed the opinion that analysts should undergo personal analysis before practicing psychotherapy. While the reasons he gave changed considerably over the following decades, Jung would always hold this position. In the early period, he regarded this analysis mainly as prophylactic. Because the keen empathy of the neurotic would quickly sense the analyst's adaptation (or maladaptation) to reality and mold to it, it was crucial for the analyst to have become free of infantile tendencies and to have achieved the moral autonomy required of patients. To the extent that the analyst's own adaptation to life remained infantile, patients would not be freed from the transference. This would lead either to interminable analysis and dependency on the analyst or to premature endings without resolution of the transference.

Jung did not, however, consider this to be the whole story of what happens in the transference. In his correspondence with Dr. Löy, he expressed his respect for what the patient brings to the therapeutic situation, including expressions of what Jung at this time termed determinants: "The psyche does not merely *react*, it gives its own specific answer to the influences at work upon it, and at least half the resulting formation is entirely due to the psyche and the determinants inherent within it" (1961b, p. 287). The analyst's psychological structures are therefore not wholly responsible for changes in the patient as the result of therapy any more than the psychological structures of parents were wholly responsible for the attitudes and character structure of their children. The patient's inherent determinants are equally important ingredients in the final product.

Archetypal Aspects of Transference

Without abandoning this understanding of transference or minimizing the importance of resolving it in analysis, Jung later argued that transference also contains an archetypal dimension. The "answer" the patient gives to the analyst's personality in the transference comes from psychic levels that lie deeper than the personally acquired imagoes and complexes. Since this understanding of transference depended on the theory of archetypes, Jung's full articulation of it came much later, even though strong intuitive hints of a symbolic view of transference can be found in his earlier writings.

The archetypal dimension of transference can be easily overlooked in favor of its personal features, although Jung felt it was a mistake to ignore the former since the two had radically different purposes in analysis. The archetypal dimension called for symbolic rather than reductive interpretation, and Jung could see the patient's religious function coming into play in the constellation of an archetypal element in the transference. The *raison d'être* of transference was now actually to create a bridge between the patient's consciousness and an unconscious transcendent "other," which, through the transference, was being temporarily projected upon the analyst. This projected "other" was a content of the collective unconscious and could not be reduced to a memory trace of actual parents or to personally acquired unconscious contents. It was directly a derivative of the archetypal layers of the psyche, and this could be seen in its mythic features, or in its godlike (or sometimes animal) qualities, or in its numinosity. Jung suggested that children project this same archetypal content upon parents, and this is what gives parents such a psychically powerful position. To interpret this dimension of transference reductively, i.e., as nothing but a carryover from childhood motivated by an infantile wish for dependency upon a parent, would be a technical error and a therapeutic blunder. It would damage the soul.

Jung would not deny that images of childhood figured strongly in the archetypal dimension of transference. But for him, childhood was here understood symbolically: In this image the unconscious was working by analogy, imaging an often still very vulnerable bond that was being created between the ego and the self. A reductive interpretation here would not only wound the patient at a highly vulnerable point, but would miss altogether the meaning and therapeutic potential in this psychological event. Here was the opportunity, as Jung saw it, for connecting to a transcendent center of authority and value that lay within the patient and yet beyond the boundaries of ego-consciousness. This would create the basis for a soul-needed religious attitude.

In working with transference at this level, the goal of analysis is shifted away from strengthening the ego through reductive interpretation of personal history toward developing an attitude of careful attention toward the unconscious and its symbolic statements. This attitude Jung called "*religio*," meaning the "careful and scrupulous observation of what Rudolf Otto aptly termed the *numinosum*" (1969c, p. 7). While the resolution of the personal levels of transference results in greater ego autonomy, with authority passing from an outer other (the analyst or parent) to the ego, the resolution of archetypal aspects of transference results in a religious attitude, with authority passing from the outer carrier of the projected imago to a sense of the inner other. The ego becomes subsumed once again under higher authority, but now to an inner authority, the unconscious, or the self.

Jung informally illustrated his ideas about how this works in a 1957 interview with Richard Evans:

> The unconscious now produces dreams in which I really assume a very curious role. In [the patient's] dreams she was a little infant, sitting on my knees, and I held her in my arms. I was a very tender father to the little girl, you know, and more and more her dreams became emphatic in that respect. I was a sort of giant and she was a very little, frail human

thing, quite a little girl in the hands of an enormous being. And the last dream of that series . . . was that I was out in the midst of nature, standing in a field of wheat, an enormous field of wheat that was ripe for harvesting. I was a giant and I held her in my arms like a baby, and the wind was blowing over that field of wheat. Now you know, when the wind is blowing it makes waves in the wheatfield, and with these waves I swayed . . . as if I were putting her to sleep. And she felt as if she were in the arms of a god, of the Godhead, and I thought, "Now the harvest is ripe, and I must tell her." And I told her, "You see, what you want and what you are projecting into me, because you are not conscious of it, is the idea of a deity you don't possess. Therefore you see it in me."

That clicked. Because, you know, she had a rather intense religious education—of course it all vanished later on and something disappeared from her world. The world became merely personal, and that religious conception of the world no longer existed, apparently. But the idea of a deity is not an intellectual idea, it is an archetypal idea. Therefore you find it practically everywhere under one name or another. . . . So she suddenly became aware of an entirely pagan image that comes fresh from the archetype. She didn't have the idea of a Christian God, or of an Old Testament Yahweh. It was a pagan god, a god of nature, of vegetation. He was the wheat himself, he was the spirit of the wheat, the spirit of the wind, and she was in the arms of that numen.

Now that is the living experience of an archetype. It made a tremendous impression on that girl, and instantly it clicked. She saw what she really was missing, that missing value which she projected into me, making me indispensable to her. And then she saw that I was not indispensable, because, as the dream says, she is in the arms of that archetypal idea. That is a numinous experience, and that is the thing people are looking for, an archetypal experience that gives them an incorruptible value. (McGuire & Hull 1977, pp. 346–47)

An archetypal transference, then, creates the opportunity for a person to contact an inner center of wholeness and value and to relate to it consciously. This brings with it a sense of religious meaning in life and becomes the basis for what Jung saw as the essence of a stable religious attitude.

The Therapeutic Function of the Transference/ Countertransference Process

This discussion of personal and archetypal aspects of transference and of their resolution tells only one side of the story of the transference/countertransference process in therapy, as Jung understood it. For while the patient is becoming emotionally involved and projecting unconscious material upon the analyst, the analyst is, in turn, becoming "infected" by the patient and often also begins to project unconscious contents in response, termed "countertransference." This insight into the analyst's psychological involvement in the therapeutic process became a cornerstone of Jung's thinking about psychotherapy, and his elaboration of its implications constitutes one of his greatest contributions to an understanding of how and why psychotherapy has a potential for healing. "One of the main features of Jung's therapy," Ellenberger noted in his massive study of dynamic psychiatry, *The Discovery of the Unconscious*, "is the great emphasis he sets from the beginning on what is now called countertransference. Jung claims that no one is able to lead someone further than he has gone himself" (p. 719).

Like transference, countertransference has entered the lexicon of techinical jargon through years of usage. If there is transference, there is bound to be countertransference, as the analyst is forced to react emotionally to the impact of transference. This reaction may be defensive and aimed at fending off disturbing affects, or it may pave the way for a dialectical process of mutual influence between analyst and patient. Of these two possible directions, Jung recommended the latter, on the grounds that the analyst's influence "can only take place if the patient has a reciprocal influence on the doctor. You can exert no influence if you are not susceptible to influence" (1966b, p. 71). This statement was made in the context of his 1929 discussion of the fourth phase of analysis—transformation—for which the transference/countertransference process was taken as central.

In his early psychoanalytic days, however, Jung's evaluation of countertransference reactions was largely negative, because they were seen as disturbances of the analyst's emotional neutrality. In the grip of a countertransference reaction, the analyst would have a harder time making rational interpretations, and, as emotions and complexes became engaged by the patient, the role of detached observer studying the mechanisms and distortions of another psyche would be more difficult to perform. In the countertransference, the analyst lost objectivity and tended to get drawn into the unconscious dynamics of the patient.

So obvious a hazard was this that it added a further reason to Jung's strong recommendation of personal analysis for anyone wishing to become an analyst. Armed with at least this amount of self-knowledge, candidates for this profession would presumably be less likely to fall naively into strong countertransference reactions and project their own unconscious complexes and needs upon the psychological material of their patients:

> Just as we demand from a surgeon, besides his technical knowledge, a skilled hand, courage, presence of mind, and power of decision, so we must expect from an analyst a very serious and thorough psychoanalytic training of his own personality before we are willing to entrust a patient to him. (1961b, p. 200)

To this requirement of personal analysis Jung added a further more general requirement:

> I know that I am also at one with Freud when I set it up as a self-evident requirement that a psychoanalyst must discharge his own duties to life in a proper way. If he does not, nothing can stop his unutilized libido from automatically descending on his patients and in the end falsifying the whole analysis. Immature and incompetent persons who are themselves neurotic and stand with only one foot in reality generally make nothing but nonsense out of analysis. (Ibid.)

Jung's concern that analysts with "unutilized libido" would respond inappropriately to the transference of patients and lose their sense of professional identity in the toils of transferential projections led him to make other similar pronouncements on the importance of analysts living a full emotional life outside of their intense relationships with patients. Throughout his career he would respect the great difficulty of psychotherapeutic work: "I have seen many cases where the patient assimilated the doctor in defiance of all theory and of the latter's professional intentions," Jung wrote in 1929 (1966b, p. 72). The combination of transference and countertransference in these cases had apparently led to the analyst's ego structures giving way under the strain.

Still, Jung would affirm—and in his later work he would stress—the value of analysts allowing themselves to be psychically infected by their patients. While countertransference always was recognized as having a dangerous potential, Jung increasingly came to regard it as a major instrument for practicing the therapeutic art of transformation.

As he abandoned the psychoanalytic ideal of the neutral analyst and adopted a dialectical model of the therapeutic relationship, Jung's understanding of the potential usefulness of countertransference began to emerge. Analysts, he recognized, will invariably respond emotionally and unconsciously to their patients' personalities, no matter how hard they try to remain neutral and indeed no matter how much of their libido is utilized in life. This is normal, even though it may include whatever pathology or infantile residue exists in the analyst's personality. By depathologizing countertransference reactions per se, however, Jung made them more useful for therapy. Countertransference need not be shunned and suppressed out of professional anxiety. Like transference, it can be useful if it is carefully observed and understood. But analysts have to learn to read their countertransference reactions as they emerge in emotion, fantasy, parapraxis, thought, and dreams and then be able to interpret them and use them for therapeutic ends. It became essential in Jung's later approach for analysts to study themselves and their own unconscious reactions to patients with the same attentiveness that they paid to their patients' psyches.

Thus Jung abandoned the effort to avoid countertransference reactions and tried instead to use them for therapeutic ends. "It is futile for the doctor to shield himself from the influence of the patient," he wrote in 1929,

> and to surround himself with a smoke-screen of fatherly and profession-
> al authority. By so doing he only denies himself the use of a highly
> important organ of information. The patient influences him uncon-
> sciously none the less, and brings about changes in the doctor's uncon-
> scious which are well known to many psychotherapists: psychic disturb-
> ances or even injuries peculiar to the profession, a striking illustration
> of the patient's almost "chemical" action. . . . Their nature can best be
> conveyed by the old idea of the demon of sickness. According to this,
> a sufferer can transmit his disease to a healthy person whose powers
> then subdue the demon—but not without impairing the well-being of
> the subduer. (1966b, pp. 71–72)

By engaging in intensive psychotherapy and becoming the object of patients' transferential projections, analysts unavoidably open themselves to the diseases of their patients. They become infected, usually via the unconscious. This observation led Jung to revise his attitude toward countertransference and his understanding of its potential for healing. While the analyst's unutilized libido could well result in over-involvement or in neurotic involvement with patients, a strong countertransference reaction might, on the other hand, lead the analyst who had internalized the conflicts of the patient to seek resolution of them within.

In *Psychological Types* (1921), Jung offered a means for explaining how countertransference can lead the analyst into this kind of inner struggle with the patient's illness:

> No matter what obstacle we come up against—provided only it be a difficult one—the discord between our own purpose and the refractory object soon becomes a discord in ourselves. For, while I am striving to subordinate the object to my will, my whole being is gradually brought into relationship with it, following the strong libido investment which, as it were, draws a portion of my being across into the object. The result of this is a partial identification of certain portions of my personality with similar qualities in the object. As soon as this identification has taken place, the conflict is transferred into my own psyche. This "introjection" of the conflict with the object creates an inner discord, making me powerless against the object and also releasing affects, which are always symptomatic of inner disharmony. The affects, however, prove that I am sensing myself and am therefore in a position—if I am not blind—to apply my attention to myself and to follow up the play of opposites in my own psyche. (1974, p. 89)

According to Jung, the demon of sickness enters the analyst when the analyst, in response to the patient's transference, first wishes strongly to heal the patient's illness. This initial response typically takes place when patients confess and thereby create a transference, when they "hand themselves over in the hope that I can swallow that stuff and digest it for them" (McGuire and Hull 1977, p. 345), as Jung colorfully put it in the interview with Evans. Soon enough, however, the analyst encounters frustration at the patient's resistance to the healing efforts. The patient does not want to give up the sickness since that would mean losing a previous one-sided adaptation to life and the sense of identity based on it. So the conflict described above begins: on the one side, the analyst's ego and wish to heal the patient; on the other, the patient's suffering and recalcitrance.

If the analyst's personality is sufficiently developed, there now exists, with the internalization of the patient's demon, a chance to resolve the conflict, at least to a greater extent than the patient has been able to accomplish. The analyst does this by opening consciousness to the compensating forces of the unconscious and allowing the unconscious to answer the conflict with a healing symbol. In this way, the analyst may come upon an irrational resolution to the war of opposites from which the patient has been suffering, and this will put the analyst in a position to answer the patient's neurosis and suffering with a response from the self rather than with formulas, interpretations, or educational exhortations.

The solution produced within the analyst is returned to the patient by way of empathic insight and interpretation as well as by a largely unconscious transmission process that Jung called "influence." The model Jung favored for discussing this effect of analyst upon patient was a chemical one (which also depicts the patient's influence upon the analyst):

> In the treatment there is an encounter between two irrational factors, that is to say, between two persons who are not fixed and determinable quantities but who bring with them . . . an indefinitely extended sphere of non-consciousness. . . . For two personalities to meet is like mixing two different chemical substances: if there is any combination at all, both are transformed. In any effective psychological treatment the doctor is bound to influence the patient; but this influence can only take place if the patient has a reciprocal influence on the doctor. (1966b, p. 71)

As Jung saw it, then, it was within the transference/countertransference process between patient and analyst that transformation takes place. Transformation in the patient depends critically on the analyst's openness to influence and to the patient's demon of sickness, then on the analyst's ability to undergo an inner transformational process and to return the result of this to the patient via the inductive effect ("influence") of his or her personality on the patient. (It should be noted that the patient is open to the analyst's influence at this level because of the initial bridge thrown between them by the transference.) This transference/countertransference loop may remain largely unconscious, or unspoken, but it is often vividly observed in the dreams of patients and analysts.

Transformation in Analysis

Transformation is a term that designates a master concept in Jung's articulation of psychological process and development. It first appeared already in his Freudian period. Throughout his writings, Jung used this term to refer to changes in the organization and direction of libido that occur during a person's passages through the stages of psychological maturation. As he worked out his disagreements with Freud, Jung's preference for the term transformation over Freud's "sublimation" became a keynote of the differences between them.

In *Transformations and Symbols of the Libido* (1912a), Jung argued for a natural process within the unconscious that resulted in a transformation of libido from an endogamous, incest constellation to an exogamous, object-related one. This reversal within instinct was caused not, as Freud held, by a threat of castration, but by a "switch" built into nature itself.

In the long course of Jung's further development, the meaning of transformation became greatly enriched with nuances and dimensions, yet it always retained the basic meaning of internally patterned libido reorganization. Like the German *Wandlung*, which ranges in meaning from superficial change all the way to transubstantiation, Jung's usage shows a range of signification from slight alterations in the dynamics between ego and the complexes on the one hand to fundamental changes in the structures of consciousness on the other.

When Jung broke with Freud and suffered his "creative illness" (Ellenberger 1970, p. 672) between the ages of 38 and 43, he experienced first-hand how a profound psychological transformation can occur at midlife. Jung's discovery for therapy in this creative period was that the process of psychological transformation could be helped by a conscious attitude of cooperation, and he sought to apply the lessons of his own experience to his therapeutic work with patients.

Jung's understanding of the meaning and purpose of psychological transformation was invariably linked to stages of development. In the first half of life, the direction of development favors the ego's autonomy and its separation from the unconscious. In childhood, adolescence, and early adulthood, transformations have the purpose of gradually channeling libido out of endogamous attachments to parents and family toward objects in the wider, impersonal world. Transformations here are intended to increase the ego's independence, to strengthen its position vis-à-vis the unconscious, to separate it from attachments to the unconscious and to foster attachments to reality that will lead eventually to family, career, and position in the social world. This encourages, or requires, the development of one-sidedness in conscious attitude and function.

The meanings and purpose of transformation at midlife and in old age are different. These are normally aimed at adaptation to the inner world, at reattaching to the unconscious and bringing into consciousness the very elements of the personality that were earlier repressed or left out for the sake of adapting to the outer world. In these later stages of individuation, images of incest have a prospective rather than a regressive meaning: They auger a psychologically necessary "return to the mothers." Transformation in the second half of life entails sacrifice as it does in the first, however not of an incestuous love object but of the superior function(s) of ego adaptation. Disssolution of conscious attitudes and of formed ego-structures is required for the sake of allowing the unconscious to enter once again into the realms of consciousness. The goal of these later phases of development is the integration of the opposites that exist in the personality from birth and get split apart during the first half of life. It is the conscious approximation to one's innate wholeness.

The details of how the process of transformation takes place, particularly in the second half of life, were described by Jung in *Psychological Types* (1921), his first major work after breaking with Freud. The process described there is consistent with the personal discoveries he made in the years 1913–18, which he reported in "The Transcendent Function" (1916b), *Two Essays on Analytical Psychology* (1966a), and *Memories, Dreams, Reflections* (1961a).

As conceptualized in *Psychological Types*, the transformational process of libido rechanneling and restructuring typically takes place in several phases. Like neurotic symptomatology, it begins with the experience of an insurmountable problem in the present. The ego cannot solve it with its primary modes of adaptation and functioning. The habitual one-sidedness of consciousness, developed to useful purpose earlier, is helpless, and a situation of persistent psychological stagnation and frustration ensues. If this goes on, libido begins to regress, abandoning consciousness and flowing back to the unconscious. The clinical picture here can vary from episodic manic flights, to anxiety and depression, general lassitude, and withdrawal from relationships and work, to existential *Angst* and feelings of emptiness.

When libido is prevented from flowing through the structures of ego-consciousness into active adaptation to life, it backs up and activates the unconscious. As libido regresses and the pressures for release increase in the unconscious, the ego suffers an *abaissement du niveau mental*. Unconscious contents, which now begin to press toward consciousness, cannot, however, break over the threshold until they gain sufficient libido. When the scales are finally tipped, unconscious material floods into consciousness. Dreams, fantasies, autonomous thoughts and images crowd into consciousness, and tasks of the outer world and attachments to it practically disappear from awareness. The ego becomes submerged in fantasy and affect, often forced to the limit of endurance by these visitations from an alien inner world. Here the ego can either cry halt and resist or it can cooperate with the transformational process under way and relinquish the defensive struggle.

The fantasies produced during this transitional period prove crucial. Fantasy, Jung asserted in *Psychological Types*, is "the specific activity of the psyche" (1974, p. 52), a direct reflection of unconscious process where the opposites form unusual and novel combinations. These combinations cannot ordinarily form in consciousness because consciousness is an inveterate discriminator and separates what is seen as incompatible.

In fantasy, symbols form. Symbols are images that combine two or more incommensurables. What is seen as impossible by consciousness— the joining of opposite attitudes (extraversion and introversion), or opposite functions (thinking and feeling, sensation and intuition), or the union of opposite aspects of the personality (masculine and feminine, persona and shadow)—can take place in the unconscious. This is revealed in fantasy. Because the unconscious contains the opposites in undifferentiated form, it can create monstrous hybrids in a fashion ego-consciousness would never imagine or design or even find satisfying in their unpolished, raw shapes. And yet these symbols will point ahead toward psychological healing and toward the next stage of development.

Because symbols combine the opposites the ego needs for resolving the original conflict, they represent a healing force in the psyche. In their vicinity, the ego often finds itself strangely comforted and energized. Symbols, moreover, are rich with libido, and this is reflected in their numinosity and near hypnotic effect. A person can draw on a symbol for orientation and adaptation and subtly repattern himself or herself on it.

As a person leaves the transitional phase and returns to adaptive' activities in the world, the former mode of one-sided functioning is significantly altered by the appropriation of the symbol. Consciousness has become transformed—reoriented and restructured from within— on the pattern of the symbol, which combines the opposites that had formerly been unreconcilable.

As consciousness assimilates the symbol into functioning, however, discrimination occurs once again, and the symbol separates into antithetical components. Certain parts of it are discarded and become repressed. This leads ego-consciousness eventually into one-sidedness again, and so the entire transformational process must repeat itself. But each time this process recurs, the ego retains more of the integration represented by the symbol. Over time it comes to approximate the psyche's totality, reflecting the psyche's paradoxical union of opposites.

Psychological transformation in analysis, as Jung saw it, implied deep-going structural change and rechanneling of libido through the mediation of a symbol, taking place typically within the transference/countertransference process. Since it is stage-related, however, transformation is limited by a person's earlier development. It is a type of change that maintains continuity with the conscious contents and integrations of the past but remolds them into a new psychodynamic pattern and amalgamates them with new contents from the unconscious. It was for Jung neither a radical kind of change from one personality structure into something totally different nor a revolutionary replacement of one archetypal dominant with another, but rather a higher form of integration.

Within the transference/countertransference process, a psychological transformation takes place in both patient and analyst. The complexity of this process Jung described as a combination of several factors: empathic adaptation to the conscious and unconscious attitudes each to the other, which involves a degree of internalization on the part of each partner; a deep response from the archetypal layers of each personality to the conscious and unconscious presence of the other; and an opening up in both persons to the realm of fantasy and to symbolic statements from the unconscious. When the conscious personality of each integrates around a new symbol and forms a new pattern for canalizations of libido, Jung spoke of transformation.

What Jung discovered through decades of analytical work was a deep-going, often largely unconscious, transformational process, symbolized in the unconscious productions of both analyst and analysand and affecting them both. Like individuation, it aimed at wholeness. The ultimate goal of this process was portrayed by images like the quaternity and the circle. Jung concluded that the many psychological transformations an individual undergoes throughout a lifetime, outside of analysis as well as within, were ultimately guided by the psyche's search for completeness. The psyche travels toward wholeness, and the task of the therapist is to assist it on this course.

It is this "higher psychotherapy" (1966b, p. 178) of transformation that Jung sought to effect for Christianity. This is what distinguished him from Christian revitalists who seek simply to rejuvenate tradition and ancient truth; from the scientific students of Christianity, who wish only to analyze it or to compare it with other traditions; from the apologists, who look for new and modern ways to defend it; and from the subverters, who want to cast it aside or to replace it with a wholly new religion. The account of how Jung went about practicing this high psychotherapy on Christianity, however, awaits the following chapters.

Chapter 3   **ON THE
RELATIONSHIP
BETWEEN
THIS DOCTOR
AND PATIENT**

Aniela Jaffé, who was intimately acquainted with Jung during the last decades of his life, wrote in her introduction to his autobiography:

> Jung explicitly declared his allegiance to Christianity, and the most important of his works deal with the religious problem of the Christian. He looked at these questions from the standpoint of psychology, deliberately setting a bound between it and the theological approach. (1961a, p. xi)

At the same time, however, Jaffé stated that from "the viewpoint of dogmatic Christianity, Jung was distinctly an 'outsider'" (ibid., p. x). This neatly summarizes Jung's ambiguous stance toward his religious tradition. He was born into it and indelibly marked by it. He felt great concern for its present and future and for its devoted members. And yet he was an outsider to its dogma and practice.

This is only the barest descriptive surface of Jung's complex relationship to his Christian background, however. The special intricacies of this relationship and of what went into creating it have never been explored in detail, nor has this biographical dimension ever been carefully related to Jung's writings on Christianity. His interpreters have by and large been content to discuss Jungian psychological theory and its applications to Christian themes apart, abstracted from this biographical context. The glaring lack of attention to this personal factor has left obscure the spirit and intention behind Jung's massive labors on Christian themes. It is quite clear that these writings arose, at least in part, out of very personal motivations, and these need to be examined in order to appreciate fully the meaning of these works.

This chapter is biographical, and in it I explore the linkages between Jung's life and his written works on Christianity. My aim here is to show that Jung's attitude toward Christianity included, as I mentioned before, a profound wish to heal it, and that his relationship to Christianity turned out to be that of a therapist to a patient. How Jung came to assume this position toward his religious heritage is the basic question I deal with here.

CHILDHOOD AND YOUTH (1875–95)

As depicted in his autobiography, Carl Jung's was an unsettling and darkly brooding childhood. Spent in large and poorly furnished manses, largely without the company of siblings or playmates, he was in the care of a mother who seemed to have two different personalities, a conventional "day-personality" and an uncanny "night-personality" (1961a, pp. 48–49). His father, a minister, he observed as reliable but powerless and unable to help him overcome his childhood terrors and somatic symptoms (ibid., p. 8) or the deep emotional disturbances rumbling through the household. Many of his childhood fears and traumas can be traced directly to "the atmosphere of the house" (ibid., p. 19), which made living there nearly "unbreatheable" for him. During a period of time around the age of six, he suffered from severe nightmares and choking fits (ibid.). D. W. Winnicott, in reviewing Jung's memoirs, ventured a diagnosis of childhood schizophrenia.

Thus, Jung's portrait of his childhood indicates emotional turmoil and conflict, and Christianity and its representatives played central roles in it. These figures were taken up in the child's logic and worked into his earliest mental organization of the world. The pattern of the thought-world he created then can be seen in his lifelong ambivalence toward Christianity, its doctrines, its official representatives, and its symbols.

Jung's early thoughts about religion and religious questions, as reported in his memoirs, seem precocious today, but these were hatched in the context of family life in the *Pfarrus*, which Brome refers to as "one of the germinal cells of German culture" (1978, p. 28). In Jung's case, the pastor's house was perhaps more than usually occupied by the influence and presence of the Swiss Protestant church. On his mother's side, there were six uncles who were parsons and a famous parson grandfather, Samuel Preiswerk (1799–1871), who had been *Antistes* of Basel, a position roughly equivalent to that of an English bishop (Hannah 1976, p. 21). (This gentleman, whom Jung of course never knew but who was the subject of many stories in the family and beyond, was said to have engaged in the extraordinary practice of consulting weekly with the spirit of his deceased first wife, in the presence of his understandably jealous and resentful second wife, Jung's grandmother [Brome 1978, p. 24].) On his father's side, there were two more parson uncles, so as far as the child's eye could see, there were staunch representatives of the Swiss Protestant church.

Before Jung turned five, a series of images and experiences came together that set the stage for his profound and lifelong ambivalence toward many elements of Christianity. This nexus of emotionally charged material—the basis for what could be called Jung's "Christianity complex"—was made of images of pious church elders in black coats burying corpses of children, of a threatening Jesuit in black dress, and of references to a Lord Jesus who, the child heard, liked to steal children from their homes while they slept. Then there were the eight parson uncles, most of whom inspired fear in the boy, and a frightful dream of an underground phallus called the "man-eater," which had strong associations with his parson father (1961a, pp. 6-23). All of this contributed to the deep sense of distrust and uneasiness the boy felt "whenever anyone spoke too emphatically about Lord Jesus" (ibid., p. 13). The church and religion, and the figures who represented them as well, had a dark side that was dangerous to the unwary. To this network of early associations Jung would much later attribute his instinctive sense of God's dark side, a subject he addressed in many of his writings on Christian themes and in numerous letters to Christian clergy.

Beside this early suspicion of "Lord Jesus" and sense of God's dark side, at the center of his Christianity complex, stood Jung's own father. Jung's memory of him formed the second major factor that colored much of his thinking and feeling about Christianity. Johann Paul Achilles Jung (1842-96) was a pastor in the Swiss Reformed church. The youngest son of a famous and widely admired Basel professor of medicine, Carl Gustav Jung (1794-1864), Paul Jung studied theology and took a doctorate in Oriental languages at the famous German University in Gottingen. Thereafter he served pastorates in Keswil on Lake Constance, where Carl Jung was born in 1875; in Laufen, a village on the Rheinfalls near Schaffhausen some 50 miles north of Zurich on the Swiss-German border; and after 1879, until his death in 1896, in Kleinhuningen, near Basel, where he also filled the position of chaplain to the Freidmatt Mental Hospital. As Jung saw him from a later vantage point, his father was a weak man. After several glorious years in a renowned German university, he "lapsed into a sort of sentimental idealism and into reminiscences of his golden student days" (1961a, p. 91). Sadly, as his son saw it, his life had "come to a standstill at his graduation" (ibid., p. 95). After that, scholarship and professional ambition apparently left him, and while he performed the conventional role of pastor, doing "a great deal of good—far too much" (ibid., p. 91), his emotional and spiritual life had withered.

The issues that began with a weak father expanded into broader territory, for Jung's father was intimately associated in his mind with Christianity and the church. For Carl, his father's weakness and suffering could not be cleanly separated from his role as a pastor and from his commitment to living spiritually within the Swiss Protestant tradition. Jung held Christianity partly accountable for his father's plight. But he also held his father accountable for shirking the task of struggling with the great spiritual issues of the age, which his son would later take up: the conflicts between tradition and modernity and between science and religion. While Paul Jung suffered the spiritual plight of modern man dumbly and blindly, his son would take it on as a conscious problem in desperate need of resolution. So healing the spiritual sources of his father's suffering became, in a deep sense, Carl Jung's vocation. In old age Jung recounted the essential kernel of his memory of a father who had died some 60 years earlier, yet who lived vividly in his son's psyche:

> My memory of my father is of a sufferer stricken with an Amfortas wound, a 'fisher king' whose wound would not heal—that Christian suffering for which the alchemists sought the panacea. I as a "dumb" Parsifal was the witness of this sickness during the years of my boyhood, and, like Parsifal, speech failed me. I had only inklings. (1961a, p. 215)

His father's weakness reached Jung's consciousness during early adolescence, around the time of his confirmation, when the lad's struggles with Christian theology and doctrine reached a high pitch. At that time, Jung later wrote, he realized that "the church is a place I should not go to. It is not life which is there, but death. . . . All at once I understood the tragedy of his [i.e., his father's] profession and his life. He was struggling with a death whose existence he could not admit" (1961a, p. 55).

At about the same time, Jung had an experience that stayed with him throughout his life. In it the themes of God's dark side, his own

Swiss Protestant religious heritage, and his father's existential dilemma come together. He could recall it vividly even in old age.

Coming out of school at noon one day, he paused in the cathedral square of Basel and gazed at the scene around him. At the center of the square stood the city's impressive cathedral, which must have been associated in his mind with his maternal grandfather, Samuel Preiswerk, who as *Antistes* of Basel probably considered it his second home. In his memoirs Jung recalled that on that day

> the roof of the cathedral glittered, the sun sparkling from the new, brightly glazed tiles. I was overwhelmed by the beauty of the sight, and thought: "The world is beautiful and the church is beautiful, and God made all this and sits above it far away in the blue sky on a golden throne and . . . . " Here came a great hole in my thoughts, and a choking sensation. I felt numbed, and knew only: "Don't go on thinking now! Something terrible is coming, something I do not want to think . . . ." (1961a, p. 36)

Fearing he was about to commit a sin against the Holy Ghost, young Carl held the dreaded thought at bay. "I cannot do that to my parents," he fretted, imagining their disappointment and grief at his eternal damnation. His anguish continued for two days and nights. Who was creating this compulsion to think a blasphemous thought? Was it God? Was it the Devil? On the third night, after concluding that "it was God's intention" after all, he relaxed and completed the fantasy:

> I gathered all my courage . . . and let the thought come. I saw before me the cathedral, the blue sky. God sits on His golden throne, high above the world—and from under the throne an enormous turd falls upon the sparkling new roof, shatters it, and breaks the walls of the cathedral asunder. (1961a, p. 39)

The immediate aftermath of this scatalogical fantasy was the surprising experience of "grace": "grace had come upon me, and with it unutterable bliss such as I had never known. I wept for happiness and gratitude. The wisdom and goodness of God had been revealed to me now that I had yielded to His inexorable command" (1961a, p. 40). To Jung, this remained one of the key religious experiences of his life. One may read this fantasy as an anal struggle with his parents in which his own omnipotence wins, or as an expression of his unconscious anger at the church, or as a displacement of his father's anger, but the important fact is that Jung survived the devastation. When, in old age, he was led to interpret it more theologically than psychologically, it was with the understanding that personal emotional struggles have a far deeper underpinning and that they also reflect archetypal energy patterns. For Jung this fantasy became a symbol of God's displeasure with traditional Christianity: God was blasting His church, and Jung, like the Old Testament prophets, was privy to His Divine displeasure. Jung here came into contact with the angry God, omnipotent and free, and this vision would later give him the strength to launch his own critique on so massive a thing as the whole of the Christian theological tradition.

It was this experience of "the miracle of grace," the sense of God's immediate presence, and the power this gave to the individual, that Jung found so utterly lacking in his father. His father, he saw, "had taken the Bible's commandments as his guide; he believed in God as the Bible prescribed and as his forefathers had taught him. But he did not know the immediate living God who stands, omnipotent and free, above His Bible and His Church . . . " (1961a, p. 40). His father refused to examine his faith in the light of modern scientific thought or, for that matter, to seek a first-hand, less cerebral experience of the source of his spiritual life. Paul Jung's understanding of "faith" was an act of willful belief in traditional teachings, and in the end, Jung felt, "faith broke faith with him" (ibid., p. 215) and left him stranded on the shores of a spiritual wasteland, without resources for renewal. His father had seemingly never witnessed God's dark side and survived the terrible experience of such awesome destructiveness. This made his religion shallow.

Jung's fantasy, and his conviction that God had paradoxically made him have it, produced a sense of grace, but it also reinforced his early childhood sense of God's dark side. God might be omnipotent and free, but he was also destructive. In thoughts like this, one can find a strong invitation to reductive analysis. Following Winnicott (1964) and a Kleinian approach, Jung can be seen as struggling from childhood onwards with a psychological disorder that included a paranoid defense against a persecutory inner "bad object." This introject (a "bad breast," represented by destructive figures of various kinds, often religious in nature) threatened his inner stability and cohesion. He defended himself against it by putting it outside of himself, into a religious system and a figure like the angry God on His throne above Basel's cathedral. By transferring the threat to the level of theological fantasy and thought, his defenses were successful in housing it in an encasement of religious paranoia.

When goodness is overshadowed by destructiveness in the self, the structures of consciousness that were created on the assumption of continuing goodness (as symbolized by the Basel cathedral in Jung's fantasy) are vulnerable, and annihilation threatens. The 12-year-old Carl Jung survived the fantasy of destruction, and, in the experience of grace, a soothing inner object (the "good breast") returned. He was strong enough, therefore, to endure the annihilating attack, perhaps because his paranoid defenses were able to depotentiate it, and then to be able to work on integrating the good and bad sides of God into a single image.

This pattern would occur repeatedly in Jung's lifetime: A severe inner attack would threaten annihilation; this persecutory inner object would be defended against by the use of paranoid thoughts and fantasies, which would function to place it "out there"; the crisis would then be followed by an experience of relief and restoration; and the final step would be an attempt to integrate the good and bad sides of the self, often in a symbolic formulation (paintings of mandalas, concepts of God as *unio oppositorum*, psychological theories).

This sketch of the workings of Jung's inner world could be filled in further to cover many of the facts of his emotional life, but it falls short at a number of points, the chief of which is its inability to recognize the archetypal dimension upon which these personal dynamics rest and which they reflect. The archetypal analysis recognizes that Jung's particular personal psychic structures (as outlined above) were keyed into deeper dynamics and energy patterns in the collective unconscious. The "bad object" is not *simply* a residue from childhood or an introject. It represents an inherent aspect of the self. Jung's experiences of death and rebirth and of incarnating the dark side of the self are based on universal patterns, which were actually paralleled in the culture and religion of his times. Many individuals pass through similar experiences, but fail to see them as clearly, or as psychologically, as Jung did. This pattern rests, then, on an archetypal substratum. So what are taken as paranoid defenses in the reductive analysis are here recognized as perceptions of a deeper level; Jung *was* witnessing the destructiveness of God in his experience of the dark side of the self, and he was attempting to integrate this vision into his thinking about Christianity.

The viewpoint that God could be destructive and want to incarnate His dark side was not much contemplated among Jung's ministerial relatives. The boy felt, too, he could not share his thoughts and fantasies with his father, because his father "would be obliged to reply out of respect for his office" (1961a, p. 52) and therefore would be of no help. So keen was his conviction that he had seen the back side of God, a deeply hidden, unacknowledged side of the One who was honored and praised in the cathedral, that church became "a place of torment" for him:

> For there men dared to preach aloud—I am tempted to say, shameless-ly—about God, about His intentions and actions. There people were exhorted to have those feelings and to *believe* that secret which I *knew* to be the deepest, innermost certainty, a certainty not to be betrayed by a single word. I could only conclude that apparently no one knew about this secret, not even the parson, for otherwise no one would have dared to expose the mystery of God in public and to profane those inexpres-sible feelings with stale sentimentalities. (1961a, p. 45-46)

When the time came for Jung to take his first communion, its banality was what struck him most forcefully. His verdict was that "it did not compare at all with secular festivals" (1961a, p. 54). Mostly old men were present, "stiff, solemn, and, it seemed to me, uninterested" (ibid.). The ceremony was traditional and correct, the bread poor in quality, the wine thin and sour. In the days following this event, it gradually dawned on the boy that "nothing at all had happened" (ibid.). What got confirmed was the boy's feeling that the church was a place of death, which in turn caused him to be seized with the "most vehe-ment pity for [his] father" (ibid., p. 55), giving Jung his first deep glimpse into what he called his father's "Amfortas wound."

Jung's sense of pity for his father should not be underestimated in considering the nature of his own ultimate relationship to Christianity. While his own confirmation experience convinced him that he was outside the Christian religion (1961a, p. 56), he nonetheless felt empathy for those who, like his father, could not afford to face their inner truths and be plunged "into that despair and sacrilege which were necessary for an experience of divine grace" (ibid., p. 55). As he later came to understand his early experiences, the cathedral fantasy had taught him that even as faith had broken faith with his father, so "God Himself had disavowed theology and the Church founded upon it" (ibid., p. 93). His father's desperate situation, therefore, reflected microcosmically the whole Christian Church's situation: Both had been repudiated by God and left stranded on dry shores without spiritual resources.

Jung later analyzed his father's predicament from another, more cognitive, angle. Here the major issue centered on Paul Jung's refusal to deal with the conflict between the claims of tradition and modernity. As his son saw it, not only had he failed to taste the fruit of primary religious experience, but he had also shirked the intellectual struggle generated in his time by the claims of modern thought. He had instead sought refuge in traditional doctrine and institutional attitudes. In order to do this, however, he had had to commit a *sacrificium intellectus*, and this, combined with his lack of primary religious experience, had produced his sadly crippled existence. What the adult Jung saw in his broken father, then, was the tragedy of a man trying to cling to the sinking vessel of traditional Christian attitudes in the swift and forceful currents of modernity.

According to his memoirs, Jung's intellectual struggle with Christianity and its doctrines began around the time of his confirmation (and, with some minor variations in theme and some interludes, continued throughout the rest of his life). Some of the themes noted in his adolescent period had origins earlier in childhood, however, and many of them were again taken up on more sophisticated levels later in life. The 13-year-old boy, for example, sought to understand the Trinity during his confirmation lessons and asked his father to introduce him to the meaning of this mystery, but all he got in response were dogmatic formulas or a shrug of the shoulders. Much later he would write an extensive essay on the doctrine of God as Trinity.

Because his father offered so little help, Carl resorted to reading. In the home's small library he found Biedermann's *Christliche Dogmatik*. This work engaged his intellect, but it offended his sense of truthfulness because the author asserted things about God's character (that He was all "good") and about His self-sufficiency (that He needed nothing outside of Himself for His Divine "satisfaction") that rang false. Nothing Biedermann said about God corresponded to Jung's own youthful experience of God's dark side, and so this theologian's exposition of Christian doctrine could not, to Jung's mind, account for the existence of evil in the world. If God was all good, why was there so much evil? So Jung concluded that this "weighty tome on dogmatics was nothing but fancy drivel; worse still, it was a fraud or a specimen of uncommon stupidity whose sole aim was to obscure the truth. I was disillusioned and even indignant, and once more seized with pity for my father, who had fallen victim to this mumbo-jumbo" (1961a, p. 59).

From a later vantage point, Jung assigned his adolescent preoccupation with religion and God's nature to his "personality No. 2" (1961a, p. 63). This personality was characterized by feelings of immortality and eternity, by a sense of immense old age and wisdom, and by a passion for fundamental truths about humankind and the cosmos. It had been a core part of him since earliest childhood. So when he left Biedermann and the theologians and turned to the philosophers in his father's library, he was looking for fellow "lovers of wisdom" who shared this perspective. But the philosophers he read proved even less satisfactory than the theologians, and gradually he realized that all of these delvings into religion and philosophy were only leading him increasingly into a state of chronic depression. He felt isolated by his own experiences, because he found no confirmation of them in his circle of relatives and acquaintances or in the works of intellectuals. And yet "it never occurred to me", he wrote, "that I might be crazy, for the light and darkness of God seemed to me facts that could be understood even though they oppressed my feelings" (ibid.).

After his fifteenth or sixteenth year, Jung's interests shifted away from religion and Christian theology to other areas, and by his nineteenth year the natural sciences and some pagan philosophers like Pythagoras, Heraclitus, and Plato had taken priority over Christian theology and philosophy. The depressions waned as Jung worked himself free of his father and Christianity, and he looked forward to pursuing his new interests at the University of Basel.

UNIVERSITY YEARS AND
EARLY PROFESSIONAL LIFE (1895–1907)

When it came time to enroll in the University and to decide on a course of study, Jung's father attempted to initiate "serious talks." Each time the pastor's advice was: "Be anything you like except a theologian" (1961a, p. 75). He was warning his son away from the pitfall in his own life. He had already allowed his son to lapse from church attendance, and for his part young Carl was only too glad to stay away. He missed nothing of it except the organ and choral music. Church-goers he disliked especially.

At the time of Jung's entry into the University of Basel, the picture one would have had of this freshman would have been of a youth more or less completely alienated from Christianity and from the church of his Swiss Protestant family and forebears. And yet he carried into university life, under a seemingly indifferent mask, the spiritual problems that his father and his father's religion had raised so acutely in his earlier years. Looking back in old age on his first 21 years, Jung perceived a direct relationship between his own youthful religious experiences and struggles and the difficulties his father was having at that time with his Christian faith. "Children react much less to what grown-ups say than to the imponderables in the surrounding atmosphere," he reflected.

> The peculiar "religious" ideas that came to me even in earliest childhood were spontaneous products which can be understood only as reactions to my parental environment and to the spirit of the age. The religious doubts to which my father was later to succumb naturally had to pass through a long period of incubation. Such a revolution of one's world, and of the world in general, threw its shadows ahead, and the shadows were all the longer, the more desperately my father's conscious mind resisted their power. (1961a, p. 90)

Jung understood himself to have been caught up in his father's personal crisis of faith, and it was only his close association with his "personality No. 2" and with the God above the cathedral that allowed him to refrain from jettisoning religion altogether. Jung later came to understand his early religious experiences as a compensatory reaction from the unconscious that suggested an answer to the spiritual dilemmas faced by his father and others who were falling victim to the religious crisis of modernity.

Jung's mother was not an explicit player in the conflict between traditional religious belief and modernity because she was not, Jung felt, as singularly committed to Christian conventionalism as his father was:

> . . . she was somehow rooted in deep, invisible ground . . . connected with animals, trees, mountains, meadows, and running water, all of which contrasted most strangely with her Christian surface and her conventional assertions of faith. . . . It never occurred to me how "pagan" this foundation was. My mother's "No. 2" offered me the strongest support in the conflict then beginning between paternal tradition and the strange, compensatory products which my unconscious had been stimulated to create. (1961a, pp. 90–91)

In the drama of Jung's struggle with Christianity, his mother appears as a dramatis persona who was supportive of his reliance on "nature" and the unconscious but did not make a substantial contribution to his investment in the Christian tradition. In clear focus at center stage, however, was the figure of his father—a man who had succumbed spiritually and physically to his and the age's crisis of faith.

Paul Jung's death in 1896, when Carl was 21 years old and still a student at the university, became a kind of paradigmatic event. In Jung's later view, his father's early death was directly attributable to religious conflicts and to the crisis in Western religion and culture. Only in long retrospect, though, did Jung come to this final understanding of his father's suffering and its meaning, for at the time of the event, he knew only that there was a deep cleavage between himself and his father.

During the last years of his father's life, Jung found him irritable and short tempered, a symptom he later ascribed to the pastor's trying to do too much good for others and trying too hard to live a pious life. Carl had kept raising troublesome questions about Christian belief, which his father was at a loss to answer adequately for either of them. Sensing something deeply amiss in his father, Carl eventually surmised that he was suffering from "religious doubts" (1961a, p. 92). Observing his father's suffering, as a Parsifal to an Amfortas, he stood helplessly by and watched the agony unfold. He could not speak the healing words, since his own experiences of God's dark side and of His grace were taboo:

> This was a great secret which I dared not and could not reveal to my father. I might have been able to reveal it had he been capable of understanding the direct experience of God. But in my talks with him I never got that far, never even came within sight of the problem, because I always set about it in a very unpsychological and intellectual way, and did everything to avoid the emotional aspects. (1961a, p. 93)

Finally their discussions about religion broke down altogether, and Jung concluded that "theology had alienated my father and me from one another" (ibid., p. 93). His father was entrapped in the church's thoughts about God, and consequently he could not allow himself to experience God directly. The church was at fault, too, because its theology had blocked the way to God. "Now I understood the deepest meaning of my earlier experience," Jung wrote, referring to the cathedral-breaking fantasy; "God Himself had disavowed theology and the Church founded upon it" (ibid., p. 93). "Theological religion," as Jung called it, was hollow, the shell of a dead tradition, and it was largely responsible for his father's pitiful condition and early demise.

What further horrified Jung was the direction his father's search for help took during his final years. Instead of going to the source of his religion for answers to his doubts, he turned to "the ridiculous materialism of the psychiatrists"! Paul Jung was reading Sigmund Freud's translation of Bernheim's work on hypnotism, *Die Suggestion und ihre*

Heilwirkung. As chaplain to the Friedmatt Mental Hospital, Pastor Jung was apparently falling under the influence of psychiatry. In looking to psychiatry for answers to his religious questions, the father was leaping from frying pan into fire, for psychiatry, in his son's opinion at least, was one of the ultimate statements of the anti-religious, materialistic attitude of modernity. At most, it could soothe the surface of consciousness, but fundamentally its attitude toward religious questions would be anathema to the religious spirit. In despair over faith, Paul Jung was looking, unknowingly and ironically, for assistance to the very forces that had helped to create his crisis of faith.

When Pastor Jung began complaining of a sensation of having "stones in the abdomen," the doctors became worried. Within months he was a complete invalid, and it was a severe blow to his self-esteem that now "Carl had to carry him round like a heap of bones for an anatomy class" (Oeri 1970, p. 185). While the medical diagnosis remained uncertain, it quickly became clear that Paul Jung was fading rapidly.

Jung was at his father's bedside when he died. His detached clinical observation of the scene bespeaks emotional withdrawal on his part, perhaps a defense against the feelings evoked by this ending to his father's ill-fated existence: "There was a rattling in his throat, and I could see that he was in the death agony. I stood by his bed, fascinated. I had never seen anyone die before. Suddenly he stopped breathing. I waited and waited for the next breath. It did not come" (1961a, p. 96). From now on Jung would contend with his father and with the source of his father's illness only in the spirit and in dreams.

The death of his father caused the location of Jung's argument with Christianity simply to become transferred from his father to other representatives of the Christian tradition. During his student years, heated and "provocative" (Brome 1978, p. 64) discussions with theological students at the university were not unusual for him. It was not only traditionalists who raised an argument from him, for proponents of various modern Protestant theological viewpoints in Basel during this period (when Ritschel was popular) did also. In all of these representatives of Christianity—including his father's vicar, an erudite church historian and theologian—Jung missed the sense of a first-hand experience of God. To him, their words were all abstract theologizing; no one spoke of actual religious experiences. Like his father, all of them were trying to solve with mere words the fundamental problems of religion in modernity. To Jung this was more than wrongheaded: It was cowardly and dishonest (cf. 1961a, pp. 97-98).

For Jung the primacy of personal experience in religious life and thought cannot be overemphasized. So much is this the central theme of his writings on religion generally that one wonders if Jung was handicapped in his capacity for understanding abstract theological thought, as he apparently was in his ability to grasp mathematical ideas (Oeri 1970, pp. 185ff.). It is surprising to find this in someone so gifted at psychological theorizing, but then it has been observed that much in Jung's psychological theory was directly related to, and even derived from, his own experience of dream and fantasy figures. His theory rarely became abstract in a mathematical or philosophical sense, except when he attempted to discuss libido in terms analogous to modern physics or when he used statistics to demonstrate synchronicity. With respect to religion and theology, this bias toward the concrete experience was even stronger. If the theologian would only back up his words and concepts with references to first-hand experience of the reality to which his words were pointing, then Jung would have been inclined to pay careful attention. But he rarely found theologians of this sort, except in ancient texts. For the most part, he showed a kind of peasantlike wariness of theologians' words, sensing an intellectual con game being played with all the fancy terminology.

E. A. Bennet told of a conversation with Jung in the summer of 1947, indicating that Jung carried this same attitude through into old age:

> [Jung] told me of a student who asked his professor, "How do you know there is a God?" The professor had no answer and came and asked Jung! This man [the professor] is a great preacher, yet it's all words, no real knowledge. C. G. Jung said, "I would have loved that question—there you have a student who can learn something." (Bennet 1982, p. 19)

This student's blunt question is the kind Jung himself would have used to challenge the theologians, as to some extent he did during his university days when already he held "the ambiguous relationship" to theological students and professors "that he was to have later with many religious ministers" (Ellenberger 1970, p. 688). Rooted in his own early religious experiences, on the other hand, Jung apparently never felt strongly tempted to join the side of the scientific materialists. His father had been more vulnerable to this temptation because of the religious doubts that grew out of his appropriation of traditional "faith," but for Carl this siren did not sing.

About the time Jung entered the university, his personality seems to have gone through a metamorphosis. From the rather reclusive, introverted youth there emerged a much more extraverted, gregarious and aggressive young man. So much was he this new person that he often managed to dominate student discussions, to the point of generating dislike and opposition among fellow students. But he was also popular and was elected president of the Zofingia Student Association, a debating and beer-drinking fraternity, where his nickname was "the barrel." In student debates Jung seemed to delight in a good fight, particularly with those whom he perceived to be captives of a narrow-minded, materialistic kind of scientism. Ellenberger and Brome both remark on the striking continuities between Jung's positions in these student discussions and his later psychological theories. Especially striking, according to his friend Gustav Steiner, was Jung's "'absolute conviction when speaking of the *soul* . . . as immaterial, transcendent, outside of time and space—*and yet to be approached scientifically*" (quoted in Brome 1978, p. 65 [italics in original]).

During these years, too, Jung continued to develop an early interest in spiritualism. For this he found little support among his university colleagues, but his mother and some relatives sympathized wholeheartedly (cf. Zumstein-Preiswerk 1975, pp. 53ff). Seances were conducted in his home with his mother and sister present, as well as several cousins, among them young Helene Preiswerk, who would become the subject of his doctoral dissertation. This interest in spiritualism, which Brome feels Jung indulged without his usual skepticism and critical thinking, corresponded to his mother's "Personality No. 2," which Jung considered to be a "natural mind" and more "pagan" than Christian (Jung 1961a, p. 50). (From this side of his mother, too, had come the suggestion, while he had been struggling in his adolescence to understand the dark side of God, that he read Goethe's *Faust*.) The primitive-mindedness and peasantlike attitude exemplified by his mother's second personality Jung would find restoring and congenial throughout his life, partly because this offered him a possible avenue beyond the conflict between tradition and modernity which had spiritually crippled his father.

Jung's program for studying the "soul" scientifically, and for doing so without falling into the bias of nineteenth-century science's materialistic assumptions, was carried a step forward in his first major work, his doctoral dissertation written at Burghölzli Klinik under Eugen Bleuler's direction. It was a study of a young medium, his cousin Helly Preiswerk, and of a number of seances conducted in her presence. As Brome points out, this work shows more sophistication than seen in

Jung's earlier university papers. During the years between the college debates and this investigation, Jung had adopted a much more skeptical and psychological attitude toward spiritualism and its practitioners. By the time of this study's completion in 1902, he had absorbed two years of intense psychiatric training and had become aware of the many possible psychopathological underpinnings and contaminations in spiritualism and occult practice. In this study of mediumship, he did not accept evidence of spirits and their transpersonal knowledge at face value but subjected these "voices" and spiritualistic phenomena to skeptical psychological and scientific scrutiny. It was the psychiatrist, not the believer, who was the author of this work. What Jung did not realize, however, was the powerful effect of Helly's romantic feelings toward him and her strong wish to please him by producing "effects" (cf. Zumstein-Preiswerk 1975, passim).

Jung still left the door ajar in this work to the possibility that even a sophisticated, psychologically oriented science could not rationally explain away all spiritualistic or parapsychological phenomena. Possibly he was inclined to leave this door open because of a personal predisposition to believe in the objective existence of spirits and souls, which kept him close to his own childhood and to his No. 2 personality, as well as to many of his mother's attitudes. His argument for not closing this door, however, was that science should not in principle ban any hypothesis from consideration; it should rather weigh evidence, collect facts, and consider all possible explanations. Jung wanted to keep modern science open enough to explore the psyche without prejudice and to probe areas of human experience that had always heretofore been accepted (or written off) as religious or mystical.

THE FREUDIAN YEARS (1907–12)

When Jung first met Freud in 1907, he still held these methodological convictions strongly, and they became a point of difference, subtle at first but ultimately very important, between the young psychiatrist of Swiss Protestant stock and the Jewish founder of the new psychoanalytic science.

From the earliest years of their association, Freud was troubled by Jung's "mysticism," much as Jung was disturbed by Freud's "materialistic rationalism." In 1909 these differences came into the open during an extensive discussion on parapsychology held in Freud's apartment. While the two men were talking, a cupboard in the apartment unexpectedly cracked with a loud report. Jung called it a "catalytic exterior-ization phenomenon"; Freud called his explanation "sheer bosh." Jung predicted that it would happen again, and a moment later there was another loud report. Freud was perplexed, but by this point the two men had reached an intellectual impasse (Jung 1961a, p. 155). Jung noted Freud's deep aversion to anything "occult" with increasing dis-may, for to him this meant that, as a science, psychoanalysis would not be in a position to investigate the soul without the old rationalistic and materialistic prejudices.

These intellectual and attitudinal differences between Jung and Freud were transposed into another key as well. Almost immediately they became assimilated to a perceived contrast between Jews and Chris-tians. As early as 1908, Freud took Jung's tendencies to accept the idea of non-material causes of material events and to balk at purely reductive interpretations of emotional and mental events as a legacy of his Chris-tian background. In a letter to Karl Abraham written July 20, 1908, Freud attempted to soften a quarrel Abraham was having with Jung by explaining that "on the whole it is easier for us Jews [to accept the psychoanalytic viewpoint] as we lack the mystical element" (quoted in Brome 1978, p. 107). He advised Abraham to understand this disadvan-tage of Jung's and to make allowances for it. So even though Jung was soon to be openly designated by Freud as a "favorite son" and an heir apparent in the psychoanalytic movement, Freud privately found trou-blesome these "Christian" proclivities of Jung's.

Freud said this, but very softly, in a letter to Jung on November 12, 1911, just a little more than a year before their final break. Com-menting on the first part of Jung's *Transformations and Symbols of the Libido*, he wrote:

> The reading for my psychology of religion [i.e., *Totem and Taboo*] is going slowly. One of the nicest works I have read (again), is that of a well-known author on the "Transformations and Symbols of the Libi-do." In it many things are so well-expressed that they seem to have taken on definitive form and in this form impress themselves on the memory. Sometimes I have a feeling that *his horizon has been too nar-rowed by Christianity*. And sometimes he seems to be more above the material than in it. But it is the best thing this promising author has written, up to now, though he will do still better. (McGuire 1974, p. 459; italics added)

Freud's tone in these comments is curious, unusually indirect and somewhat ironic. Jung's work was anything but "well-expressed" or "definitive." It was brilliant, but, as the author himself knew only too well, it was also chaotic. It "was written at top speed, amid the rush and press of my medical practice, without regard to time or method. I had to fling my material hastily together, just as I found it," Jung wrote later about this early work (1950, p. xxiii). Freud's avuncular tone of generosity and support, laced with irony that derived from his deep misgivings about Jung's thinking, was an attempt to cover the fundamental difference between his and Jung's attitudes toward the unconscious and its contents. And this difference, in both of their minds, reflected a difference between Jews and Christians. This way of framing their differences must have seemed natural for both men, for both would carry it forward into their later acrimony.

In his ill-timed, but nevertheless delicately balanced and subtly ironic, comments of 1934 in the *Zentralblatt für Psychotherapie*, Jung wrote, as though still in reply to Freud's letter of 1911:

> The Jewish race as a whole—at least this is my experience—possesses an unconscious which can be compared with the "Aryan" only with reserve. Creative individuals apart, the average Jew is far too conscious and differentiated to go about pregnant with the tensions of unborn futures. The "Aryan" unconscious has a higher potential than the Jewish; that is both the advantage and the disadvantage of a youthfulness not yet fully weaned from barbarism. In my opinion it has been a grave error in medical psychology up till now to apply Jewish categories— which are not even binding on all Jews—indiscriminately to Germanic and Slavic Christendom. Because of this the most precious secret of the Germanic peoples—their creative and intuitive depth of soul—has been explained as a morass of banal infantilism, while my own warning voice has for decades been suspected of anti-Semitism. This suspicion emanated from Freud. He did not understand the Germanic psyche any more than did his Germanic followers. (Jung 1964, p. 166)

At first this reads a bit like bombastic Aryanism, but closer inspection reveals quite the opposite. To say that the "Aryan unconscious has a higher potential than the Jewish" was not a compliment to the Aryans; rather it meant that their consciousness and their culture were more primitive. Aryan consciousness and culture had not yet made its way out of barbarism, and this was both a drawback and a potential strength. After disclaiming the accusation of anti-Semitism, an imputation incidentally that would have rung favorably in the ears of the German authorities of the time, Jung makes his statement that Freud was to blame for this misapprehension. To say that it was Freud who had planted and nurtured the rumor that Jung was anti-Semitic seems, in this context, to be a double irony, as though Jung were saying to the Nazi anti-Semites: It was a Jew who said I'm on your side, but I'm not! At one stroke Jung repudiated both Freud and German anti-Semitism. What he *was* saying, positively, had to do with an old and familiar theme: The soul should not be reduced to purely instinctual or materialistic sources but should be studied without bias or prejudice and allowed to reveal its nature in a positive, therapeutic climate of acceptance.

Behind Freud's very early aversion to Jung's mysticism there may well have lurked his suspicion that it hid a latent anti-Semitism. Eventually mysticism would become Christian zeal, and pogroms, crusades, and missionaries would not be far behind. Unfortunately, as both men discovered, the Christian/Jewish cultural differentiation could be used for many purposes, not all of them in the interests of pure science, and Freud was not above using it to discredit Jung's thought, as Jung was obviously not altogether above using it to discredit Freud's.

What Freud had identified as Jung's mysticism, however, was not at all what Jung himself would have attributed to the influence of Christianity. This mystical trend grew out of his (and his mother's) personality No. 2, which was more pagan than Christian. It was rooted not in Christianity but, if anywhere culturally, in Germanic paganism, a nature religion. The Christian side, on the other hand, Jung identified with his father and his uncles, and it was anything *but* mystical. To Jung it was characterized by cold, formal adherence to doctrine and by the absence of religious feeling or personal appropriation of religious symbolic reality. In many ways Protestant Christianity was, in Jung's mind, closer to Freud's attitude—dogmatic, rationalistic, and narrow minded.

The fortuitous resemblance between the architecture of Jung's father complex and Freud's attitudes became a source of endless misunderstandings between the two. From their correspondence and from a number of Jung's comments elsewhere, it is plain that Jung experienced Freud through the effects of a strongly constellated father transference, which created intense emotional and empathic reactions as well as distortions on his part and filled him with ambivalent feelings toward his mentor. He could always appreciate Freud's genius and objective stature, but in time he came to see him predominantly as he had his own father, a weak and almost pathetic victim of his own psychology and cultural heritage.

Jung's relationship to Freud and to psychoanalysis, and its outcome, betray the same pattern we find in his relationship to his father and to Christianity. Jung repeated with Freud what he had done with his father. The strong ambivalence that arose within the context of his childhood toward the heavily Swiss Protestant Jung family and their religious tradition arose again when he entered into a similar situation of intense involvement with Freud's "family," the psychoanalytic movement. At the center are the two father figures, Paul Jung and Sigmund Freud. Moreover, both of these "family involvements" concluded with Jung's taking a therapeutic position toward the father figure. Both situations, then, share the features of (a) Jung's unwillingness (or inability) to identify completely with the father of the family, (b) his attempts to stave off the father's influence and to highlight his shortcomings, and, finally (c) his urgently felt impulse to heal the father's illness and to therapeutize his family's tradition.

Jung's transference to Freud began quickly and intensely. On October 28, 1907, some eight months after their first encounter in Vienna and a few weeks after receiving a handsome photograph from Freud, Jung confessed that he was experiencing a troublesome emotional reaction: "I have a boundless admiration for you both as a man and a researcher," he wrote, and then tried to explain why he had delayed responding to Freud's previous letters. (Throughout their correspondence, Jung's delays were understood as signals of ambivalence.) "I bear you no conscious grudge," he continued, acknowledging what Freud had called his "self-preservation complex" (Freud's relevant letters are missing) and trying to locate its source and meaning in his psychology. "It is rather that my veneration for you has something of the character of a 'religious' crush. Though it does not really bother me, I still feel it is disgusting and ridiculous because of its undeniable erotic undertone." Finally Jung tried to explain the genesis of the discomfort he was experiencing toward Freud: "This abominable feeling comes from the fact that as a boy I was the victim of a sexual assault by a man I once worshiped. . . . *I therefore fear your confidence.* I also fear the same reaction from you when I speak of my intimate affairs" (McGuire 1974, p. 95).

The molestation incident in childhood to which Jung alluded has not been uncovered by his biographers. Worthy of special interest is Jung's use of the phrase "religious crush" to describe his feelings for Freud. The religious element harks back to childhood, to father, and to the boy's earliest longings for and fear of religious forces. Jung would later use Rudolf Otto's term "numinous" to refer to this type of feeling and to the experience of the holy. Like the underground phallus ("the maneater") in Jung's early childhood dream and like the angry God enthroned above Basel's cathedral, Freud was "numinous" and therefore evoked religious awe and fear, an ambivalent reaction to a highly valued, dangerous, and power-filled being. The erotic element in Jung's feelings may have represented a desire to merge with Freud, who was an "idealized object," and thereby to gain similar stature and value for himself (cf. Homans 1979).

In a subtle and deftly precise way, Jung's religious awe of Freud must have played on Freud's view of himself as the founder of a new era in human consciousness and have provoked dogmatic, almost Moses-like, pronouncements from him. In his memoirs, Jung recalled a particularly critical scene, one of several, when Freud spoke authoritatively about absolute guidelines to his "eldest son . . . anointed . . . as my successor and crown prince" (McGuire 1974, p. 218). The part that Freud played in this scene must have resonated deeply with Jung's experience of dogmatic religion in his childhood:

> I can still recall vividly how Freud said to me, "My dear Jung, promise me never to abandon the sexual theory. That is the most essential thing of all. You see, we must make a *dogma* of it, an unshakable bulwark." He said that to me with great emotion, in the tone of a father saying, "And promise me this one thing, my dear son: that you will go to church every Sunday." In some astonishment I asked him, "A bulwark—against what?" To which he replied, "Against the black tide of mud"—and here he hesitated for a moment, then added—"of occultism." First of all, it was the words "bulwark" and "dogma" that alarmed me; for a dogma, that is to say, an undisputable confession of faith, is set up only when the aim is to suppress doubts once and for all. But that no longer has anything to do with scientific judgment; only with a personal power drive.
>
> . . . I knew that I would never be able to accept such an attitude. What Freud seemed to mean by "occultism" was virtually everything that philosophy and religion, including the rising contemporary science of parapsychology, had learned about the psyche. . . .
>
> Although I did not properly understand it then, I had observed in Freud the eruption of unconscious religious factors. Evidently he wanted my aid in erecting a barrier against these threatening unconscious contents. (1961a, pp. 150–51)

Incidents like this reversed Jung's evaluation of Freud. From the powerful godlike figure he had been—the object of a "religious crush"—

he turned into the defensive protector of a belief system that was being threatened by modern science. While Freud was playing the role of lawgiver, Jung was responding to a frightened father figure in need of help to keep his religious doubts in check. With Freud, as with his own father, Jung came to feel called upon to speak the healing words of a Parsifal to an ailing Amfortas.

In an illuminating analysis of the Jung-Freud relationship, Alexander points out that it was precisely what Jung found intolerable in his father that he ultimately also found intolerable in Freud: Both relied on dogma, and both required their sons to believe and have "faith" rather than to understand. As the founder of psychoanalysis, Freud had become a Mosaic, oedipal father. Out of his need to make up for *his* father's weakness and deficits, Freud was driven to strive for achievement and success and to identify with heroic figures such as Hannibal, Alexander the Great, and ultimately Moses (Alexander 1982, pp. 1010-11). Freud felt, moreover, that Jung held an unconscious death wish toward him as a father figure because he was heroic and successful, while Jung felt that Freud was an authoritarian and dogmatic father who could not tolerate deviations from his sons. Both of them operated on so many distorted perceptions of the other that their final break seems, in retrospect, more or less inevitable.

Jung's training in psychoanalysis, meanwhile, had made him acutely aware of his father-burdened, projection-laden attitude toward Freud. Joseph Henderson (1982) has expressed the view that it was Jung's awareness of this psychological situation that led him to hold back emotionally from Freud. According to Henderson, Jung recognized his strong inclination to succumb even more deeply to the transference and, fearing it, deliberately shielded himself from Freud's importuning rather than yield to his frequent overtures for more intimacy. Jung's delays in responding to Freud's letters and his persistent greeting throughout the correspondence to Freud as "Professor" can be seen as efforts to maintain distance.

Jung's transference to Freud did awaken his awareness of the importance of the father imago, and in 1909 he published a small paper on this subject in the *Jahrbuch für psychoanalytische und psychopathologische Forschungen*, in the first issue of this Freudian journal, entitled "The Significance of the Father in the Destiny of the Individual." This paper made the basic psychoanalytic point, illustrated by case material from patients, that a person's family milieu has lifelong determinative effects on character structure and emotional patterning, as well as on lifestyle and on basic decisions regarding mate, family life, and vocation. This short but, for our purposes, very significant paper was written while Jung's transference to Freud was at the height of its idealization phase. Indirectly it also reflected Jung's growing awareness of the importance of his father in his own history. Jung's main point in the paper is over-determined, possibly as a result of the transference to Freud, because the evidence he cites does not actually support his contention that fathers are particularly crucial in their children's destiny, but that parents and families are. Nevertheless, Jung insisted that "it is usually the father who is the decisive and dangerous object of the child's fantasy, and if ever it happened to be the mother I was able to discover behind her a grandfather to whom she belonged in her heart" (1961b, p. 323, n.26). Jung later regarded this brief essay important enough to revise in considerable depth, and in 1948, some 40 years after its first publication, he added the archetypal perspective to the original personalistic interpretation.

In the revised version, the theme of the paper becomes the importance of the archetypal base on which a child's projection of "fatherhood" first rests. This, and not the actual father, is the principal influence in a person's life. It is this archetype, Jung argued, and not a memory image or introjection of an actual father, that is the "destiny maker." This "god" whom a person obeys and serves throughout life is first projected on a father, then on other father figures, and, finally, it may come to represent God Himself apart from any particular carriers of the projection. In this view, Jung's "religious crush" on Freud indicates that for him Freud was the carrier of an archetypal transference. Jung experienced Freud, during this phase, as the god at the center of a new religious cult—psychoanalysis—and himself in the role of ambivalent devotee.

In the 1908 version of this paper even more so than in the 1948 revision, Jung closely joined the themes of psychology and religion. He agreed with Freud, he wrote, that "all 'divine' figures have their roots in the father-imago" (1961b, p. 315). He argued later, however, that this imago was based on an archetype, which has a "dual aspect": "it is capable of diametrically opposite effects on consciousness rather as Yahweh acted towards Job—ambivalently" (ibid., p. 321). In Jung's life, one can draw a straight line from his father to Freud to his writings on Yahweh in *Answer to Job*. The ambivalent effects on consciousness of the father archetype—which unites the image of the personal father, images of other father-figures, and the *imago dei*—were exemplified for

Jung in the story of Job and Yahweh, as well as in the relationship between sons and fathers generally, and in *Answer to Job* Jung explored the archetypal dimensions of the oedipus complex. There Jung's anger and passionate concern toward the God of Judeo-Christian tradition reflect precisely this ambivalent attitude toward the "Father," as Jung adopted the position of an angry Job against an arbitrary, power-driven Yahweh. At one level he was trying to force God to develop a greater degree of consciousness and self-integration, while at other levels he was dealing once more with his own father and with Freud. In reading beyond the personal levels to the archetypal, however, he was seeking to achieve a cultural task and not merely a personal "working through" of unresolved issues.

Jung's ambivalence toward Freud indicated the constellation of the father archetype. On the one hand, he saw Freud as a great man, a world-shaking pioneer, an awesomely powerful figure at the center of a new religious cult. On the other hand, he viewed Freud as inwardly split and neurotic, unable to face his doubts and therefore dogmatic, touchy, and defensive about authority, and out of touch with (or distrustful of) the unconscious. In these respects, Jung's image of Freud came to resemble the image of his father, and it also resembled his later evaluation of the Father at the center of the patriarchal Judeo-Christian tradition. Like Paul Jung and Sigmund Freud, Jung would see this Divine Father as being in need of a therapeutic transformation to heal His internal duality, which again must be understood in both personal and archetypal/collective terms.

As relations deteriorated between Jung and Freud and as their long-suppressed conflicts broke into the open, Freud became incensed that Jung was threatening to diagnose his psychological blind spots and to treat them through the mails. Jung's letter of December 18, 1912— an explosive reply to Freud's earlier mention of a "slip" of Jung's pen that indicated, he felt, Jung's ambivalence toward being one of "his" followers in the dispute with Adler—accused Freud of

> sniffing out all the symptomatic actions in your vicinity, thus reducing everyone to the level of sons and daughters who blushingly admit the existence of their faults. Meanwhile you remain on top as the father, sitting pretty. For sheer obsequiousness nobody dares to pluck the prophet by the beard . . . . (McGuire 1974, p. 535)

Jung would not be an obsequious son. He vowed to point out the illness and neurotic weaknesses in the father, *for his own good*. And this, he claimed, was a "token of friendship." On January 3, 1913, in response to this threat of impending therapy, Freud removed himself from the relationship: "Take your full freedom and spare me your supposed 'tokens of friendship'" (ibid., p. 539), he wrote, therewith ending their correspondence.

In a letter also dated January 3, 1913, which crossed with Freud's termination letter, Jung repeated his therapeutic intention, now spoken almost as a New Year's resolution: "So if I offer you the unvarnished truth it is meant for your good, even though it may hurt" (McGuire 1974, p. 540). Jung was fully prepared to continue the relationship on this new basis, with himself now in the more masterful therapist's role. While it would take him 30 years more to be able to say fully what was wrong with Freud and psychoanalysis, his conscious intention was clear enough: He wanted to help Freud therapeutically by confronting him and analyzing his complexes and in this way possibly healing his neuroses. As disagreeable as Freud was about accepting this treatment and as unpalatable as Jung must have known it was to Freud's closely attached disciples, he persisted in it, and at their last meeting, which took place at the Munich Congress in September 1913, this attitude was remarked on by Lou Andreas-Salomé:

> At the Congress the Zurich members sat at their own table opposite Freud's. Their behavior towards Freud can be characterized in a word: it is not so much that Jung diverges from Freud, as that he does it in such a way as if he had taken it on himself *to rescue Freud and his cause* by these divergences. (Andreas-Salomé 1964, p. 168; italics added)

THE POST-FREUDIAN PERIOD (1913–21)

In the six years of Jung's personal relationship with Freud, his feelings traveled through an arc from a "religious crush" to a wish to heal a neurotically split, fearful, tragically limited father-figure. This reversal of a strong idealizing transference into what could be seen as a kind of therapeutic attitude was in important respects a replication of his relationship with his own father. Jung's father, too, must have earlier felt what Freud now felt, as his intellectually aggressive adolescent son assaulted his weakened theological positions. No more than Paul Jung was Freud able to receive and to use Carl Jung's ministrations, and probably both felt him to be an insensitive and ungrateful son. While Carl felt misunderstood and the victim of his fathers' defenses, helpless and unable to speak the healing words, his fathers felt equally victimized by Carl's brutality. "'So we are at last rid of them,'" Freud wrote to Abraham later in 1913, "'the brutal, sanctimonious Jung and his disciples'" (quoted in Brome 1978, p. 154). Brome remarks on the "entirely new and ruthless note" (ibid.) in this comment of Freud's. It was a note that could have rather likely been sounded at times by Jung's father too, not to mention by Yahweh and His theologians later on in Jung's therapeutic career.

From the published Freud-Jung correspondence, it is evident that the decisions to reduce and finally to break off personal relations were at every point initiated by Freud, who was reacting to Jung's behavior, to his letters, to his publications, and to the stories of others about him. Freud's letter of January 3, 1913, was his last personal correspondence with Jung. From Jung's letter of the same date, it is clear that Jung would have continued to struggle in this relationship, in the hope perhaps that eventually the older man would hear his words and change. Jung's departure from the psychoanalytic movement and his resignation as president of the International Psychoanalytic Society was a relief to Freud and placed full control of the movement back in his own hands.

For Jung the break with Freud and with psychoanalysis precipitated a life crisis of vast dimensions. "I felt as though I had been banished from my father's house," he later told Joseph Henderson (private communication), and during the five years following 1913 he entered what he called a "confrontation with the unconscious." In it he had to come to terms with his own heroic ambition (as symbolized in one dream by the figure of Siegfried, in German legend the son of Sigmund!) and find his own inner authority for his future work as a psychological theorist and psychotherapist. He would have to find another father, within.

One's attention is arrested in the autobiography by Jung's statement that the basic question he faced after this banishment from his "father's house" and the psychoanalytic cult was *religious*:

> About this time I experienced a moment of unusual clarity in which I looked back over the way I had traveled so far. I thought, "Now you possess a key to mythology and are free to unlock all the gates of the unconscious psyche." . . . And promptly the question arose of what, after all, I had accomplished. I had explained the myths of peoples of the past; I had written a book about the hero, the myth in which man has always lived. But in what myth does man live nowadays? In the Christian myth, the answer might be, "Do *you* live in it?" I asked myself. To be honest, the answer was no. For me, it is not what I live by. . . . "But then what is your myth—the myth in which you do live?" At this

point the dialogue with myself became uncomfortable, and I stopped thinking. I had reached a dead end. (1961a, p. 171)

At this point in Jung's life, the question might well have been asked in other terms: If you do not live by the myth of *psychoanalysis*, what is your myth? In psychoanalysis Jung felt he had discovered the "worship" of sexuality—Sexual Eros was god, and Freud was his prophet. From the start Jung had been uneasy with this emphasis and had been unable to accept Freud's dogma, just as he had been unable to accept the dogmas of Christianity which his father had preached. As he had found Christianity to be one-sided in its affirmation of a purely good, loving God and its denial of His dark, destructive side, so he had found psychoanalysis to be one-sided in its affirmation of sexuality as the primary force in psychological life and its denial of a power drive (Adler) and of a spiritual drive as equally fundamental tendencies of the psyche. Jung felt he could not be an adherent of either dogmatic system of thought because of their denial of what he knew from experience to be factual. But he could not, and did not, simply walk away from either of them and develop his own independent, and altogether new, myth either. Rather, he turned back to them and reflected on their partialness while holding up to them a vision of wholeness. In this reaction, he attempted to portray and to communicate wholeness where he found partialness, not for the purpose of abolishing either system of thought but for the sake of pointing them toward their own potential wholeness.

Jung's first major published work after *Transformations and Symbols of the Libido* was *Psychological Types* (1921), a book that can be read as his attempt to present the fragmented psychoanalytic movement with a theory that could include and heal its internal splits. The original germ of this massive work saw the light of day briefly in 1913, when Jung gave a talk entitled "Zur Frage der psychologischen Typen" (translated in 1916 as "A Contribution to the Study of Psychological Types") at the Munich Congress. It was at this meeting that Lou Andreas-Salomé perceived Jung as trying to "rescue Freud and his cause" (Andreas-Salomé 1964, p. 168).

In this paper Jung was struggling with reconciling the differences between the Freudian god of sexuality and the Adlerian god of power, religions of two very different types. He concluded by saying: "The difficult task of creating a psychology which will be equally fair to both types must be reserved for the future" (1974, p. 509). By the time Jung had elaborated the ideas in this talk into the full presentation of the "critical psychology" that *Psychological Types* was, he had passed through the period of his "creative illness" and had developed his own approach to the psyche and to psychotherapy. While *Types* is a brilliant exposition of a highly complex theory of consciousness and a summation of Jung's psychological thought to date, it is also a sustained commentary on Freudian theory and psychoanalysis as partial truth. In this work Jung was trying to transcend the differences among Freud, Adler, and himself by formulating a theory of psychological wholeness.

Psychological Types is a confession of the subjectivity of psychologizing. When human beings attempt to study their own or others' mental and emotional processes, distortions are inevitable because the student brings his or his own biases to the investigation. The only way to approach objectivity is to recognize the inevitable distortions and to understand how they work. Then one can compensate by filling in the gaps with opposing or alternate perspectives. No one perspective, and therefore no single dogma or theory, tells the whole truth about the human psyche, though each may offer a partial or relative truth. Jung was especially fond of an analogy from physics, where light can be studied equally well as particle or wave, both being theoretically defensible and useful, yet neither wholly sufficient. So it was, he argued, with Freud's theory of libido as sexuality and Adler's theory of it as power drive: Both contribute useful insights, but neither alone tells the whole story of the nature and dynamics of libido.

This perspectivalism in *Psychological Types* was balanced, however, by Jung's own theory of individuation and psychological wholeness. His view of libido as neutral psychic energy, the flow and channeling of which account for the differences among the eight psychological types, was built into a model of the mind that saw it as a unified system striving for wholeness and integration, but achieving this only partially. The theory he put forward explained why there were differing psychological perspectives, how they functioned within the psyche as a whole, and the kinds of distortion characteristic of each. Behind the perspectivalism, therefore, lay a vision of wholeness, an overarching perspective on the perspectives. And it was *this* vision of psychological wholeness that represented Jung's "wish to heal" and his converted transference reaction to Freud and to psychoanalysis.

In the therapist's countertransference, as I described Jung's view of it in the previous chapter, the doctor takes the patient (in this case, Freud and his psychoanalytic system) into himself psychologically, and this stimulates a conflict within. This conflict reflects the patient's internal conflict. In this instance, Jung's internal struggles would have reflected the conflicts within psychoanalysis (e.g., Freud vs. Adler), but now translated into conflicts between his own psychic structures or drives (sexuality vs. power, extraversion vs. introversion). This conflict Jung suffered through during the period of his "confrontation with the unconscious" following his break with Freud.

Through this experience of introjection and internal struggle, the unconscious of the therapist responds by offering a resolution to the conflict. So there emerges within the therapist's psyche a solution that synthesizes the constellated opposites and transcends the conflict. In psychotherapy, this solution is returned to the patient by way of inter-pretation, empathy, and unconscious influence. In *Psychological Types*, Jung was presenting Freud and the psychoanalytic movement with his solution to the one-sidedness and internal splits he had found in them. This volume represented the fruit of Jung's long struggle with an internalized Freud and the answer of his psyche to the conflicts he had undergone during the previous 15 years.

Throughout his later writings, Jung consistently affirmed the rela-tive truth and usefulness of Freud's theory and treatment methods (as he did Adler's), but he also stressed their partialness. And this would be precisely the approach he would eventually take to his father's religion as well. Christianity was not false and a mere relic of the superstitious past, as Freud had seen it. It was not untrue, but it was partial.

Psychological Types also contains a commentary on Christianity and a discussion of *its* typological one-sidedness. Like Freud's theory, Jung pointed out, Christianity is extraverted because it stresses the subject's relation to, dependency on, and ethical obligations toward the object, toward an external other. God himself is seen as an "Object," a wholly other "Thou," and He is required to be loved as such. Secondly, Christianity affirms "feeling" above "thinking" and an unseen world above the material world: This indicates its preferred functions to be "feeling" and "intuition" (over "thinking" and "sensation"). Christi-anity was characterized, therefore, as an "extraverted feeling-intuitive type." As a collectivity, it would tend to value similar types and tend to reject or devalue other contrary types.

This accounted, Jung argued, for Christianity's difficulty with in-cluding and integrating within its dominant tradition (a) mystical ele-ments (mystics tend to be introverted intuitive types), (b) speculative philosophy such as Gnosticism (such speculators tend to be introverted thinking types), (c) experimental science (such scientists tend to be extraverted sensation-thinking types) and other equally discordant typological tendencies. In contrast to this bias of Christianity, Eastern religions such as Buddhism, Hinduism, and Taoism are fundamentally introverted in attitude, and therefore show very different biases. They are equally one-sided, only in a different respect. Both the extraverted and the introverted religions need to develop their contrary attitude and inferior functions if they are to approach wholeness.

JUNG'S MISSION IN THE SECOND HALF OF LIFE (1922–61)

While Jung's dialogue with Freud's psychology never disappeared completely from his writings, it diminished drastically in importance and urgency in the years following his publication of *Psychological Types*. At the same time, his father reemerged as an important figure in dreams, and his dialogue with Christianity and its representatives gradually took on greater importance. Between 1921 and 1936, Jung delved into non-European cultures and religions, and while Christianity remained a growing concern, it did not occupy the foreground of his attention, as it would in his last decades. After 1938, Jung turned his attention fully to the crisis in European culture, and during the last 20 years of his life he became intensely engrossed with questions raised by modern European thought and particularly by the question of the present status and future existence of Christianity.

Brome, as well as Jung's other biographers, notes that all the major shifts in Jung's life were accompanied, or stimulated, by dreams. This is true for the theme we are tracing here. In the years between 1920 and 1950, Jung had a number of significant dreams that had a direct bearing on his relationship to Christianity. Several of them included his father as a key figure. His record of these dreams and his interpretations give us the essential clues for understanding his attitude in the later critical dialogue with Christianity. (As far as I am aware, Jung recorded no dreams of Freud after the break in 1913.)

In *Memories, Dreams, Reflections*, Jung reported three dreams of his father in detail; several others he summarized. Elsewhere (Bennet 1982, p. 98) some further details about these have come to light and still other dreams of his father are mentioned. All of these father dreams bear on the question of the nature of Jung's relationship to Christianity because of the close association between his father and Christian tradition, but there is an explicit and especially intimate interconnection between Jung's late dreams of his father and his careful examinations of Christian theology and care of souls.

Jung records the first of these dreams in relation to his father's death. Twenty-one years old when his father died, Carl then moved into his father's vacant bedroom. There he had a recurring anxiety dream: His father was coming home and would find him occupying his room. In these dreams, the victorious oedipal son (his mother had said shortly after her husband's death, "He died in time for you"! [1961a, p. 96]) was frightened and ashamed. His father was not angry at him, however; he had recovered from his illness and was simply coming home again. Later Jung interpreted these dreams as telling him what was transpiring with his father in the afterlife (ibid., pp. 96–97).

The next dream of his father, recorded in more detail, was fixed to a precise date in Jung's memory. It occurred in 1922, just a few weeks prior to his mother's death. Jung had not dreamed of his father since 1896, the year of his father's death. Now Paul Jung appeared again, having just returned from a long journey, rejuvenated, and without the aura of paternal authority. Carl was thrilled to see his father again and eager to fill him in on everything he had accomplished in the meantime. Particularly, he wanted to tell him about his recently published book, *Psychological Types*. But it turned out that his father had come for a professional consultation: He wanted some information and advice about marriage!

Following his mother's death a few weeks later, Jung took this dream as premonitory: His father was preparing himself to resume a relationship with his wife "on the other side" and wanted some advice about how to improve what had formerly been a difficult marriage.

This dream confirms what has been said already about the relation of son to father at this point in Jung's life. In the adult Jung's unconscious, the early family relationship of son to father had become fully transformed into a therapeutic relationship of doctor to patient, the father now seeking the son's advice and psychological counsel. This dream picture of Paul Jung coming to his son for assistance, and in effect asking for therapy, is of a piece with the picture of the son carrying his broken father about in his arms during the last months of his life. Both scenes indicate the achievement of a therapeutic position in Jung's attitude toward the paternal: The son is doctor to his father's patienthood; the father is patient to his son's doctoring.

It is astonishing that the obvious oedipal themes in these dreams are almost entirely uncommented upon by a man who had once been the crown prince of the psychoanalytic movement. The earlier set of dreams Jung apparently did consider from the oedipal viewpoint—Is father returning to punish the victorious son?—but he rejected this interpretation because the father was not angry or threatening, nor did he want to reclaim his old space (or spouse). Of course Jung could have dug further toward the dream's latent content, but he chose not to do so. Nor did he look at these dreams as compensatory or in any other way having a bearing on his subjectivity. Oddly, he preferred to take these dreams as objective portraits of the afterlife. He did not say why he chose this approach, but the most obvious explanation for introducing occult mysteries precisely where Freud would have nailed down the Oedipus complex is that Jung wanted to make a clear statement that the psyche is not strictly subjective. The psyche reaches beyond subjectivity to realms of being that are not only figures of the personal unconscious.

The other two major father dreams recorded in *Memories* occurred some two to three decades later. One took place in the early 1940s, the other around 1950. These two dreams are much more symbolic than the earlier ones, and they are also more indicative of the substantive issues taken up in Jung's discussion of the Christian care of souls and Christian theology. Whereas the point of the earlier father dreams was the relationship between father and son, the later dreams make reference to broader cultural and religious concerns, which were a concurrent preoccupation in Jung's conscious life. They also extend our appreciation of the critical position held by the father imago in Jung's deeply engaged encounter with the question of the fate of Christianity and of Christians in the modern world.

The first of these father dreams took place in the context of Jung's life in the early 1940s. Despite the terrifying reality of war in Europe and the constant threat of invasion, Jung undertook a schedule of lecturing and writing with added intensity during this period (cf. Hannah, pp. 266-87). There was additional free time in his practice, and he felt burdened, with much still to say and to write. The central themes in his writing and lecturing during these early war years were explicitly associated with the Christian tradition. The two major works of these years give evidence of this new focus: "A Psychological Approach to the Dogma of the Trinity" (begun as a spontaneous lecture at the Eranos Conference in 1940, then revised and published in 1942) and "Transformation Symbolism in the Mass" (given as an Eranos lecture in 1941 and published in 1942). Before this Jung had never written an essay focused exclusively on Christian doctrine or rite. These two papers would be the forerunners of much more similar work. Jung identified the first of his two late father dreams as a "herald" of what was to come (1961a, p. 213).

The dream ran as follows: Jung discovers a large wing of his house that he has never visited before, which contains a zoological laboratory. This belongs to his father; it is his workroom. His father is now an ichthyologist, and the workroom contains every kind of fish imaginable. Then Hans, a country boy, shows Jung still another room. This one belongs to his mother. Two rows of chests hang from the ceiling, each containing two beds for visiting spirits ("ghostly married couples") to sleep in. Another door is opened, and Jung finds a brass band loudly playing dance tunes and marches in a large hall. In the dream he is struck by the strong contrast between the spirit of worldly joviality in the outer hall and the practice of spiritual mysteries in the silent inner chambers (1961a, pp. 213–14).

Possibly more important than this dream itself, which shows up so well the contrast in Jung's personality between his jovial, extraverted personality No. 1 and his mystical, introverted personality No. 2, is the interpretation he gave it. He found that it confirmed his vocation as a healer of Christian souls and as a therapist to the Christian tradition.

Jung took the dream's idea that his father was an ichthyologist as a reflection of his father's actual identity as a Christian pastor, a "caretaker of Christian souls" that had been caught in "Peter's net." The fish represented the souls in a pastor's keeping. His mother too, he wrote, was evidently "burdened with the problem of the 'cure of souls'" in the dream (1961a, p. 214). This dream, Jung felt, put the burden of the care and cure of Christian souls on his own shoulders, since the presence of the parental figures symbolized his own unconsciousness and their tasks represented the work he had yet to do, tasks that were still latent in his unconscious and were only now beginning to reveal themselves. This was the meaning to him of the "discovery motif" in the dream.

Jung's associations to fish led him to reflect on the Grail legend and the Fisher King, which in turn aroused the thought of his father as "a sufferer stricken with an Amfortas wound." The type of suffering that Jung had witnessed in his father's life exemplified "that Christian suffering for which the alchemists sought the panacea" (1961a, p. 215): This was the suffering of wounded souls whose access to nature and to its healing powers had been cut off.

Jung himself was immersed in the study of alchemy at this time. For him, alchemy had come to represent the equivalent in Western European tradition of his own analytical psychology in modernity (1961a, p. 212): Both worked outside of the collective mainstream, and each was searching for the *lumen naturae*, the hidden sparks of consciousness ("light") within the depths of the unconscious ("nature"). The conviction took hold in Jung that his own work, a psychology of the unconscious, was an effort akin to the alchemists' search for a panacea, a quest to find a therapeutic release for the suffering of souls caught in the net of a one-sided, strangulating Christian tradition. This was the same net that had crippled his father's spirit.

The beginning of Jung's intensive exploration of the religious meaning of European alchemy dated from a dream he had in India in 1938, which had presented him with the theme of the quest for the Holy Grail. This dream, the last major turning point in Jung's vocational life, had launched him on the path that he would travel during his last two decades. His purpose became no less than the therapeutic transformation of Christianity and Western culture.

The crispness and clarity of this purpose had meant a sharp refocusing of Jung's perennial interest in religion. Since the early 1920s, and indeed to some extent since his late psychoanalytic period, Jung had taken a lively interest in Eastern religions and in the religions of "primitive peoples." His psychological concept of the self had a major taproot in his reading of Eastern philosophical and religious texts. In the 1920s, when he began elaborating this concept, Jung was collaborating with Richard Wilhelm, the German Sinologist who had translated the I Ching into German, and he was also working with the famous Indologist Heinrich Zimmer, who became a close friend as well. Jung's broad interests in Eastern and primitive religions—in the 1920s he visited Africa twice as well as the American Pueblo Indians in New Mexico, primarily to learn about their religious beliefs and attitudes— were consistent with his earlier interests in spiritualism and in religious experience.

Until 1938, then, Jung's interest in the religious life, and more specifically in the "religious function" within the human psyche, had taken precedence over his concern for any particular religious tradition, including Christianity. Christianity had in effect been left behind with childhood, and it had been Jung's more impersonal scientific interests— and not a commitment to a therapeutic goal—that had led him to express some thoughts on Christianity in such works as *Transforma-*

tions and Symbols of the Libido (1912–13), *Psychological Types* (1921), and *Psychology and Religion* (1938). In these works and in the frequent seminars he conducted in England, the United States, and Switzerland, Jung had commented on the repressions of Christianity (in the Polzeanth/Cornwall Seminar of 1923), on its typological one-sidedness (in *Types* and elsewhere), and on the complementariness to Christianity of other religious traditions and attitudes, such as Islam and Buddhism. In these earlier writings and lectures, Christianity had by no means been ignored or left out, but nowhere had Jung developed a sustained interpretation of Christianity's history or symbols and rituals, nor had he before tried to engage Christian tradition in a transformational dialogue. It was only after 1938 that Jung forcefully bent his energies directly toward Christianity and its therapy.

Ironically, this new purpose snapped into place while Jung was on a trip to India. There he saw for the first time the actual cultural manifestations of the two ancient religious traditions, Hinduism and Buddhism, whose texts had fascinated him for decades. In that exotic setting, he had a dream that would channel his energies entirely toward the West. From then on, his most important works were addressed to Western religion and culture. Studies of the *I Ching*, of Chinese alchemy, of Tibetan Buddhism and Tantric Yoga, of the Upanishads and of primitive religions were all behind now, and his attention was thrown completely onto what he perceived as a profound crisis in Western religion and culture.

In the 1938 India dream, Jung found himself with some Swiss friends on an island off the south coast of England. The island was long and narrow in the north-south direction, and on the south end of it stood a medieval castle. Jung and his friends were gathered in the castle's courtyard, admiring the bell tower and a staircase visible inside it. They understood this to be the Grail castle. Candles lit the stairway, and they anticipated witnessing the Grail celebration that evening. Beside Jung stood a German professor "who strikingly resembled old Mommsen" (the famous German professor of history). He and Jung carried on a learned conversation about the Grail legend. But as they talked, it became evident that the professor was speaking about a remote past, as though lecturing about history in a dusty classroom and not recognizing the immediate surroundings.

Suddenly Jung discovers that he is standing on a wall covered by an elaborate iron trellis. From there he spots in the foliage a tiny iron gnome, "a *cuccullatus*." Then the scene changes, and now he and the others, but not the old professor, are outside the castle. Jung realizes the Grail has still to be found and is urgently needed for that evening's celebration. It is reputed to be in the northern part of the island, hidden in an uninhabited house. It is *his* task to bring the Grail to the castle. As he sets out northward, he discovers that the island is divided in two by an arm of sea. The sun sets, it is cold and desolate, and his companions fall asleep. He concludes that he must go on alone. He must swim the channel and find the Grail. The dream ends with Carl Jung plunging into the icy water.

Jung's commentary on this dream in *Memories* ran as follows:

> Imperiously, the dream wiped away all the intense impressions of India and swept me back to the too-long-neglected concerns of the Occident, which had formerly been expressed in the quest for the Holy Grail as well as in the search for the philosophers' stone. I was taken out of the world of India, and reminded that India was not my task, but only a part of the way—admittedly a significant one—which should carry me closer to my goal. It was as though the dream were asking me, "What are you doing in India? Rather seek for yourself and your fellows the healing vessel, the *servator mundi*, which you urgently need. For your state is perilous; you are in imminent danger of destroying all that centuries have built up." (1961a, pp. 282–83)

While this dream and Jung's interpretation of it need to be set against the backdrop of events in Europe in 1938, his associations to it extended considerably beyond the meaning of Nazism and World War II. In Jung's mind, the outbreak of barbarism in Europe was symptomatic of a spiritual disease in the soul of modern man: Modern man had lost the vision of transcendence and had traded the soul's values for the rational intellect's instrumental powers. It was a Faustian dilemma. The search for the Holy Grail was for the modern psyche's healing, for a panacea that would provide it with a sense of depth and meaning. This, Jung felt, could come only through first-person experience of the divine, through a new revelation of being, not through determined belief in traditional doctrines.

The cul-de-sac his father had entered, because he wanted to rest content with belief in Christian dogma, had entrapped the tradition itself: It was now without life because it was not renewing itself in the original source of its vitality. Modernity had overthrown the religious sensibility of Western men and women and now required either abandonment of traditional Christian belief and faith altogether (replacing them with belief in human reason and in science) or a *sacrificium intellectus*, which rendered persons like Jung's father broken and frightened victims of an age they could not understand. The absence of a containing and ordering *mythos* had left Western culture bereft of resource for healing the modern soul and for giving modern persons a sense of transcendent purpose and meaning. If Christianity was to continue as the central religious expression of Western culture, it had to be willing to submit to a thorough-going process of transformation, which would mean assimilating the gains in consciousness achieved by modernity (the ego-strengths represented by science) and reconnecting to the living spirit (in Jung's terminology, the "collective unconscious") by abandoning rigid commitments to already formulated and developed structures of belief. This would open the doors to new and perhaps unorthodox, but nevertheless life-giving, revelations.

Jung returned to Europe from India in 1938 fully committed to the quest for a *servator mundi*. This was the personal context of his dream of the soul-curing rooms in the unexplored wing of his house, which occurred a few years later and was taken as a message by Jung that he "was still not conscious of an essential aspect of [his] task" (1961a, p. 216). The consciousness of this would unfold over the following decade, as Jung increasingly took on the task of therapeutizing Christianity.

TO THE HIGHEST PRESENCE

Around 1950 Jung (1961a, pp. 217ff.) had another major dream in which his father again played a key role. If the earlier dream of his parents' soul-curing rooms presaged his work on the Christian tradition in *Aion* (1951) and in his late magnum opus *Mysterium Coniunctionis* (1955), this latter dream prefigured the central theme of *Answer to Job* (1952), a work that of all Jung's writings most clearly expressed his intensely emotional relationship to Christianity and to its central symbol, the Godhead. Again, as this dream and Jung's interpretation of it demonstrate, his relationship to his father and his relationship to Christianity and its theology were deeply intertwined, even at the advanced age of 75.

In this dream, Jung is paying a visit to his long-deceased father. His father is once again a curator, not of fish this time but of an eighteenth-century mansion containing the sarcophagi of famous persons. He is a distinguished scholar. Two other psychiatrists are also present. From a shelf his father takes a heavy old Bible bound in shiny fishskin and begins interpreting a passage from the Pentateuch, but his exposition is so swift and learned that Jung and the other two psychiatrists cannot follow it. In fact, his intensity and the excitement over the flood of ideas pouring into his mind lead the other two psychiatrists to suspect a pathological condition. (These figures, Jung commented, represent the limited medical viewpoint.)

Then the scene changes. Father and son are outside in front of the house, and they hear noises in a nearby shed. Jung's father says the shed is haunted by poltergeists.

Entering the house again, they come into a large second-storey hall, "the exact replica of the *divan-i-kass* [council hall] of Sultan Akbar of Fatehpur Sikri." The room is circular, the shape of a mandala. At the center, on an elevated base, is the seat of the sultan; around the rim are seats for his counselors and for the court philosophers. From the raised center there is a steep stairway that leads to a small door high up on the wall. His father points to it and says, "Now I will lead you into the highest presence." Then he kneels and touches his head to the floor, Moslem style. Jung follows suit, but his head does not go all the way to the floor; there remains "perhaps a millimeter to spare." It suddenly dawns on Jung that this door leads to the chamber of Uriah, King David's betrayed general (1961a, pp. 217–19).

Again, it is as much Jung's interpretation of this dream as the dream itself that is important for understanding Jung's relationship to his father and to Christianity. His father, who had in fact been trained as a scholar of Near-Eastern languages but had not used this education productively in his pastoral career, is associated in the dream with the Biblical tradition. In fact, in the dream he is seen as the scholar and hermeneut he never became in life. Upon reflection, Jung interpreted this image of his father as a signal that his own unconscious was engaged in the task of interpreting the Bible. Here lay his own unfinished business: interpreting the Christian God-image in the context of its Semitic, Old Testament background.

By the time this dream occurred, Jung had already been interpreting Christianity intensively for some ten years, but he had not paid particular attention to the Biblical background. This dream, he observed in his memoirs, presaged his *Answer to Job*, which was to be a passionate interpretation (like that of the dream-father) of the God-image in Judaism (Yahweh), its transformation in Christianity, and its evolution in the two millennia following. Jung's ambivalence toward Yahweh should, in terms of his own understanding of the effects of the father archetype upon consciousness, be taken as a sign of his archetypal transference to the Biblical God.

This dream's second major point of significance for Jung lay in the contrast between the attitudes of father and son toward the "holy." In bowing to the "highest presence," his father's head touches the floor, indicating complete submission; Carl's head, however, does not succumb entirely. Jung pointed out that this indicated a fundamental, lifelong attitude: his determination "not to be a dumb fish." Even in the presence of the sacred he would retain a mental reservation. This, he expounded, was precisely also the stance of Job, who refused to accept his friends' conventional doctrines on sin and punishment but rather reserved judgment to himself and even went so far as to make God answer for *His* deeds. *God* can be at fault and in need of greater consciousness and further development. This commitment to the individual human being's judgment (Jung's strongest affirmation of an ego psychology) barely disguised "the idea of the creature that surpasses its creator by a small but decisive factor." Uriah, the innocent victim and a prefiguration of Christ, was a symbol of the same value that Job represented. Jung himself identified with this lineage of defiant innocents, whereas his father represented the more docile (and traditional) attitude toward authority and toward the conventional image of God. This dream stated Jung's attitude toward Christianity, the religious tradition of his father: The God who is the symbolic center of Christianity's life and faith is as much in need of transformation as His human worshipers. This was, as we have seen before, Jung's attitude to his other two father figures, Paul Jung and Sigmund Freud.

As had been the case with the other two dreams of this late period—the Holy Grail dream and the "cure of souls" dream—this dream of his father as Biblical interpreter reflected Jung's already deep involvement with Christianity and also strengthened his resolve to continue working at its therapy. By now he was doing what his father had left undone: addressing himself to the cure of Christian souls and to the task of finding the panacea for Christian suffering. Also, he was interpreting the Biblical tradition. But above all, he was preparing to face up to the task his father had fearfully evaded—that of confronting the Christian tradition and its symbolic center, the Godhead, with the full force of his own personality, which he would do in his *Answer to Job.*

JUNG'S THERAPEUTIC
STANCE TOWARD CHRISTIANITY

Beginning in 1938 with the Holy Grail dream, Jung entered into a new conscious relation to Christianity and the Christian tradition. His attitude can best be grasped by reference to therapy and to its goal of psychological health and wholeness. The seeds that grew and blossomed in this relationship had been planted many years earlier in the soil of his childhood and the relationship with his father. With Freud and psychoanalysis Jung repeated what he had done with his father and his father's religion. Later, in his relation to Christian tradition, this pattern of transference would again come into full expression. Moreover, as Jung had risen above the strife of conflicting viewpoints in psychoanalysis and presented that movement with an image of wholeness in his work on psychological types, so he would stand back from Christianity while he interpreted its history and doctrines and then come forward with a vision of its potential wholeness in such writings as *Aion, Answer to Job,* and *Mysterium Coniunctionis.* The truly stupendous output of thought and writing on Christianity during his last two decades was motivated largely by a therapeutic impulse, which had important roots in his feelings for his one-sided, spiritually defeated father.

I have no wish to reduce the meaning of Jung's writings on Christianity simply to an expression of his father complex, for it is clear that he was genuinely concerned with the massive cultural crisis created by a waning of his religious tradition. On the other hand, it is also evident that Jung's concern with Christian tradition and symbols had a personal motivation. Jung's own understanding of the complexity of projection and perception in the transference/countertransference process can accommodate the dual realization, that while his writings on Christian themes were indeed dealing with the cause of his father's spiritual illness (and therefore with Jung's strong feelings about his victimized parent), they were also an attempt to treat a profound problem in Western culture—the conflict between tradition and modernity—which both his father and he had inherited. Jung's therapeutic attitude toward Christianity, therefore, had an intensely personal aspect, as well as an objective, cultural aspect. Jung's early wish to heal his father—the wish of a Parsifal to speak the healing words to a King Amfortas whose wound was torturing him and making his life a misery—passed over ("transferred") first to Freud and psychoanalysis and finally came to rest on Christianity. If the physician was born from an ailing Swiss parson, he went on until he found his true patient in the original source of his father's disease—modern Christianity.

There is a view of Jung as a misguided, "haunted prophet" (Gedo 1983, Stern 1976), and in this interpretation we see Jung's therapeutic challenge to Christianity as an expression of grandiose, narcissistic inflation. How could he presume to take the position of healer to a whole religious tradition! Brome points out that in Jung's lifetime there were a "hostile handful" of critics who felt that in *Answer to Job* "Jung had now appointed himself psychiatrist to God, diagnosed a divine sickness and successfully cured the Patient by applying his own theories" (Brome 1978, p. 254). Victor White implied this same criticism in his acid remarks on that work. But finally this view, as titillating and stimulating as it may be, comes to grief because it does not include an accurate assessment of Jung's own self-awareness. It vastly underestimates his psychological stature and consciousness and ends up falsifying his life by denying his hard-won self-awareness and his critical faculties. Jung was not naively a prophet, but he certainly did take risks and did expose his personality to public scrutiny. But since he assumed the position of physician to an ailing religious tradition, he was required to reveal himself in this fashion to his patient. A "doctor of souls" cannot hold back. In addition to the personal factors at work in his treatment of Christianity, he revealed a detailed account of its disorder, its developmental history, and its potential for further development toward wholeness. The details of this diagnosis, treatment, and prognosis I will present in the following two chapters.

Chapter 4 **DOCTOR JUNG'S TREATMENT OF CHRISTIANITY**

In 1941, as part of the 400th anniversary of Paracelsus' death, Jung was invited to give a lecture in honor of this fellow Swiss physician. "Paracelsus as a Spiritual Phenomenon" was delivered in Einsiedeln, the birthplace of Paracelsus and an important European pilgrimage site some 50 miles southwest of Zurich. The editors of Jung's *Collected Works* comment that this paper "stands out as a separate study with a powerful appeal, perhaps because Jung could identify himself rather closely and sympathetically with that dynamic and explosive personage, his own countryman" (1967, p. v).

As Jung portrayed Paracelsus, he

was a well-intentioned, humble Christian. His ethics and his professed faith were Christian, but his most secret, deepest passion, his whole creative yearning, belonged to the *lumen naturae*, the divine spark buried in the darkness, whose sleep of death could not be vanquished even by the revelation of God's son. The light from above made the darkness still darker, but the *lumen naturae* is the light of the darkness itself, which illuminates its own darkness, and this light the darkness comprehends. Therefore it turns blackness into brightness, burns away "all superfluities," and leaves behind nothing but "faecam et scoriam et terram damnatam" (dross and scoriae and the rejected earth).

Paracelsus, like all the philosophical alchemists, was seeking for something that would give him a hold on the dark, body-bound nature of man, on the soul which, intangibly interwoven with the world and with matter, appeared before itself in the terrifying form of strange, demoniacal figures and seemed to be the secret source of life-shortening diseases. The Church might exorcise demons and banish them, but that only alienated man from his own nature, which, unconscious of itself, had clothed itself in these spectral forms. Not separation of the natures but union of the natures was the goal of alchemy. (1967, pp. 160-61)

This statement about Paracelsus and alchemy contains the key for understanding Jung's own writings on Christian doctrine and tradition, because it states the goal of his psychotherapy: not the separation but the union of two natures, body and spirit. This therapeutic aim will guide us through the labyrinth of Jung's commentary on Christianity.

The present chapter contains the heart of my enterprise. Earlier chapters have explicated Jung's model for psychotherapy and explored his personal relationship to Christianity. Now I will harvest the ideas planted there and apply them to a reading of Jung's six major works on Christianity and its cultural tradition: "A Psychological Approach to the Dogma of the Trinity" (1942), "Transformation Symbolism in the Mass" (1942), "Introduction to the Religious and Psychological Problems of Alchemy" (1944), *Aion* (1951), *Answer to Job* (1952), and *Mysterium Coniunctionis* (1955). My intention is to show how each of these works reflects Jung's overall therapeutic intention and how each represents the phases of therapeutic analysis as described in Chapter 2. These works represent Jung's final and perhaps his greatest effort as a doctor of souls: the psychotherapeutic treatment of Christianity and its culture.

JUNG'S THERAPEUTIC INTERPRETATION OF CHRISTIANITY'S GOD SYMBOL

In commenting on the spiritual significance of Paracelsus for Christendom, Jung quoted another favorite alchemical author, Michael Maier:

Of this *filius regius* [who is hidden in the sea and cries out for deliverance] Michael Maier says: "He lives and calls from the depths: Who shall deliver me from the waters and lead me to dry land? Even though this cry be heard of many, yet none takes it upon himself, moved by pity, to seek the king. For who, they say, will plunge into the waters? Who will imperil his life by taking away the peril of another? Only a few believe his lament, and think rather that they hear the crashing and roaring of Scylla and Charybdis. Therefore they remain sitting indolently at home, and give no thought to the kingly treasure, nor to their own salvation." (1967, p. 145)

As Jung copied these lines into his lecture, he must have thought about his India dream of 1938, in which *he* was the one preparing to plunge into the cold waters in quest of the Holy Grail and the panacea for the king. As a personal gloss for Jung on "king" in this alchemical text, we can read: father, Christian cultural dominant, the God-image of Western culture. In another context, Jung interprets the "king" in alchemy as the "Christian dominant, which was originally alive and present in consciousness but then sank into the unconscious and must now be restored in renewed form" (1970c, p. 332).

Like the alchemists, whom he regarded as seeking to redeem God from entrapment in nature by delving into the darkness of *materia*, Jung wanted to heal the soul-sickness of Christianity by uncovering a more complete symbol of wholeness within the darkness of the human psyche. Against the partialness and one-sidedness of Christianity, he would set his vision of psychological wholeness. This vision and its contrast to Christian theology and practice was first spelled out in the essay, "A Psychological Approach to the Dogma of the Trinity."

This work began as an extemporaneous response to an Eranos lecture given by the Swiss mathematician, Andreas Speiser, in 1940 (Hannah 1976, p. 270). These remarks were subsequently expanded and published in the *Eranos Jahrbuch* of 1940-41. This paper was later revised and again expanded for publication in 1948. The final version is consequently a refined and carefully considered statement. Its fundamental theme, which was strongly present in the first spontaneous remarks at the Eranos Tagung in 1940, derived from Jung's psychotherapeutic response to the symbol that lies at the core of Christian doctrine, namely the symbol of God Himself. In those remarks, and even more so in the final essay, Jung sounded the major themes that were to be played and elaborated in the rest of his later works on Christian thought and practice.

We have noted from his autobiography that Jung's interest in the Trinity dated back to his confirmation years, when his father disappointed him by being unable to explain the meaning of this difficult doctrine to this rather bullishly inquisitive son (1961a, p. 53). The intervening 50 years had been occupied with psychological studies and practice and with intensive work on mythology, comparative religion, anthropology, and symbolism. By the time Jung began to write his essay on the Trinity, he was 65 years old—more than 10 years older than his father had been when he had died—and he brought to this task all the extensive learning and experience of his professional life.

The introduction to the Trinity essay clearly shows that Jung, even at this advanced stage of life, felt somewhat uneasy and perhaps presumptuous about subjecting this core symbol of Christianity to psychological analysis. He was anything but an inflated "prophet" in the presence of this sacred doctrine. He was concerned that it might be an act of hubris to discuss the sacrosanct heart of his own (and his father's) religious tradition from the viewpoint of his psychological understanding and psychotherapeutic concern. Pointing out that he had analyzed non-Christian religious symbols in this fashion, though, he brusquely remarked that "what is sauce for the goose is sauce for the gander" (1969c, p. 109), as the translator renders Jung's own untranslatable "*was dem einen recht ist, soll dem andern billig sein*" (1948, p. 323), and presses on with his interpretation, anticipating a sharply critical reaction from his Christian audience.

Jung's anxiety at the outset reveals that this essay is not a purely scientific-psychological study of an ancient religious doctrine or a hermeneutical bridge to assist modern man to understand more deeply the meaning of ancient texts. Had that been the case, there would have been little cause for worry. But because this psychological interpretation of the Trinity contains a more clinical and critical intention, Jung knew it would be upsetting to the "patient." Jung interprets the Trinitarian doctrine of God as he would the dream or the psychological structures of a patient. From experience, he could anticipate a mixed reaction to this procedure. Analysis and interpretation will disclose shortcomings and deficits in the patient; they will diagnose an unhealthy condition; they will propose therapeutic change and will not simply confirm and support the patient's conscious attitude and underlying structures of attitude and belief. Jung the therapist would support the patient's further evolution toward wholeness, but not the status quo or nostalgic longing for retrieval of past glories. So there would be resistance. And Jung the therapist would have to be prepared to analyze this defensive reaction or to override it in the interest of the patient's future wholeness.

In the Trinity essay, Jung was lifting up the core of Christian belief, the doctrine of God, for psychological analysis. All of his major writings on Christian themes, it should be noted, are centrally concerned with the doctrine of God and its transformative evolution. I am presenting here a rather lengthy discussion of the Trinity essay because it contains, at least in brief, the complete content of Jung's critical interpretation of Christianity and of his therapeutic design for its future development. The Trinity essay contains a diagnostic statement regarding Christianity, a psychological interpretation of its conscious and unconscious psy-

chological structures and dynamics, the kernel of a historical/recon-
structive statement of Christianity's "childhood" and early development, and a challenge to Christianity to submit to a therapeutic transformation and to enter the next stage of its individuation process.
Absent from the surface of this essay is the transference/countertrans-
ference dynamic between patient and doctor; it exists in the unconscious at this point. It will become more evident, because more conscious, later in Jung's writings.

The Argument of the Trinity Essay

Jung begins his discussion of the Trinity by adducing a number of
pre-Christian parallels to the Trinitarian conception of God: Babyloni-
an, Egyptian, and Greek. These are in most cases triads of separate gods
and goddesses, but the structure of their relationship is based on the
archetype that also underlies Christian Trinitarian doctrine. Various
examples of such triads are mentioned: Anu-Bel-Ea, Sin-Shamash-Adad,
Sin-Shamash-Ishtar among the Babylonians; God-king-*ka* and Osiris-
Horus-Isis among the Egyptians; and, at a more abstract level among
the Greeks, the number symbolism in Pythagorean philosophy and in
Plato's cosmology. The existence of these numerous parallels of the
Christian conception indicates the archetypal background to Trinitarian
patterns of thinking about the Divine. The Christian doctrine of the
Trinity, therefore, is an expression of the archetypal structure of the
human mind. The archetype, Jung writes, "is 'that which is believed
always, everywhere, and by everybody'" (1969c, p. 117), because it is an
elemental feature of human mentation. Conceiving by "threes" is an
instance of this.

Greek philosophy speculated at some length about the symbolic
significance of primary numbers. "One" indicates the state of original
unity; "two" signifies division, therefore conflict, separation, individuation, discrimination between right/left, good/evil; "three" resolves the
conflict and overcomes polarity, restoring unity on another level. Jung
understands this Pythagorean speculation to show a dialectical process
beginning in potentiality, moving forward through division and conflict,
and resolving in the realization of potential. Platonic mathematical speculation and philosophy, however, introduced the problem of the
"fourth," which Jung sees as critical. To move from plane surface
geometry to three-dimensional reality, which is equivalent to moving
from potentiality to actuality, Plato said that simple pairs of opposites

must be joined by two "means." Four elements are therefore necessary to create reality. Extending this, Jung argues that without the fourth dimension there can be no concrete realization of potentiality in time and space, only the abstract conception of it. So the "fourth" indicates the critical presence (or absence) of "reality" in physical, political, social, down-to-earth terms. Jung points out that Plato himself was unable to include this dimension in his life and teachings, and that his perfect abstractions failed when he tried to introduce them into social and political life:

> The step from three to four brought him sharply up against something unexpected and alien to his thought, something heavy, inert, and limited, which no "*may ov*" and no "*privatio boni*" can conjure away or diminish. Even God's fairest creation is corrupted by it, and idleness, stupidity, malice, discontent, sickness, old age and death fill the glorious body of the "blessed god." Truly a grievous spectacle, this sick world-soul. . . . (1969c, p. 123)

Jung concludes this section of the Trinity paper by reflecting on Plato's theory of creation in the *Timaeus*, where the demiurge is said to have mixed two pairs of opposites (divisible-indivisible and different-same) twice, creating a quaternitarian world-soul. Plato was impelled toward a quaternity, Jung argues, because an "unconscious *spiritus rector*" (1969c, p. 127), which represented the action of a quaternitarian archetype, was guiding his thought. This archetype, as distinct from the Trinitarian one, seeks inclusive totality and comes to rest only in actualized wholeness.

In the essay's second section ("Father, Son, and Spirit"), Jung advances the view that the Church Fathers, in laboring to design the great Christian doctrines such as the Trinity, the *homoousia* of Father and Son, and the Virgin as Theotokos, were likewise guided by an unconscious *spiritus rector*. Busily, almost antlike, they were working out an archetypal ground plan for Christian thought. Each of these fundamental doctrines rests on, or represents, an archetypal pattern that can be found in other (often unrelated) cultures and religions and can arise spontaneously in human thought and imagery in any time and place where conditions are favorable. In the doctrine of the Trinity, then,

> the archetype reasserted itself, since . . . archetypal ideas are part of the indestructible foundations of the human mind. However long they are forgotten and buried, always they return, sometimes in the strangest guise, with a personal twist to them or intellectually distorted . . . but

continually reproducing themselves in new forms representing the timeless truths that are innate in man's nature. (1969c, p. 130)

It was not the influence of religious or philosophical tradition, therefore, that directed the minds of the Church Fathers as they elaborated the Trinitarian doctrine; it was, rather, a psychic factor, the archetype. To comprehend fully the doctrine of the Trinity, then, it is necessary to understand the archetypal factors that guided and motivated the creation of this doctrine.

Father, Son, and Holy Ghost: this is the "psychological datum" to be analyzed and interpreted. "Father" logically implies "child." That his child is a "Son" rather than a "Daughter" is the first clue to the meaning of this datum. It is fundamentally male. The "Holy Ghost" is more puzzling, in that it is "supernatural." While called a "person," the Holy Ghost is not imagined in human form. It represents something Father and Son have in common, their "mutual life." In medieval thought, Jung amplifies, the "corpus" and the "spiramen" were separate, the latter being the life or soul ("anima") that inhabited the body for a time and then left. In Egyptian thought, this same entity was represented by the *ka*, the life-spirit, the "animating principle of men and gods" (1969c, p. 131). In Christian doctrine, this archaic form of thought reasserts itself: the Holy Ghost "is hypostatized procreative power and life-force" and is therefore a "hypostatic representation of an abstract thought (two-dimensional triad)" (ibid., p. 132).

By elevating the Holy Ghost to the status of a "third person" in the Godhead, and not simply regarding this as a relation between Father and Son, Christianity demonstrated its extraordinary valuation of masculine "spirit": the "father-son relationship is thus lifted out of the natural order (which includes mothers and daughters) and translated to a sphere from which the feminine element is excluded" (1969c, p. 132). Thus the feminine is doctrinally excluded from the realm in which the mystery of Divine Life takes place. This, Jung claims, implies a male initiation mystery from which women must be expelled. Its function, in fact, is to separate the male initiand from his mother. "The celibacy of the priesthood is a continuation of this archetypal idea" (ibid.).

The "invisible figure" named Holy Ghost, then, is "a 'spirit' that is the very essence of masculine life" (1969c, p. 133). Thus, "Father-son-life (or procreative power), together with rigorous exclusion of the Theotokos, constitute the patriarchal formula that was 'in the air' long before the advent of Christianity" (ibid.).

Jung then shifts from this archetypal amplificatory interpretation of the Trinity's three Figures to an interpretation of the Trinity as a dynamic progression from one to three. This second line of interpretation, based largely on the Pythagorean and Platonic idea of the one-two-three dialectical progression discussed earlier, threads through the work alongside the structural one.

In this dynamic interpretation, "Father" represents the first stage of psychological and cultural development. This is the origin and beginning of things. It is characterized by psychological oneness, by lack of conflict and criticism, by the absence of moral discrimination and reflectiveness. In this stage, as it pertains to religious sensibility, God and man "form a unity, unclouded by criticism" (1969c, p. 134) or complaint. It is the world of childhood, of simple faith and trust in the Father, an age of "pristine oneness with the whole of Nature, no matter whether this oneness be beautiful or ugly or awe-inspiring" (ibid.). This state of pre-moral consciousness Jung places historically in the pre-Christian era.

The appearance of the Son introduces a second factor; beside the One now is the "Other." This second stage is characterized by criticism, conflict, and psychological differentiation. A critical attitude is born. Creation now comes to be regarded as imperfect, and "the goodness and almightiness of the Father cannot be the sole principle of the cosmos" (1969c, p. 134). Indeed, nature is seen as so imperfect that it needs to be redeemed. In Western history, this age began when the Greeks started criticizing the world and when "gnosis," which "ultimately gave birth to Christianity" (ibid.), took over cultural and religious consciousness. The critique of nature and of the world raised questions about the origins of evil in the cosmos; it also created the longing for redemption and for restoration of oneness with the Father, which characterized the Western mind in the centuries surrounding the birth of Christianity. But consciousness had advanced too far to return to uncritical acceptance of nature. The gates to paradise were closed.

Dynamically, this second stage represents a development out of and beyond the One. One, which is original unity, divides into two—one and the other—and this division represents an advance for consciousness. A new stage of self-consciousness and self-knowledge is created. The Son reveals the Father, and God gains definition as "Father" because now there is a "Son." Increased consciousness makes definition possible; before, the One was undefinable.

The third stage, represented by the appearance of the Holy Ghost, is the culminating step in this dynamic progression. In this stage, the opposition that was created in the second stage is resolved. The internal opposition of that stage culminates in intense suffering and splitting apart (abandonment), which then is resolved in the perfect peace of the three. Harmony returns between reunited Father and Son. The Holy Ghost is the legacy of this resolution, left among mankind to continue the work of peace, comfort, and life-renewal.

Jung concludes the second section by again emphasizing that the Christian doctrine of Father-Son-Holy Ghost is rooted in archetypal factors and patterns and has many pre- and non-Christian parallels. This in no way detracts from the value and authenticity of the doctrine. Indeed, it recommends its authenticity. But it does mean that the essential features of this core Christian doctrine reflect human psychological structures and development.

Having argued that the doctrine of God as Trinity rests on archetypal foundations and represents them, Jung turns to the Christian sources of this doctrine. The New Testament contains no explicit Trinitarian teachings, he notes, but the implicit outlines of this doctrine lie just beneath its surface. This indicates that the archetype was constellated but not yet manifest or fully conscious at the time of the canonical writings. This archetype was gradually raised into consciousness by the Church Fathers as the Apostolic Age advanced, culminating in the creeds of the third and fourth centuries and finally in the Creed of the Lateran Council of 1215.

This, the shortest section of the entire essay, is also its least interesting and significant. Jung clearly was not greatly interested in tracing the nuances of Christian theological history. His only purpose here is to argue that Trinitarian doctrine developed in the Church's thinking from a latent to a manifest state, becoming a clearer expression of the archetypal image that had been unconsciously intended all along. The Trinity doctrine is not, according to Jung, the product of rational concept-building but rather the result of an uncovering process.

With this Jung concludes his scholarship. In the fourth section, he turns to further psychological reflections on the Trinity and its three Persons. The fourth and fifth sections of the essay constitute roughly half of its content, and in them Jung extends the ideas presented earlier and states the core of his critical psychological analysis of Christianity.

He opens the fourth section ("The Three Persons in the Light of Psychology") by affirming again that Christian doctrine, like all other fundamental religious ideation, is not the product of rational thought and logic but rather the elaboration in consciousness of underlying unconscious archetypal forms and patterns. This fact makes religious doctrine very difficult for the rationalistic modern person to comprehend or appreciate. The psychologist, on the other hand, equipped with the knowledge of symbolism and its psychological meaning, has the intellectual tools for comprehending and explaining these ideas. Without affirming or denying the metaphysical claims made for religious doctrines by the proponents of a religion's belief system, the psychologist nevertheless may stay open to the possibility that archetypal ideas and images might be correlated with the larger structures of reality.

That said, Jung begins his exposition. The "history of the Trinity presents itself as the gradual crystallization of an archetype that moulds the anthropomorphic conceptions of father and son, of life, and of different persons into an archetypal and numinous figure, the 'Most Holy Three-in-One'" (1969c, p. 151). This doctrine may have reflected "a patriarchal order of society" in ancient times and may have referred to historical figures and events, but the motive force behind the crystallization of doctrine into this specific form was provided by an archetype creating its characteristic pattern. This is why the doctrine was considered a revelation: It was not created by man through efforts of thought and reflection, but rather appeared to the Church Fathers as an object of belief, to be fought for and upheld. To be sure, it was elaborated and clarified by argument and reflection, but it was accepted by the Christian community because it rang true, because it resonated with believers' deep psychic structures. The "holiness" of this doctrine is a sign of its archetypal nature.

Having discussed some of the details of how the Christian Trinitarian conception of God is an expression of an archetype, Jung turns next to the figure of Christ. In a subsection entitled "Christ as Archetype," he argues that the specific features of the historical Jesus very rapidly disappeared in a mass of aroused archetypal projections. Jesus the man was assimilated to an archetype in the minds of early Christians:

> At a very early stage . . . the real Christ vanished behind the emotions and projections that swarmed about him from far and near; immediately and almost without trace he was absorbed into the surrounding religious systems and moulded into their archetypal exponent. He became the collective figure whom the unconscious of his contemporaries expected to appear, and for this reason it is pointless to ask who he "really" was. (1969c, p. 154)

Beside the symbolic Christ, therefore, the historical Jesus has little significance, for the symbol was what attracted peoples and nations, not the human being. In the symbol they found hope and healing. But which archetype was it, specifically, that wrapped itself around the man Jesus?

Jung's method for answering this question is amplification. First collecting the mythic and metaphorical statements about Jesus, Jung then compares them with other similar archetypal motifs and finally relates them to the projective contents and images of modern, contemporary people. He finds that the statements about Jesus Christ contain

> essentially the same symbolism . . . [that] occurs in individual dreams or in fantasy-like projections upon living people (transference phenomena, hero-worship, etc.). The content of all such symbolic products is the idea of an overpowering, all-embracing, complete or perfect being, represented either by a man of heroic proportions, or by an animal with magical attributes, or by a magical vessel or some other "treasure hard to attain". . . . This archetypal idea is a reflection of the individual's wholeness, i.e., of the self, which is present in him as an unconscious image. (1969c, pp. 155–56)

The historical Jesus, therefore, was assimilated to the archetype of the self, which was constellated in the group unconscious of his time and place. For the people who found salvation in Christ, Jesus "realized the idea of the self" (ibid., p. 156) ("So verwirklichte Christus die Idee des Selbst" [Jung 1948, p. 384]).

Having said this, however, Jung introduces his analytic critique. While Christ clearly symbolizes the self, embodying a power and an authority greater than the conscious human ego, he does not represent the self fully: "the Christ-figure . . . lacks the nocturnal side of the psyche's nature, the darkness of the spirit, and is also without sin. Without the integration of evil there is not totality . . . " (1969c, p. 156). Christ is a true, but only partial, symbol of the self, and his appearance on the human stage can be compared with the "mean" in the "first mixture" in Plato's story of creation. As the mean between the Indivisible (Father) and the Divisible (Holy Spirit), Christ's manifestation results in the triad that comes into being through the first mixture and "is not yet reality. Consequently a second mixture is needed" (ibid., p. 157).

The realization that the Christian doctrines of Christ and the Trinity exclude the "dark side" of reality, and therefore leave the archaic instinctual portion of human nature—the "old man"—untransformed, lies at the heart of Jung's psychological critique of Christianity.

The transformation of humanity promised by Christ and envisioned in a multitude of ways by Christianity has never been fully realized in history. Christianity's vision of transformed human beings, as exemplified by the life of Jesus, has remained an ideal; it has not become reality.

Not that Christianity has not wanted to transform the whole person. The doctrine of incarnation clearly expresses an attempt to include humanity fully in the transformative process. The "indwelling of the Holy Spirit," moreover, is meant to continue the work of mankind's redemption. But the evidence of history weighs on the side of failure.

It is to the third Person of the Trinity that Jung now turns, and his interpretation of the Holy Spirit is perhaps the darkest, most obscure, and most complicated in the entire work. He starts by wondering why the Trinitarian conception of God did not follow the model of the human family: father, mother, son. That Christian thinking did not follow this pattern means that the archetype underlying the Trinitarian conception and guiding its development was not the same factor that underlies human mating and family-making patterns. But the conception of the Holy Spirit did not derive from pure, non-naturalistic logic either, because logic, if it followed Plato, would not have led to a Godhead involving Itself with human reality and "remaining behind," as it does in the doctrine of the Holy Spirit. A Platonic Trinity would have excluded humanity altogether in favor of formal perfection.

In the figure of the Holy Spirit, Jung argues, the human element is included in two ways. First, the Paraclete remains among the human community and works to transform humans into gods. (The words of Jesus, "Ye are gods" (John 10:34), is one of Jung's favorite quotations.) Second, the Holy Spirit arises out of the struggle between Father (unity) and an at least partially human Son (duality). He is the uniting "third," resolving the tension between the other two (1969c, pp. 158–60). "The Trinity, therefore, discloses itself as a symbol that comprehends the essence of the divine *and* the human" (ibid., p. 161).

In the rather tortured argumentation of these pages, Jung is trying to show that the Holy Spirit symbolizes "the transcendent function," which in his psychological theory refers to a psychic factor, or a developed attitude, that remains in fairly continuous contact with both conscious and unconscious processes. This attitude comes into being through resolution of an energetic conflict between them. It is a term implying high-level psychological integration through the development of a bonding force that unifies the split between conscious and unconscious.

At the conclusion of this section, Jung drops an idea that will be expanded later in this paper and developed much more extensively in other works: Christian doctrine, as developed and formulated over the span of centuries, represents the collective psyche's "compensation" to the era in which it emerged. This compensation includes the emergence of the Trinitarian doctrine of God: "The symbol of the Trinity . . . was destined to serve as a saving formula of wholeness in an epoch of change and psychic transformation" (1969c, p. 162). For the historical period in which this doctrine crystallized, therefore, it served to symbolize wholeness and to lay the ground work for a new step forward in psychological evolution. But this leads to the question of its relevance for *our* epoch, for the twentieth century and hereafter. Have Western men and women developed past the point where this doctrine adequately symbolizes wholeness? To this question Jung turns in the next section.

"The Problem of the Fourth" is the title of the essay's fifth, and by far longest, section. Here Jung introduces the idea of the quaternitarian pattern and compares it to the Trinitarian. Images of quaternity, he argues, are based on an underlying archetypal structure, as are those of a Trinity. This archetype found expression in ancient times in pre-Platonic (Pythagorean) Greek thought, in primitive modes of ritual action and symbolization, and in non-Western religions such as Buddhism (e.g., the "four elements, four prime qualities, four colours, four castes, four ways of spiritual development" [1969c, p. 167]). In modern times, it has appeared structurally in Schopenhauer's thought and in Jung's own theory of psychological types. The quaternitarian pattern implies "completeness," in distinction from "perfection," which is implied by Trinitarian patterns. In a "complete judgment," all aspects of a situation are taken into account by using all four psychological functions (thinking, feeling, sensation, intuition). Following ancient and classical symbolic conceptions, Jung points out that "the ideal of completeness is the circle or sphere, but its natural minimal division is a quaternity" (1969c, p. 167).

If reality divided falls into four parts, what becomes of the "Fourth" when the central conceptualization of a religion's God includes only Three? One aspect of reality has been left out. And here Jung takes up the topic of evil and Christianity's ways of dealing with it. To his mind, evil is the element of reality that Christian doctrine generally, but especially in its Trinitarian thought, excludes from the horizon of the real. Evil obviously does not meet the requirements of perfection, which are implicit in all Trinitarian thinking.

Clearly though, Christianity has recognized the need to face the question of human and cosmic evil. But it has done so, Jung argues, (a) by repressing it, as in its doctrine of *privatio boni*, which claims that evil is the absence (or privation) of good and has no further ontological status; or (b) by displacing it into the figure of the Devil, the eternal adversary of Christ, who as "prince of this world" rules over the repressed shadow aspects of Christian life. The first theological move, while it is more easily squared with Trinitarian attitudes, denies reality; the second, while it tends to run in the face of Trinitarian (and monotheistic) doctrine by moving toward a dualistic view of good versus evil, nevertheless offers a more accurate account of existence. In neither case, however, is evil integrated into the doctrine of God. God remains all good.

As "prince of this world," the Devil symbolizes the power of the repressed material world. This realm includes the "lower man," the body and its appetites and instincts. In the recent doctrine of the *Assumptio Mariae*, however, Jung saw an attempt on the part of dogmatic Christianity to take a radical new step toward integrating the repressed. By including the *body* of the Virgin within the inner chambers of the celestial realm, Christianity was expanding away from a purely spiritual (and masculine) conception of God toward a symbolic image that would include human flesh and its vulnerability to sin and corruption within the doctrine of God: "The *Assumptio Mariae* paves the way for the divinity of the Theotokos (i.e., her ultimate recognition as a goddess), but also for the quaternity. At the same time, matter is included in the metaphysical realm, together with the corrupting principle of the cosmos, evil" (1969c, p. 171). So along with the elevation of the Virgin's body into heaven comes, ironically, the Devil. In this evolution of dogma, Jung sees Catholic Christianity struggling to evolve toward a statement of wholeness, from a Trinitarian symbol to a quaternitarian one. This development represents a movement in the collective psyche toward a statement of full reality and human wholeness.

At this point, Jung injects the scandalous suggestion of including evil within the doctrine of God: Satan as a fourth figure in the Godhead. The Devil, Jung argues, represents God the Father's eternal adversary, and this figure should be placed back in the symbolic realm whence he originated. Evil and its symbolic agent, Satan, belong to the core of Christian theology, as is actually evidenced in the doctrine of creation, where disobedience and resistance are intrinsic to the unfolding development of autonomous spiritual beings. At a more metaphysical level, the Devil is "conceived to be the soul of matter, because they [i.e., matter and the Devil] both constitute a point of resistance without which the relative autonomy of individual existence would be simply unthinkable" (1969c, pp. 171-72). As Lord of this world and author of the fall and original sin, moreover, the Devil's work leads to the necessity for God's further manifestation in the incarnation. Again, this situates the representative of evil dynamically at the heart of Christian doctrine, making Satan responsible for forcing the incarnation.

It is in relation to Christ himself, however, that the figure of Satan comes into sharp prominence in the biblical tradition. The Old Testament Satan foreshadows him, but "the real devil first appears as the adversary of Christ" (1969c, p. 173). Christ and Satan, both sons of God (ibid., n.19), are a pair of hostile brothers. "Once the indefinable One unfolds into two, it becomes something definite" (ibid., p. 193), and this "definiteness" is the "two"—Christ and his arch opponent, "the Lord of this world," the Antichrist. "The act of love embodied in the Son is counterbalanced by Lucifer's denial" (ibid.); as sons of God, both equally reveal aspects of God Himself. When the One divides into Two, the oppositions latent within the One become manifest. So the Devil "too is a divine 'procession'," and it is this aspect of God that "became Lord of this world" (ibid.). The opposition between these two aspects of God, Christ and his brother, the Antichrist, is symbolized astrologically in the sign of Pisces, under whose aegis the Christian era has existed since its origin.

If Christ and the Devil are equally powerful but opposite emanations of God the Father, the resolution of their conflict has not been possible so far in the Christian era because it has been too intense. The two Christian millennia have formed an age of radical splitting and intense conflict between good and evil:

> This opposition means conflict to the last, and it is the task of humanity to endure this conflict until the time or turning-point is reached where good and evil begin to relativize themselves, to doubt themselves, and the cry is raised for a morality "beyond good and evil." In the age of Christianity and in the domain of trinitarian thinking such an idea is simply out of the question, because the conflict is too violent for evil to be assigned any other logical relation to the Trinity than that of an absolute opposite. In an emotional opposition, i.e., in a conflict situation, thesis and antithesis cannot be viewed together at the same time. This only becomes possible with cooler assessment of the relative value of good and the relative non-value of evil. Then it can no longer be

doubted, either, that a common life unites not only the Father and the "light" son, but the Father and his *dark* emanation. The unspeakable conflict posited by duality resolves itself in a fourth principle, which restores the unity of the first in its full development. The rhythm is built up in three steps, but the resultant symbol is a quaternity. (1969c, pp. 174–75)

The three stages include, then, four "actors": the Father (the stage of uncritical unity), His two Sons (the conflict stage), and the Holy Ghost (the stage of reconciliation and restored unity).

A quaternitarian doctrine of God not only represents the resolution of conflict between good and evil within Christianity, but it also includes the natural world within the doctrine of God. Whereas the Trinitarian conception of God keeps Him "off the ground" and up in the realm of spirit, abandoning nature, matter, the feminine, and the world as worthless and draining these aspects of existence of all ultimate meaning and value, the quaternitarian conception locates God also in this world and in nature, and includes these areas within the domain of Divinity. The God-image that results from this greater integration represents all of reality, imperfections included.

Suturing the split in the God image also helps to heal the conflict on the level of human consciousness. The human condition stretches between the heavenly realm of spirit, wherein the Trinity and aspirations of perfection dwell, and the realm of instinct and physical existence, which "is in thrall of the Lord of this world" (1969c, p. 177). Because humans suffer from this condition of self-division, drawn upward by spirit and pulled downward by instinct and body, they have sought to find a way to resolve it. "Seekers" devoted "their lives to a work whose purpose it was to redeem the 'four-horned serpent,' the fallen Lucifer, and to free the *anima mundi* imprisoned in matter" (ibid., p. 178). The psychological work of understanding and integrating the unconscious, Jung argues, is equivalent to the religious work of the Gnostics and alchemists who searched for the light hidden in the darkness of matter and attempted to reunite the light and dark sides of God through the inspiration of the Holy Ghost (ibid.).

One great advantage of the quaternity over the Trinity is its realism. It accepts "the existence of a power opposed to God, namely 'this world' and its Lord," and it recognizes "the existence of this power as an undeniable fact by fettering trinitarian thinking to the reality of this world":

The Platonic freedom of the spirit does not make a whole judgment possible: it wrenches the light half of the picture away from the dark half. This freedom is to a large extent a phenomenon of civilization, the lofty preoccupation of that fortunate Athenian whose lot it was not to be born a slave. We can only rise above nature if somebody else carries the weight of the earth for us. What sort of philosophy would Plato have produced had he been his own house-slave? What would the Rabbi Jesus have taught if he had had to support a wife and children? If he had had to till the soil in which the bread he broke had grown, and weed the vineyard in which the wine he dispensed had ripened? The dark weight of the earth must enter into the picture of the whole. (1969c, p. 178)

Quaternitarian thinking would ground theologizing in the reality of this world and force it out of its idealistic trajectory into facing the limitations imposed by nature. Indeed, it would require building these limitations right into the conception of its ground plan and aim, which is "wholeness." The movement from Trinitarian to quaternitarian theology, therefore, would be a movement from idealistic intellectualization to a more realistic recognition of life as lived by actual humans. The cross, which lies at the center of the Christian story and *is* a quaternity symbol, affirms the centrality of brokenness, evil, and limitation in human experience (1969c, p. 179) and so is in line with a possible quaternitarian theology.

Quaternitarian theology would also provide a way to extract meaning from human conflict and from the plagues of moral evil and physical corruption that constantly dog human existence. Whereas Trinitarian theology leads inevitably to repression and to the denial of evil's power and reality, quaternitarian theology would accept the existence and power of evil and find God's hand at work there as well. This theology would see mankind as caught up in a double movement of God's self-revelation. On the one side appears the bright God, on the other the dark God. Both good and evil derive from the same source, and both reveal something about God's reality. As an instrument of God's self-revelation, mankind too exemplifies both sides of God. The human conflict between light and dark, between self-transcendent and egoistic motivations and strivings, is also a manifestation of God's polarity. And the human struggle to reconcile these opposites is mankind's participation in the divine drama of reconciliation. Quaternitarian theology would place great meaning on mankind's conscious suffering of the conflict between good and evil and on the attempt to reconcile them into a state of wholeness rather than repressing one in favor of the other.

This section of the Trinity essay (5.1, "The Concept of Quaternity") contains the essential content of Jung's proposal for reconstructing the Christian doctrine of God and Christian theology along quaternitarian lines. In the next section, "The Psychology of the Quaternity," he expands his thoughts in a less theological and more psychological way. There he treats theological doctrine "as an expression of the psyche, rather as if it were a dream-image" (1969c, p. 180).

As an expression of the psyche, the Trinitarian conception of God can be interpreted in reference to three stages of psychological development. The first (the "father stage") is childhood, when a person is "dependent on a definite, ready-made pattern of existence which is habitual and has the character of law" (1969c, p. 181). This is a stage of passive acceptance, and it lacks critical reflection. The second stage occurs "when the son starts to put himself in his father's place" (ibid.). Jung does not name this stage oedipal, but the implication is clear. This stage, which is full of conflict and criticism, produces higher consciousness: Now a person makes choices and does not simply obey an authority. Habit is discarded for individual preference and decision. This stage is reflected in Jesus' attitude toward the Pharisaic guardians of the law. What is gained in this stage—"reason and reflection" (ibid., p. 183)—results in a separation from the father and in attainment of an independent conscious standpoint.

The second stage is transitional, however, to a third, in which the son becomes a father. So that this will not become simply repetitious of the father's patterns, the gains made in the second stage need to be included in the third. The second stage consolidated the son's separate, autonomous, independent ego position over against the father; the third stage brings this ego position along but connects it back to the father. Psychologically this means recognizing that the ego is master of some things but not of all, and that it is not the sole originator of all its thoughts, feelings, and fantasies: "Accordingly, the advance to the third stage means something like a recognition of the unconscious, if not actual subordination to it" (1969c, p. 183). In the third stage, a person relinquishes "exclusive independence" in favor of "voluntarily submitting to a paternal authority, either in psychological form [i.e., the self], or factually in projected form, as when he recognizes the authority of the Church's teachings" (ibid.). The third stage is entered, Jung points out, usually through experiences that "have a numinous character, and can take the form of conversions, illuminations, emotional shocks, blows of fate, religious or mystical experiences . . . " (ibid., pp. 183–84).

Jung mentions some pitfalls of the third stage, when egos become subsumed under a higher authority. Collective mass movements such as National Socialism, the Jehovah's Witnesses, and the Oxford Groups are highlighted. Equally dangerous, however, is "getting stuck in the transitional stage of the Son," which is characterized by an excessively critical, ego-assertive attitude. As a definition of psychological maturity, Jung offers the following:

> The criterion of adulthood does not consist in being a member of certain sects, or nations, but in submitting to the spirit of one's own independence. . . . This third stage . . . means articulating one's ego-consciousness with a supraordinate totality, of which one cannot say that it is "I," but which is best visualized as a more comprehensive being, though one should of course keep oneself conscious all the time of the anthropomorphism of such a conception. Hard as it is to define, this unknown quantity can be experienced by the psyche and is known in Christian parlance as the "Holy Ghost," the breath that heals and makes whole. (1969c, pp. 184–85)

The third stage, which in Trinitarian theology is represented by the emergence of the Holy Ghost, symbolizes achieved adulthood: the conscious relationship between a firmly established ego and a supraordinate self.

In this section (5.2) of the essay, Jung interprets the Trinity as a developmental dynamic for both individuals and the Judeo-Christian culture as a whole. With regard to historical cultural developments, the first stage of the Father represents Yahweh and Old Testament attitudes and thought; the second stage of the Son is the succeeding generations and the New Testament revisions; and the third stage of the Holy Spirit is the post-New Testament phase of Christian history. Each stage is a phase of psychological development in which consciousness and collective attitudes consolidate until they are ready to move on to the next one.

One interpretive question remains: Has Christianity as a collective, organized religion, or have the majority of individuals in it, actually completed the developmental sequence represented by the Trinitarian symbol? Or does this symbol represent a still-unfulfilled promise of development? At several points in the Trinity essay (and elsewhere in his writings), Jung implies that Christianity has fallen short: It has remained in the second stage, or at times has even regressed to the first stage, but it has definitely failed to carry out the promise of development represented by the Paraclete. The full realization of "God within," as implied by the Johannine saying, "Ye are gods" (John 10:34), would represent the fulfillment of the third stage, and this has not taken place in Christianity. The religion as a whole and the majority of its adherents have therefore not completed the psychological evolution implicit in the Trinity doctrine.

This opinion is restated in the final part of this section (5.3), under the somewhat misleading heading of "General Remarks on Symbolism." Here Jung explicitly introduces the theme of therapy into his discussion.

From comparative studies, he recapitulates, the Trinity can be shown to be based on an archetypal structure of the human psyche. These comparative studies also routinely indicate that a "fourth element" is missing in Trinitarian formulations. Without this fourth element, the realm of idea and concept lacks genuine linkage to reality. For Christianity, this has finally resulted in the Trinity doctrine's fading, among other things: It has lost meaning for common believers and even for the Church's teachers. To overcome this loss of the symbol's meaning, reconstruction is necessary. Psychotherapeutic reconstruction functions to overcome a dissociation that has taken place between present states of consciousness and past ones that have slipped into the unconscious. "This split can only be mended if consciousness is able to formulate conceptions which give adequate expression to the contents of the unconscious" (1969c, p. 188), and this is the role of reconstructive interpretation. So in this essay on the Trinity, Jung is performing a therapeutic task for Christianity by reconstructing the Trinity symbol and by interpreting it in a language that the modern, psychological person can assimilate. He is retrieving lost or repressed symbolic meanings for contemporary Christianity and is thereby helping it to overcome the split that has been created in the course of its history.

To achieve therapeutic results, reconstruction and interpretion must adequately express the unconscious. Jung argues that at one time the Trinity doctrine, "plus the incommensurable 'fourth,'" must have offered "a saving, healing, wholesome effect" (ibid.). For modern persons, for whom this symbol has become unconscious, a type of psychological reconstruction and interpretation that honors this doctrines's archetypal foundations and understands its symbolic language is required if this symbol of wholeness is to function again. The healing effects of the archetype of wholeness and of its symbolic expression cannot be evoked through purely rational, abstract formulations. A symbolic equivalent is needed, and this is the purpose of symbolic interpretation.

The traditional Christian symbol for wholeness, its God-image, has faded and lost its power to convince and to heal, and without this symbol, "wholeness is not represented in consciousness" (1969c, p. 188) for Western men and women. As a consequence, modern consciousness falls into a vacuum and exists "at the mercy of all the utopian fantasies that rush in to fill the gap . . . " (ibid.). The loss of a convincing God-image results in the dangerous vulnerability of the modern person to "-isms" that promise, and offer visions of, wholeness. Modern godless-ness has resulted in a state of consciousness that feels functional at best, rings insubstantial and hollow at par, and falls prey to demonic posses-sion at worst.

Symbols of the self and of psychological wholeness nevertheless continue to appear for modern men and women, often in dreams. The task of the psychotherapist is to assist persons to understand them and to relate to their symbolic value. Often this symbolism, which is typi-cally quaternitarian, is so mundane that it may be easily overlooked by the dreamer ("three men and a woman, either sitting at a table or driving in a car, or three men and a dog, a huntsman with three hounds, three chickens in a coop from which the fourth has escaped, and suchlike" [1969c, p. 189]). The knowledgeable analyst will, however, recognize this kind of symbolic evidence of the self's existence.

If modern clinical evidence shows that the self is characteristically symbolized by quaternitarian images, an explanation is needed for why Christianity formulated its God-image as a Trinity: "One is driven to ask how it came about that a highly differentiated form of religion like Christianity reverted to the archaic triad in order to construct its trinitarian God-image" (1969c, pp. 190–91). This symbol needs expla-nation: Why did Christianity conceive of God as Three and not as Four? The answer to this is again based on clinical evidence, Jung asserts: When Trinitarian rather than quaternitarian symbols are pro-duced by an individual's unconscious, clinical experience shows that "there is so much unconsciousness, and such a large degree of primitiv-ity to match it, that a spiritualization appears necessary as a compensa-tion. The saving symbol is then a triad in which the fourth is lacking because it has to be unconditionally rejected" (ibid., p. 191).

Applying this to the reconstruction of Christian history, Jung argues that the doctrine of the Trinity was formulated during a period in Western cultural history when the further development of consciousness required the repression of the "fourth"—the "old Adam," instinctual nature, egoistic assertion and striving. Christianity therefore elaborated a symbol that was of partial psychological wholeness but was required to be so for developmental reasons. Christianity's partial or incomplete God-symbol, the Trinity, is therefore a residue of an earlier developmental stage in Western culture when the requirements for further psychological development were such that repression of the fourth element was needed for the sake of other psychological gains.

While this type of partialness was required for the sake of strengthening the altruistic and spiritual side of human nature over against the egoistic and instinctual, and, incidentally, also eventuated in the great scientific triumphs of the West, it has also produced a serious split in the psyche. And this is what concerns Jung as a contemporary doctor of souls. The psychological doctor's responsibility in modern times is to recognize and to interpret "the symbols aiming at wholeness" (1969c, p. 191) and to help patients toward a "synthesis of conscious and unconscious" aspects of the self (ibid., p. 192). Symbols of wholeness present a way to integrate the repressed and atrophied portions of the self. This therapy, moreover, requires "a conscious confrontation" between ego-consciousness and the unconscious, and "this is not possible unless one understands what the unconscious is saying" (ibid.). Hence the need for symbolic interpretation. And this is what Jung is seeking to do in this essay for his patient, Christianity.

Jung closes this section by commenting on the relative merits of modern Protestantism and Catholicism and on their resistance to his ministrations. Protestantism "proclaims doctrines which nobody understands, and demands a faith which nobody can manufacture"; Catholicism, on the other hand, "possesses a richly developed and undamaged world of dogmatic ideas, which provide a worthy receptacle for the plethora of figures in the unconscious," but in the modern world it is increasingly the case that a person "slips out of this form" and falls into "fanatical atheism" (1969c, p. 192). Neither branch of Christianity relates effectively to modernity, and neither has much regard for the doctor's efforts to heal its dissociation between spirit and nature and to restore a link between modern consciousness and the timeless, archetypal images of wholeness.

In the Conclusion, Jung rehearses his argument once more, adding, however, a thought that will become more salient in later works, especially in *Answer to Job*. The continuing presence of God among mankind as the Holy Ghost means that humanity is included in the divine process, and this "means that the principle of separateness and autonomy over against God—which is personified in Lucifer as the God-opposing will—is included in it too" (1969c, p. 196). Lucifer is an archetypal image of the self-assertive will, of human egohood. This "rebellious will," the shadow brother of the "light Son," Christ, is necessary for self-actualization.

> An object that has no will of its own, capable, if need be, of opposing its creator, and with no qualities other than its creator's . . . has no independent existence and is incapable of ethical decision. . . . Therefore Lucifer was perhaps the one who best understood the divine will struggling to create a world and who carried that will out most faithfully. For, by rebelling against God, he became the active principle of a creation which opposed to God a counter-will of its own. (Ibid.)

Likewise the human ego, backed by the Luciferian insistence on autonomy and freedom and self-assertion, is a necessary dynamic element in a person's unfolding actualization of psychological wholeness. Without this element there would be only potential, and the self would remain latent, an abstraction.

Jung's own strong identification with this Luciferian spirit appeared in his dream of approaching the "highest presence" where his father bows and touches his head to the floor, while Jung refrains from touching his own forehead to the ground: "There was perhaps a millimeter to spare" (1961a, p. 219). This spirit of independence, which was also a motive force in Jung's original separation from his father and from his father's faith and later led to his break with Freud, states itself forcefully once again in the late work, *Answer to Job*. In a personal sense, Jung's argument for including Lucifer in the Godhead was a bid for a place of his own in the very tradition he often so strenuously opposed. The bad son would turn out to be the best son after all, bringing back the healing medicine to an ailing paternal tradition. Here lies the subtle transference dynamic beneath the surface of this essay's content.

The Trinity Essay as Therapy

As a part of Jung's therapeutic design on Christianity, the Trinity essay is primarily a diagnostic, reconstructive, interpretive statement, representing the early phases of therapy. The transference/countertransference dynamic is present but quite unconscious. We see Jung's therapist eye falling on the moribund religious tradition of Western modernity. The remaining adherents of this religion no longer experience the effect of its symbolic meanings, and they follow the traditional forms out of habit, if at all. Jung's own father, Pastor Paul Jung, was a prime illustration of this malaise.

As a physician of souls, Jung asks what is wrong. Christianity is no longer psychologically functional. It no longer supplies or shows vitality. Its present-day members are dissociated from past structures of meaning, much like patients cut off by amnesia from childhood and youth. The therapist begins to work on closing this split between past and present, between traditional symbols and modern modes of thought.

This therapeutic operation calls for remembering, for reconstructing the past so that its meaning and inner life can once more glow and be experienced and be understood in the present. The first stage of psychotherapeutic treatment is remembering (cf. Ch. 2, above).

This phase of treatment not only requires remembering factual history and recalling significant historical events, but it also requires bringing the inner meaning and emotions of the past to consciousness. Once there was a child who, through time, developed certain features and inner structures that became encoded in the psycho-symbolic matrix of a personal history. These encoded events represent the stages of emerging personhood. Crystallized in symbolical expressions that capture key moments in the developmental sequence, these images signal the inner meaning of that history. Once they also provided a sense of direction and meaning. The person who has arrived in the second half of life—as Christianity has—often has lost touch with the dreams of youth, and the symbols that patterned and channeled libido then no longer are conscious or feel meaningful. In fact, they are neglected, misunderstood, and often even shunned with embarrassment as the follies of youth.

This is the situation with Christianity in modern times, according to Jung. It has forgotten the meaning of many of its major symbols, and some of them have been discarded as an embarrassment in this age of scientific rationality. The symbol of the Trinity represents a key internal development in the history of Christianity, its meaning once having helped organize the symbolic world of many believers. Once this symbol sustained the Christian psyche and communicated a revelatory message with power and authority. But no longer. Even Jung's father, a doctor of divinity and a pastor, could give no credible account of its meaning, let alone benefit from it in his own spiritual anguish.

So the doctor of souls takes up this central symbolic statement of his patient, as he would the archetypal dream of a patient's childhood or youth, and brings it close for scrutiny and interpretation. He reconstructs the stage of psychological development in which it arose, the attitudes that it compensated, and the historical meaning of its emergence into consciousness. He interprets its meaning structurally and dynamically: with the method of amplification, he elucidates the underlying archetypal structures that it symbolizes; using the theory of compensation, he shows its developmental significance, which speaks to how it served the purpose of increasing consciousness at the time of its appearance. From this there emerges a picture of the patient's psychological development.

The doctor's account also includes a diagnosis of the patient's present condition, which requires a discussion of the aspects of psychological wholeness that were repressed or left out of consiousness because of this developmental history and therefore now may be the cause of psychological symptoms. Moreover, these repressed contents indicate where the seeds of future development lie. The next stage will come about through a structural transformation that integrates these shadow aspects. In the case of Christianity, this new structure of wholeness will be expressed by a quaternitarian symbol. The Christian doctrine of God, which is this religion's master symbol for conscious wholeness, must consequently change from a Trinitarian to a quaternitarian symbol. The doctor cannot predict precisely what the new symbol of wholeness will look like, since this must be revealed through the spontaneous symbolization process of the psyche itself. The new symbol of integrated wholeness will come about of its own accord, and the doctor's only duty is to be aware of when it happens, and then to help the patient understand and assimilate it.

In this very carefully worked out essay, Jung detailed his position on the contemporary problems of Christianity (diagnosis), on its developmental history (reconstruction), and on its core structures of consciousness and its central "dream" (interpretation). He also assumed the psychotherapeutic stance of waiting patiently for the next stages of development to unfold.

AN ARCHETYPAL INTERPRETATION
OF A CHRISTIAN RITUAL: THE MASS

Jung's next major work on a Christian theme, "Transformation Symbolism in the Mass," was drafted in 1941. This paper was prepared for the Eranos Conference that followed the one where he had extemporized on the Trinity in response to the mathematician Speiser's presentation. The range of concerns discussed in this paper is much more circumscribed than in the previous one. Principally an interpretation of the Roman Catholic Mass, it was entitled "Das Wandlungssymbol in der Messe" (slightly mistranslated in the English *Collected Works*; more accurate would be "The Symbol of Transformation in the Mass"). This paper was delivered some two months prior to the talk on Paracelsus referred to above. In it Jung's growing preoccupation with alchemy is evident.

"Transformation Symbolism in the Mass" is divided into four sections: a brief introduction; a description of the ritual itself; parallels from primitive religions (principally Aztec) and from alchemy and Gnosticism (the visions of Zosimos); and a final, major section entitled "The Psychology of the Mass." It is only in the fourth part that Jung employs his psychological concepts to interpret the meaning of this Christian ritual.

Rather than treating the Mass in its entirety, Jung focuses on one specific theme, variously named sacrifice, dismemberment and renewal, and transformation. What he wants to discuss is principally the archetypal substratum underlying the action of the Mass. This he calls "the archetype of sacrifice" (1969c, p. 265). This same archetypal pattern, he argues, supports the phase in a person's individuation process when the ego is brought into a critical new relation to the self. The psychological purpose of the ritual of the Mass is seen as facilitative of the matured ego's coming into relation to the self, thereby uniting its experience of the temporal world with perceptions of the eternal, joining the mundane with the divine, and fostering the "communion of the living Christ with his flock" (ibid., p. 267).

The central drama of the Mass is God's sacrifice of Himself, in the form of His Son, for mankind. Jung relates this theme to primitive practices of slaying a king who has become impotent or can no longer guarantee fertility for his land. At the heart of Christianity and of the Mass is such a story of king-slaying: The Son is sacrificed by the Father, who is also the Son, for the sake of His people, in order to restore their well-being. This is necessary because God is guilty of letting His people down: "God's guilt consisted in the fact that, as creator of the world and king of his creatures, he was inadequate . . . " (1969c, p. 271). Consequently, God must undergo transformation, and to the transformational process belongs, archetypally, the image of dismemberment (ibid., p. 272).

The Mass functions to reach out to the congregation, to include the people in the process of God's transformation, which is being enacted on the divine plane (1969c, p. 273). Through the Mass, mankind participates by means of projection and identification (*"participation mystique"*) in God's self-transformation.

Jung fully acknowledges the Gnostic tone of his interpretation of Christ's sacrifice and of the Mass, but he defends a moderate Gnosticism on the grounds that it is more psychological than the orthodox consensus: Gnosticism perceived the archetypal mystery behind the scenes of the historical events in the life of Jesus (1969c, p. 273). Therefore, Jung argues, "the Docetism of the Acts of John appears more as a completion of the historical event than a devaluation of it" (ibid., p. 283). The very real danger of the Gnostic position, Jung acknowledges, is psychological inflation, which seems indicated in the case of the author of the Acts of John ("one of the most important of the apocryphal texts that have come down to us" [ibid., p. 273]): John's "overweening attitude arises from an inflation caused by the fact that the enlightened John has identified with his own light and confused his ego with the self" (ibid., p. 287). "Recognizing the danger of Gnostic irrealism, the Church . . . has always insisted on the concretism of the historical events . . . . [This is the] justification for postponing the elevation of man's status until after death, as this avoided the danger of Gnostic inflation" (ibid.). The conventional Christian emphasis on history, therefore, is a salutary defense against the danger of psychological inflation.

The Mass, Jung argues, provides a careful balance between proximity to and distance from the self. On the one hand, the transformational process of dismemberment and renewal is taking place entirely in and through the divine persons; on the other, congregants participate in this action through *participation mystique* and therefore also experience the transformational process taking place in the self. Making this connection to the self is identical to what Jung elsewhere describes as the goal of the individuation process. It is identical with the psychological aim of Christian Gnosticism as well:

> This Gnostic Christ . . . symbolizes man's original unity and exalts it as the saving goal of his development. By . . . bringing order into chaos, by resolving disharmonies and centring upon the mid-point, thus setting a "boundary" to the multitude and focusing attention upon the cross, consciousness is reunited with the unconscious, the unconscious man is made one with his centre, which is also the centre of the universe, and in this wise the goal of man's salvation and exaltation is reached. (1969c, p. 292)

This same process and outcome are experienced by persons in psychotherapy when they enter into a conscious relationship to "a compensatory ordering factor which is independent of the ego and whose nature transcends consciousness" (1969c, p. 294). This factor is no more miraculous than is "the orderliness of radium decay, or the attunement of a virus to the anatomy and physiology of human beings" (ibid.). It is a part of nature. What *is* extraordinary is that humans can become conscious of this ordering factor, while other organisms seem to lack this capacity: "Presumably it would also be an ecstatic experience for a radium atom to know the time of its decay is exactly determined, or for the butterfly to recognize that the flower has made all the necessary provisions for its propagation" (ibid.). The human species seems to be the only one with this sort of self-consciousness.

The Therapeutic Intention of Interpreting the Mass

In comparison with the earlier Trinity essay, "Transformation Symbolism in the Mass" is less critical of the one-sidedness of Christianity and also much less sharply focused on the present need for its transformation. It is almost entirely reconstructive and interpretive. In it, Jung returns to the origins of Christian religion, to the early events and archetypal themes behind its later mature manifestation, and to its numinous, sacred center. Starting with the Mass, which is "a still-living mystery" (1969c, p. 203), he interprets the meaning of the sacrificial offering in Christianity from a psychological viewpoint. The statement made by the Mass is amplified by comparing it with similar rituals and symbolic statements from other religions, and its deeper meanings and significance are sounded for their psychological value and import.

Jung finds the central psychological meaning of the Mass to reside in the vivid, evocative protrayal of a dismemberment-renewal process. Through being connected to this unconscious process, persons are renewed spiritually by the Mass and drawn into relation to the self. Since this is the deepest meaning of the Mass, and since this ritual represents the very heart of Christianity's vision and message, this also states the ultimate purpose of the Christian religion as a whole: to make the mystery of the self available to ordinary persons and to democratize the mystery of the individuation process, which had earlier always been the guarded privilege of royalty and special elites (1969c, p. 295).

This essay, which in so many ways seems weaker and less challenging to Christianity than the former one, appears to have the purpose, within the framework of Jung's therapy of Christianity, of stating the core meaning and values of its existence, as these are represented in its own symbolic system. The doctor has probed to the core of the patient's symbolic universe, taken up the mainspring of the earliest and deepest motivations and of the factor that formed the dominant pattern of libido organization, and presented an interpretation of its meaning. This has a number of therapeutic functions. It reconnects the patient to childhood origins and thereby overcomes the repressions that have created amnesia or loss of identity. Dynamically, it creates a bridge for ego-consciousness to the layers of the unconscious that contain images and values which have fallen away or become repressed. Possibly it allows the patient to catch a glimpse of the self, thereby restoring vitality and a sense of purpose.

Jung's reputation as a Christian revitalist results from works such as this, which are principally hermeneutical and not critical. This represents only a phase of therapy, however, and not the essence of Jung's overall approach to Christianity. By itself, this kind of interpretation would have little transformational impact on Christianity. But as an aspect of the larger work of therapy, it occupies an important place. It is a key interpretaion of a central feature of the patient's psychology. In it, Jung is functioning as hermeneut, reconnecting modern Christianity to the archetypal sources of its past existence and to its ultimate origins in the self, reminding Christianity of its fundamental *raison d'être* and purpose. Christianity came into the world to democratize the individuation process. This is its telos.

THE INTERPRETATION OF
CHRISTIAN HISTORY AND ITS REPRESSIONS

Jung's understanding of alchemy played an important part in his interpretation of the Mass. Ultimately, he felt, alchemy and Christianity were two aspects of the same human endeavor, namely, the transformation and development of consciousness. But, like a pair of rival siblings, they became shadow brothers and were incapable of working together, although they shared the same aim.

Since the late 1920s, Jung had been immersed in the study of European and Oriental alchemy. His great India dream in 1938 confirmed his sense that his vocation would be fulfilled only through retrieving the meaning of alchemy for modern Western consciousness. His own psychological and psychotherapeutic efforts were sharply prefigured, he felt, in this alchemical material. In many ways, Jung identified with the Hermetic underground tradition in European cultural history. In alchemy's often conflicted and compensatory relationship to Christianity, he saw a reflection of the relation of his own psychology and therapy to modern Western scientific culture. Jung's voluminous interpretive writings on alchemy are therefore an essential part of his engagement with Christianity and Western culture.

In 1944 Jung published *Psychology and Alchemy*, the first of several major works on this subject. This book was divided into three parts. The origins of Parts II and III dated back to the Eranos Conferences of 1935 and 1936. Part I, entitled "Introduction to the Religious and Psychological Problems of Alchemy," was written last, in 1943, and is the only portion of the book to be considered in detail here.

The overall intention of *Psychology and Alchemy* was to validate the concept of the collective unconscious and the existence of a spiritual process spontaneously at work within it. The introductory essay, written after this task had been substantially completed, touches on many of the themes discussed in the papers on the Trinity and the Mass. It goes further, however, and relates modern psychotherapy to the type of therapy offered by traditional Christianity, and then argues that the therapy offered by Christianity has the drawback of shying away from the integration of the shadow. *Psychology and Alchemy* is both an exposition of Jung's aims and methods of psychotherapy and a critical commentary on the Christian tradition and its method of curing souls.

Jung opens this fascinating discussion by reflecting on the problem of the "interminable analysis." Certain patients, he says, seem unable ever to terminate treatment, and the doctor wonders why, despite symptom relief, improved functioning, and reduced personal transference, they cannot leave. Consciously and unconsciously, he goes on, they are seeking a goal not yet reached and one that may never be fully appropriated: "that hidden and as yet unmanifest 'whole' man . . . " (1968a, p. 6). They are seeking wholeness, maximum integration of the psyche, and this is a substantially different goal from functional improvement. This is, moreover, a *longissima via*, a very long road.

This goal is identical to the *imitatio Christi*, in Jung's understanding of it as the attainment of selfhood and wholeness which was symbolized by the life of Christ. Common misunderstandings, however, converted that Christian ideal into a flagrant imitation of externals. Rather than following the pathway toward "developing and exalting the inner man" (1968a, p. 7), it became a practice of superficial formalisms.

This outward preference of form over substance characterizes Western attitudes generally. The East offers an instructive contrast, where the subject is all and the object world is illusory. In the West, the value and awareness of the psyche tend to be reduced to zero, and the individual soul suffers from this sharp discount. In comparison, the value placed on collective history and external facts is enormously high. While Christianity recognizes the soul's significance, and thus stands on the side of valuing the human psyche and the inner life beyond the inclinations of the other forces active in the Western attitude, it too has been influenced toward externalism and formalism and has tended to neglect the value of the individual psyche, preferring instead outward, formal observances and statements. When the sacred is projected completely outward upon external, historical or theological "objects," the consequence is that subjective reality and attitudes remain unformed and uninfluenced by it. Hence we confront the astounding fact that Europeans, after many centuries of Christian influence, seem untouched inwardly by its message: "Christian civilization has proved hollow to a terrifying degree: it is all veneer, but the inner man has remained untouched and therefore unchanged" (1968a, p. 12).

While Christianity has had all the necessary symbols—in the figure of Christ and in its various doctrines and rites—for facilitating the individuation process and for relating the ego to the self, it has failed to do so because it has not concentrated its efforts enough on the inner person:

> Too few people have experienced the divine image as the innermost possession of their own souls. Christ only meets them from without, never from within, the soul; that is why dark paganism still reigns there, a paganism which, now in a form so blatant that it can no longer be denied and now in all too threadbare disguise, is swamping the world of so-called Christian civilization. (1968a, p. 12)

This failure was declared in 1943, in the midst of German Nazism's flagrant disregard of values held high by Christian culture throughout the preceding centuries. Christianity's efforts and methods have failed to Christianize the soul, Jung declares, because they have not solidified the inner religious function within the Western psyche. Christianity has failed to educate the soul, and it has also failed therefore to cure the soul of its tendencies to split and fragment.

One thing Christianity has lacked is an effective method for relating the heights and glories of its doctrines to the everyday experience of men and women who "are incapable of establishing a connection between the sacred figures and their own psyche: they cannot see to what extent the equivalent images are lying dormant in their own unconscious" (1968a, p. 13). Psychology, Jung claims, knows how to bridge this gap. Disclaiming the wish to invent a new religion or to construct a new heresy—"Psychology is concerned with the act of seeing and not with the construction of new religious truths" (ibid.)— Jung says that psychology can describe the God-image in the individual human soul and uncover the archetypal roots of religious doctrine. It can demonstrate how the same factors underlying doctrine are manifest in the dreams and visions of contemporary men and women, and it can show how the goal toward which religious doctrines point can be approached by the modern individual (ibid.). Psychology opens "a way . . . for reason and feeling to gain access to those other images which the teachings of religion offer to mankind" (ibid., p. 15).

Psychology can therefore assist theology, because "the archetypes of the unconscious can be shown empirically to be the equivalents of religious dogmas" (1968a, p. 17). The human psyche reflects the *typos* (imprint) of a God-image. While religion looks to the imprinter, psychology studies the imprint. The *typos* itself, however, is more variegated and less definite than are the many religious representatives of it (Christ, Purusha, the Atman, Buddha, etc.). The *typos*, an archetype, is indeterminate and expresses itself in many forms and images, all of which imply, to one extent or another, the same essence: human wholeness. This is what the psychological term "self" refers to as well: "a term on the one hand definite enough to convey the essence of human wholeness and on the other hand indefinite enough to express the indescribable and indeterminable nature of this wholeness" (ibid., pp. 17–18).

The Christ-symbol, which is "perhaps the most highly developed and differentiated symbol of the self, apart from the figure of the Buddha" (1968a, p. 19), differs, however, from the fullest possible expression of the self in one serious respect. The essence of the self "is a union of opposites" (ibid.): individual/universal, masculine/feminine, light/dark, good/evil. The allusion to Christ's androgeny is "the utmost concession the Church has made to the problem of opposites. The opposition between light and good on the one hand and darkness and evil on the other is left in a state of open conflict, since Christ simply represents good, and his counterpart the devil, evil" (ibid.). The Christ-symbol, therefore, falls short of expressing the human person's wholeness and consequently cannot perform the central psychological function of symbols, which is to heal conflicts and to overcome splits between opposites in the psyche. Instead, the Christ-figure tends to exacerbate the splits, because it leaves the *scoriam* of human nature that is "evil"—the "lower man," the "old Adam"—essentially unredeemed (ibid.).

Because Christian doctrine leaves the tension between good and evil unresolved, its adherents are driven to find ways of avoiding, or denying, the part of their nature that is identified as sinful, evil, and corrupt. Christian doctrine and symbolism do not provide a way to resolve the impasse in the human soul between light and dark, spirit and instinct, transcendent and egoistic strivings. Practices such as confession of sin and doctrines such as moral probabilism derive from the need to go on living, but they offer no real solution to the conflict between good and evil.

Christian doctrine is in part responsible for creating this deep and almost total cleavage between good and evil, and it has had to find ways to mitigate the psychological damage created by this. Moral probabilism relaxes the tension and could possibly lead ultimately to the constellation of a healing symbol that would include and contain the good/evil opposition. But the weight of Christian tradition, anchored in its masculine vision of God and its Trinitarian doctrine, militates against a resolution of this split at the symbolic level. And here once again Jung identifies the major flaw in Christian thought as being its exclusion of the "fourth" and its consequent denial of the possibility of genuine redemption of the "'whole' man" (1968a, p. 6).

This part of the argument stated, Jung begins his discussion of the relation of alchemy to the dogmatic Christian tradition, revealing now the direction of his main thrust and also the reason for his intense interest in alchemy. Alchemy, he declares, operated on the axiom of Maria Prophetissa: "'One becomes two, two becomes three, and out of the third comes the one as the fourth'" (1968a, p. 23). This preoccupation of alchemy with the "fourth" reflects its concern for the redemption of matter and for the release of the soul that is locked in the embrace of *physis*. Alchemy was doing the work that Christianity avoided, redeeming the part of human nature rejected by the Christian builders and finding God within the rejected *scoriam*.

> The point is that alchemy is rather like an undercurrent to the Christianity that ruled on the surface. It is to this surface as the dream is to consciousness, and just as the dream compensates the conflicts of the

conscious mind, so alchemy endeavors to fill in the gaps left open by the Christian tension of opposites. (Ibid.)

The study of alchemy is the study of Christianity's unconscious, therefore, and, like dreams, the images of alchemy reveal the compensatory reaction of the unconscious toward the dominant attitude of Christian consciousness. Alchemy developed images, for example, that indicated the reaction of the unconscious, the "chthonic feminine," to the historical (pre-Christian) cultural shift toward masculine domination. With the constellation of the father-son dominant first in classical and then in Christian culture, there was a simultaneous repression of the mother-daughter pattern of earlier matriarchal consciousness. In alchemy the unconscious revealed a reaction to this change in the form of a compensatory image, that of the mother-son, the *prima materia* (mother) and the *filius macrocosmi* (son). The drama of this alchemical relationship compensated the father-son drama of Christian theology. Alchemy produced the image of another "son," not Satan, "not the antithesis of Christ but rather his chthonic counterpart, not a divine man but a fabulous being conforming to the nature of the primordial mother. And just as the redemption of man the microcosm is the task of the 'upper' son, so the 'lower' son has the function of a *salvator macrocosmi*" (1968a, p. 24).

These two sons were never joined in a single myth or symbol, but their dual constellation, the one from the father's world reaching downward in the incarnation, the other from the mother's world reaching upward in the symbolism and work of alchemy, represent an attempt to bridge the gulf that had deepened during earlier millennia (1968a, p. 24). On the principle that the unconscious reflects the face turned toward it, the unconscious produced—because of the non-hostile attitude of the alchemists—an image that was not intransigently hostile to the upper son of God. The *filius philosophorum* of alchemy is clearly the son of the rejected primordial mother, but his benign attitude toward the Christian son represents

a sign that the chthonic underworld, having been rejected by the spirit and identified with evil, has the tendency to compromise. There is no mistaking the fact that he is a concession to the spiritual and masculine principle, even though he carries in himself the weight of the earth and the whole fabulous nature of primordial animality. (Ibid., p. 25)

The answer from the mother-world, heard and communicated through the images of alchemy, "shows that the gulf between it and the father-world is not unbridgeable" (1968a, p. 25). Unity is possible, and this can come about through joining the Christian Trinity with the divine unity discovered by alchemy, which also sometimes has a Trinitarian structure but more often is quaternitarian. (The wavering between Trinity and quaternity "amounts to a wavering between the spiritual and the physical" [ibid., p. 27]).

At this point, Jung somewhat surprisingly turns away from this historical line of thought and returns to the theme of therapy. Individuals who come into therapy are usually torn by rifts and conflicts in the self that call for resolution, but Christian tradition, and indeed modern psychotherapists as well, have little direct help to offer. Resolution of these problems must come from the self. Help arrives in the form of a symbol of the patient's own indestructible center. The therapist observes dream and fantasy images of circling around this center and of working toward a union of opposites. And by following this complex and often serpentine network of images, the journey toward individuation is begun, which will lead finally to conscious awareness of the indestructible center, the self. This therapeutic journey requires a person to recognize and accept his or her own individual being, the good as well as the bad aspects of it, for "one can miss not only one's happiness but also one's final guilt, without which a man will never reach his wholeness" (ibid., p. 30). On this route of self-discovery, good and evil intermingle and together weave a pattern, for "both belong to the chiaroscuro of life" (ibid., p. 31). So the conscious encounter with the shadow and the integration of it into self-awareness belong inherently to the individuation process.

The interjection at this point of these comments on psychotherapy is not accidental. Therapy is the model operative in Jung's mind for relating alchemy and his own work to the Christian tradition. Like working with a patient who has to face guilt and limitation and accept the shadow in order to approach conscious wholeness, Jung tells the Christian tradition that to develop further it must accept *its* unconsciousness, which is the rejected "fourth," and it must include this element in its doctrinal awareness and conscious functioning. In therapy, the doctor interprets dreams to facilitate the work of integrating the unconscious: In commenting on Christianity, Jung used alchemy because it spoke for the unconscious of Christianity: "Whereas in the Church the increasing differentiation of ritual and dogma alienated consciousness from its natural roots in the unconscious, alchemy and astrology were ceaselessly engaged in preserving the bridge to nature, i.e., to the unconscious psyche, from decay" (1968a, p. 34). As physician to the Christian tradition, then, Jung interprets the message of alchemy to the patient, Christianity, as he would interpret dreams to an analysand.

Although alchemists generally spoke of themselves as conventional Christians, their thought departed considerably from the Christian consensus and returned to the symbolic origins of dogma. By going back to the unconscious, where Christian dogma had originated many centuries earlier, they exposed themselves to the danger of psychic possession and inflation, but this "*descensus ad inferos*" (1968a, p. 36) also eventually led them to a formula for uniting the opposites in a way that Christianity had failed to do. The alchemical tradition expressed this union in the symbol of the *hieros gamos*, or "chymical wedding," where "the supreme opposites, male and female (as in the Chinese *yang* and *yin*), are melted into a unity purified of all opposition and therefore incorruptible" (ibid., p. 37). The alchemists were able to produce what the Christian consensus and its dogma had failed to achieve: a symbolic statement of psychological unity. This healing symbol was the gift of the unconscious to the Christian dominant.

The Therapeutic Purpose of Interpreting Christianity's Psychodynamics

Better than any other single statement of Jung's, the introductory essay to *Psychology and Alchemy* explains his fascination with alchemical symbolism and the meaning of his labor to bring its significance to light. It was true that he felt the images of alchemy confirmed his theory of the collective unconscious and the individuation process, but beyond that he considered the meaning of alchemy to lie in its compensatory relation to Christianity. It was at the time of his Holy Grail dream in India, after which he took up the vocation of searching out the panacea for the ailing Christian tradition, that he became most absorbed in studying Western alchemy. For Jung the study of alchemy was the study of Christianity's unconscious, and this would eventually redound to the therapeutic benefit of the patient.

In the papers on the Trinity and the Mass, Jung was interpreting commonly accepted doctrines and images of Christian tradition, the equivalent in analysis to interpreting a patient's conscious structures and the more easily accessible aspects of personal history. The study of alchemy and its relation to Christianity, on the other hand, is equivalent to interpreting a patient's unconscious, the compensatory dreams and fantasies. These are the elements of the person that have been repressed, or have been left out of the conscious attitudes and patterns of identity. With the interpretation of alchemy, Jung was entering a new phase of his therapeutic treatment of Christianity. In this phase, the therapist interprets the historical relation of the unconscious to conscious aspects of the personality. This results in a reconstruction of the history of repression and ego-defense, and also in an understanding of the dynamics of unconscious strivings toward individuation and the ego's resistance to them. This is a combination of the second and third phases of analysis—elucidation and education—as described in Jung's 1929 paper. In the phase of elucidation, the analyst pieces together the historical development of a conscious dominant attitude, including the history of repression of aspects of the self; during education, the analyst attempts to enlarge the patient's consciousness so as to facilitate the integration of unconscious aspects. This is directed toward making room in consciousness for the compensatory action of the unconscious to have therapeutic effect. Jung's arduous efforts to interpret the images and meaning of alchemy within the context of a discussion of Western spirituality and religion was, therefore, his attempt to open a bereft and strife-torn Christian consciousness to the healing influences of the unconscious.

AION: THE RECONSTRUCTION OF CHRISTIANITY'S DEVELOPMENTAL HISTORY AND CRITICAL INTERPRETATION OF ITS CENTRAL SYMBOLS

The papers on the Trinity and the Mass and the Introduction to *Psychology and Alchemy* fall into Jung's first three phases of a psychotherapeutic treatment. *Aion: Researches into the Phenomenology of the Self,* published in 1951, is a further detailing of Jung's therapeutic labors, and this too falls within the scope of these phases. In the Foreword, Jung writes that his readers have asked him to explain "the relations between the traditional Christ-figure and the natural symbols of wholeness" (1968b, p. x), so in this work he will take up this question, which had been broached but not fully treated in his earlier papers. More broadly, this work compares and contrasts Christian doctrine and symbolism with other expressions of human wholeness. As a therapist ("I write as a physician," he confesses [ibid.]), Jung was concerned with the health of modern people "who in the confusion and uprootedness of our society were likely to lose all contact with the meaning of European culture" (ibid.). Additionally, he was concerned with the health of Western culture itself and with the declining effects of its central religious expression of wholeness, the Christ-symbol.

In *Aion*, Jung demonstrates in detail many of the points he strongly suggested in the earlier papers and essays. The central argument is as follows. The Christ-symbol, which lies at the center of Christianity, came into being because an archetype of the collective unconscious was constellated in the times of Jesus of Nazareth. The stories and images that gathered around the historical Jesus eventually created a symbol that compensated the collective consciousness of the times. This Christ-symbol represented the self, but only partially, because the self was split into good and evil components. The resulting religion and its doctrine created a tradition, and ultimately a culture, in which the splits and unreconciled oppositions of the originating images were lived out by multitudes of men and women. From independent scientific studies of comparative symbolism and from unconscious images and symbolic statements of contemporary (and historical) persons, a picture of the self's structure emerges that shows the shortcoming of the Christ-symbol. The self is best represented by symbols that unite the opposites, while the Christ-symbol represents only one side, the other being shown by his enemy, the Antichrist or Satan.

This argument is familiar from the earlier papers, but *Aion* adds a great deal of historical and interpretive detail.

How *Aion* carried Jung's therapy of Christianity a step further needs still to be considered. Jung described a vivid hypnogogic image that appeared to him at the beginning of what we can call his "therapeutic confrontation with Christianity and Western culture" period (1938–60). The image occurred to him in 1939, while he was immersed in alchemical studies and also leading a seminar on Loyola's *Spiritual Exercises*:

> One night I awoke and saw, bathed in bright light at the foot of my bed, the figure of Christ on the Cross. It was not quite life-size, but extremely distinct; and I saw that his body was made of greenish gold. The vision was marvelously beautiful, and yet I was profoundly shaken by it. (1961a, p. 211)

Jung interpreted this vision as a symbol that combined the Christ of traditional Christianity and the *filius macrocosmi* of alchemy. Here the sons of heaven and earth were united. The unconscious had produced precisely what Jung said the tradition of Western Christianity lacked, a symbol marrying spirit and matter. For Jung this was a symbol "of Christ as a union of spiritually alive and physically dead matter" (ibid.). This symbol sutured the split between these elements in the Christian psyche.

The meaning of this image, which was constellated as a result of Jung's own "shamanic" suffering of his Christian heritage, is what he would present to modern Christianity as the cure for its illness and as the goal of its development toward wholeness.

Immediately following the discussion of this vision in his memoirs, Jung comments that in *Aion* he wanted

> to show the development, extending over the centuries, of the religious content which he [Christ] represented. It was also important to me to show how Christ could have been astrologically predicted, and how he was understood both in terms of the spirit of his age and in the course of two thousand years of Christian civilization. (1961a, p. 211)

Aion is Jung's most detailed reconstructive study of Christianity's origins and history, but it also puts forward his critique of Christianity and proposals for its transformation. In *Aion*, Jung held up against the Christ-symbol a counterproposal for a doctrine of wholeness that would be represented by a theological symbol uniting the opposites split assunder by Christian tradition. Needless to say, this symbol also represented the healing of Jung's own inner psychic splits.

A brief note on the history of the volume *Aion*. It was originally published with a study by M.-L. von Franz, *Die Passio Perpetuae*, which was supposed to describe the "psychological transition from antiquity to Christianity" (1961a, p. ix, n.l). *Aion* picked up the discussion at that point: "My investigation seeks . . . to throw light on the change of psychic situation within the 'Christian aeon'" (ibid.). *Aion* was conceived to be a psycholgical interpretation of Christian history within the context of the evolution of Western consciousness from pagan Greece to modern times.

The opening chapters (I-V) of *Aion*, which provide perhaps the clearest account anywhere in Jung's writings of his understanding of basic psychological concepts such as the ego (I), the shadow (II), the anima and animus (III), and the self (IV), were added after the more substantial portions of the volume had been written. To understand the argument, Jung felt, the reader needed a brief survey of his psychological theory and terminology (Hannah 1976, p. 300), and it is small wonder that he thought so, because this is probably his most difficult lengthy work. Hannah (ibid., p. 301) claims that it was also the least understood at the time of publication. Chapters II and III derive from a 1948 paper, "Schaten, Animus, Anima," published in the *Wiener Zeitschrift für Nervenheilkunde*, later translated into English and published by the New York Psychological Club in 1950. Chapters IV and V, "The Self" and "Christ, a Symbol of the Self," derive from the Eranos lecture of 1948, "Concerning the Self."

Aion is a blend, therefore, of psychological theory, history of religious symbolism, psychological interpretation of Christian tradition, and creative psycho-theologizing. For Jung, this was not an unusual potpourri, but one does feel that in *Aion* he occasionally indulged his penchant for esoteric amplification beyond the limits of coherent argumentation. Consequently the thread of his main thought is often lost in a welter of poorly related detail. Nevertheless, it is plain that what Jung intended to do in *Aion* was to develop further the themes raised in his earlier works on Christianity and to discuss and criticize more thoroughly the ways in which Christianity has dealt with the problem of opposites.

In chapter V, "Christ, A Symbol of the Self," Jung sets forth the main argument. A brief review of the Christian doctrines of Christology and redemption in the writings of St. Augustine and other Church Fathers, Jung writes, makes it obvious that "*Christ exemplifies the archetype of the self*" (1968b, p. 37, italics in original). The term self, he says, refers to the God-image within and symbolizes human wholeness. "There can be no doubt," he continues, "that the original Christian conception of the *imago Dei* embodied in Christ meant an all-embracing totality that even includes the animal side of man" (ibid., p. 41). Having said this, he returns to the oft-repeated caveat: "Nevertheless the Christ-symbol lacks wholeness in the modern psychological sense, since it does not include the dark side of things but specifically excludes it in the form of a Luciferian opponent" (ibid.). In the course of Christian theology's development, beginning with Origen, the "dark side of things" was deprived of substance and came to be regarded as mere *privatio boni*, an absence of good. This was the product of denial, which caused an aspect of human psychological reality to be repressed and lose its relationship to consciousness, to disappear from the world of substance into the realm of shades and shadows, into the unconscious.

By way of contrast, Gnostic myth and thought did not repress evil.

Unlike the conventional Christians, the Gnostics stayed close to empirical psychological life and experience, so their conceptions are closer to modern psychology's findings, where light and dark form an indissoluble unity and the self is "an archetypal quaternity bound together by inner antinomies" (ibid., p. 42). "In the Christian concept, on the other hand, the archetype is hopelessly split into two irreconcilable halves, leading ultimately to a metaphysical dualism—the final separation of the kingdom of heaven from the fiery world of the damned" (ibid.).

The conscious identification with one side of the self through the assimilation of the Christ-symbol constellated a figure, the Antichrist, who represented the other side, and the early predictions of the Antichrist's coming followed "an inexorable psychological law whose existence, though unknown to the author or the Johannine Epistles, brought him a sure knowledge of the impending enantiodromia" (1968b, p. 43). So the "intensified differentiation of the Christ-image" brought about "a corresponding accentuation of its unconscious complement, thereby increasing the tension between above and below" (ibid.).

This early stage of Christian history (its infancy and early childhood, so to speak) laid the foundational pattern for the ensuing millennia. Spiritual striving for perfection culminated in the image of the medieval Gothic spire. This was reversed in the Renaissance when the opposite tendency, "the materialistic earth-bound passion to conquer matter and master the world" (1968b, p. 43), took hold of the European spirit, and striving for a heavenly goal was exchanged for earthly conquest. This change from "the vertical [attitude] of the Gothic style" to the "horizontal perspective (voyages of discovery, exploration of the world and of nature)" (ibid.) of the Renaissance represented a return of the repressed, an enantiodromia, which led to the Enlightenment and finally to a "situation today which can only be called 'antichristian' in a sense that confirms the early Christian anticipation of the 'end of time'" (ibid.). The opposites revealed symbolically at the beginning of Christian history (in the Christ-Antichrist polarity) have been lived out in the subsequent 2,000 years of European cultural history, and this has taken place according to the psychological law of opposites: First one opposite gains the upper hand, then the other.

Another way Jung interpreted Christian history in *Aion* centered on the dynamics of repression. In the course of its doctrinal development, Christianity repressed evil from its self-awareness. Theologically it denied evil the status of ontological reality, in the doctrine of God as *Summum Bonum* and in the understanding of evil as *privatio boni*.

Christ, too, came to be looked upon as having no shadow. All evil was personified by Satan, but then Satan's reality was denied in the doctrine of evil as *privatio boni*. Christianity could take no responsibility for evil in the world since it was identified with the good God. And this would encourage Christians, too, to split off their shadow impulses and project them into the "others," namely pagans, heathens, unbaptised children, etc.

Jung's vehement attack on the *privatio boni* doctrine is a complex, and perhaps philosophically muddled, argument. (It was the major stumbling block in his discussions with the theologically sophisticated Victor White.) In *Aion* he developed his repudiation of it by referring extensively to the works of Church Fathers and teachers such as Basil the Great, Dionysius the Areopagite, John Chrysostom, St. Augustine, and St. Thomas, showing how they twisted logic and common sense for the sake of a theology that would see God as only good, as the *Summum Bonum*. Jung would prefer a doctrine of God as *Unio Oppositorum*, because this would take evil into account a) without splitting or creating a theological dualism, b) without blaming humans for all evil, and c) without repressing evil or denying its power and reality. This would encourage shadow integration among the adherents of Christianity as well.

The argument for this position is psychological, and it is twofold. First, the categories good and evil are judgments of consciousness and are therefore relative and easily prey to distortion. What appears to be absolutely good or evil to one person may not appear so to another. Second, from a psychological viewpoint human wholeness appears inevitably to be a mixture of good and evil, with now one side predominating, now the other, but neither side ever exclusively in control. To say, therefore, that anyone or anything is absolutely good or absolutely evil is a distortion by conscious judgment, which will inevitably be accompanied by the opposite judgment being placed on someone or something else (equally a distortion). This is the essential dynamic of psychological splitting. Theological doctrines that divide good and evil so sharply, as some of Christianity's doctrines have done, encourage believers similarly to make black/white discriminations about aspects of themselves (instinct vs. spirit, for example) and about others ("us" vs. "them" in politics and society). This describes a psychologically unhealthy condition. So the *Summum Bonum* and the *privatio boni* doctrines of Christianity are symptoms of an illness whose origins lie at the beginning of the religion itself. It is a deep, early, and perhaps irremedial pathological condition that is built on, and encourages, fundamental flaws in the human personality.

Jung's psychological argument in *Aion* tends to get lost in a clutter of endless documentation and esoteric reference. It is cogent, however, and not hard to comprehend if seen as an interpretation of a patient's history and based on psychological theory and psychotherapeutic concern. To this point in *Aion* (Chapter V), Jung has further explicated his diagnosis of Christianity and has added detail to his earlier reconstructions of the patient's history. He has also elucidated the dynamic relationship between conscious and unconscious elements of the Christian personality, and he has identified a central psychodynamic issue, the repression of the shadow.

Jung concludes Chapter V by placing before the reader, and the patient, a vision of psychological wholeness that contrasts with Christianity's vision of perfection:

> The Christ-image is as good as perfect (at least it is meant to be so), while the archetype [of the self] (so far as known) denotes completeness but is far from being perfect. It is a paradox, a statement about something indescribable and transcendental. Accordingly the realization of the self . . . leads to a fundamental conflict, to a real suspension between opposites . . . and to an approximate state of wholeness that lacks perfection. To strive after teleiosis in the sense of perfection is not only legitimate but is inborn in man as a peculiarity which provides civilization with one of its strongest roots. This striving is so powerful, even, that it can turn into a passion that draws everything into its service. Natural as it is to seek perfection in one way or another, the archetype fulfils itself in completeness, and this is a [teleiosis] of quite another kind. Where the archetype predominates, completeness is *forced* upon us against all our conscious strivings, in accordance with the archaic nature of the archetype. The individual may strive after perfection . . . but must suffer from the opposite of his intentions for the sake of his completeness. (1968b, pp. 68–69)

What Jung is advocating, ultimately, is self-acceptance. Self-acceptance requires the recognition, without guilt and remorse, that one is not, and in principle cannot become, perfectly pure and single-minded.

Chapter 5 states the main features of the argument in *Aion*. The remainder of the book consists largely of further psychological interpretations of the origins and history of Christianity. Beginning with the birth of Christianity under the sign of the fishes (Pisces), Jung interprets the psychological situation into which this new religion was born and the archetypal elements active in its history. Summing up the case before elaborating details, Jung gives us the full sweep of his vision:

> The course of our religious history as well as an essential part of our psychic development could have been predicted more or less accurately, both as regards time and content, from the precession of the equinoxes through the constellation of Pisces. The prediction . . . was actually made and coincides with the fact that the Church suffered a schism in the sixteenth century. After that an enantiodromian process set in which, in contrast to the "Gothic" striving *upwards* to the heights, could be described as a horizontal movement *outwards*, namely the voyages of discovery and the conquest of Nature. The vertical was cut across by the horizontal, and man's spiritual and moral development moved in a direction that grew more and more obviously antichristian, so that today we are confronted with a crisis of Western civilization whose outcome appears to be exceedingly dubious. (1968b, p. 95)

With this astrological reading of Christian tradition, Jung felt he had purchased an archetypal viewpoint that corresponded to his psychological interpretation of Christian history as governed by a dynamic of splitting, repression, and enantiodromia. Attaching this astrological amplification to the psychological argument provided an account of the archetypal background of Western religious history and cultural development, and this is the equivalent, in Jung's therapeutic, to an amplificatory interpretation of a patient's personal history. Concrete historical details are placed in a context of deeper structure, thereby showing their relation not only to the causal nexus out of which they arose but also their prospective meaning. Amplificatory interpretation as a therapeutic technique serves to save, or to restore, meaning and to ground individual experience in archetypal pattern.

In *Aion*, Jung was struggling to express a vision of Western cultural and religious history that is grounded in an archetypal individuation process. The archetypal pattern shows an inevitable pattern of evolution of consciousness from original undifferentiated wholeness (identified as the pre-Christian pagan era) to a higher level of consciousness when the opposites are set into tension and conflict (the Christian era) to differentiated, regained wholeness when the opposites are reconciled (the modern age and beyond). This third stage would be represented by images of quaternity.

Within the range of this wider historical framework, Christianity, which shows an internal development of its own, plays a role in the development of its larger cultural context and the collective consciousness of that culture. Moreover, just as an individual's inner development is conditioned by family history and culture, in addition to growing from an archetypal base, so Christian tradition and the evolution of its doctrine are conditioned by larger cultural forces and are not only expressions of an archetypal process of evolving consciousness. In *Aion* Jung places the details of Christianity's history within the perspective of the evolution of consciousness in Western culture, showing the reciprocal effects between culture and religion within an overarching developmental process that includes both Christianity and Western culture.

While Chapters VI through XI of *Aion* contain this interpretation of Christian history and Western culture, Chapter XII returns the focus to the present. From here on, Jung is looking toward future developments in Christianity that would maintain continuity with its past structures but would also represent a transformation and move Christianity ahead into the next phase of its development.

Jung opens this phase of his analysis with a diagnosis of the contemporary cultural and religious scene. He begins by observing that science and faith parted company in the eighteenth century, the one becoming an objective study of nature, the other increasingly a subjective confession of faith. On the one side, science excluded psyche, the subjective factor, which is however an implicit aspect of all human knowing; on the other side, Christian doctrine may be a "highly differentiated symbol that expresses the transcendent psychic—the God-image and its properties" (1968b, p. 174), but its meaning has been lost to modern man. So the Western contemporary person is left without a means for maintaining contact with the human soul and for experiencing the unconscious in symbolic form. Science rejects soul, and religion no longer expresses it effectively.

In this condition, people

> begin looking round for exotic ideas in the hope of finding a substitute, for example in India. This hope is delusory, for though the Indian symbols formulate the unconscious just as well as the Christian ones do, they each exemplify their own spiritual past. . . . Though we can learn a lot from Indian thought, it can never express the past that is stored up within us. The premise we start from is and remains Christianity . . . . (1968b, p. 175)

Adopting the ideas of Eastern religions offers no solution, in Jung's view, to the spiritual dilemmas of Western modernity. Patients must begin with their own specific past and expand on that. One cannot abandon a specific historical heritage without loss of soul.

The hermeneutical problem, however, is immense. "The bridge from dogma to the inner experience of the individual has broken down. ... Dogma no longer formulates anything, no longer expresses anything; it has become a tenet to be accepted in and for itself, with no basis in any experience that would demonstrate its truth" (1968b, p. 178). This breakdown of the bridge between doctrine and experience is characteristic of modernity, where scientific rationality and secular consciousness have become utterly alienated from the archetypal, symbolic layers of the unconscious. Christian symbols no longer evoke or express the archetypal images of the psyche in a way that modern persons can find credible. Since Christianity no longer supplies a home for the human psyche, modern persons have been cast adrift. And "when a living organism is cut off from its roots, it loses the connection with the foundations of its existence and must necessarily perish. When that happens, anamnesis of the origins is a matter of life and death" (1968b, p. 180). Here is the concern of the physician. Anamnesis in this case is therapy through hermeneutics—"re-establishing the connection between conscious and unconscious" (ibid.)—through the methods of historical reconstruction and amplification.

A hermeneutic of Christian doctrine that would be effective in modern times, however, must relate to the modern level of consciousness and must therefore include the scientific world-view. The healing of the split in the modern psyche requires a symbol that will bridge the abyss between ancient symbolic themes and current attitudes toward life, nature, and culture.

The "old myth needs to be clothed anew in every renewed age if it is not to lose its therapeutic effect" (1968b, p. 181). If the modern, Western, scientific attitude is to be reconnected to the unconscious without losing its achieved, conscious position, the means for doing this must fall "along the lines traced out by history, and the upshot will be a new assimilation of the traditional myth" (ibid.). Jung the physician would not support a new symbol that did not maintain continuity with the Western cultural and religious tradition. On the other hand, however, he would insist that it include the scientific world-view with its horizontal perspective and its concentration on nature rather than spirit. This amounts to saying that the Three of traditional Christianity must move through a transformation to Four, which includes the scientific horizontal attitude.

To suggest how this might be done and eventuate in a new religious symbol, Jung backs up and discusses the fish image in Christian iconography. In early Christian tradition, he points out, Christ was represented by the fish. This image arose spontaneously from the collective unconscious in response to the impact of the Christ figure, and "in this way Christ became an inner experience, the 'Christ within'" (1968b, p. 183). This kind of correspondence between an inner unconscious reaction, which produces an image (the fish), and an outer historical development in religious tradition is necessary if a religious figure or doctrine is to become effective as a symbol. The fish image helped the Jesus figure deepen into a genuine symbol, the Christ.

In modern times, Jung continues, there is "a new symbol in place of the fish: a psychological concept of human wholeness" (ibid.). For the modern person, the *concept* of the self, namely of human wholeness, functions as the fish image did. This concept is an image that has arisen within modern consciousness and, if joined to a historical development in religious tradition, could produce a symbol that would provide a way for human consciousness once again to experience psychic wholeness.

The remainder of *Aion* is devoted to a discussion of this new inner image, the self. As he did with the fish image, Jung begins his discussion by amplifying the idea of the self. The chapter in which he carries this out, "Gnostic Symbols of the Self," makes the point that images of the unconscious that depth psychologists consider to be images of the self were anticipated in Gnostic images and myths. To enrich the modern concept of the self, Jung cites images, stories, and ideas from Gnostic writers. Why Gnosticism? Because, first of all, it is within the historical stream of Western religious, cultural tradition; but also because, secondly, unlike developing Christian orthodoxy, it remained closely in contact with nature and with the unconscious. What the Gnostic materials show, in vivid imagery, is how

> in contradistinction to the ego, another goal or centre [comes into being] which is characterized by all manner of names and symbols: fish, serpent, centre of the sea-hawk, point, monad, cross, paradise, and so on. . . . The innumerable Gnostic designations for the Anthropos . . . make it quite obvious what is meant: the greater, more comprehensive Man, that indescribable whole consisting of the sum of conscious and unconscious processes. This objective whole, the antithesis of the subjective ego-psyche, is what I have called the self, and this corresponds exactly to the idea of the Anthropos. (1968b, p. 189)

In Christian Gnosticism, of course, the Anthropos was identified as Christ, who would then, too, have been an image for the inner "'complete' man, the self" (1968b, p. 200). By reaching back to Gnosticism and to the figure of the Gnostic Christ, Jung is establishing a link between tradition and modernity, between a self-figure in Western cultural history and the self-concept of modernity.

The purpose of trying to link the self concept of modern consciousness up with Western Christian tradition is essentially psychotherapeutic. The Christian aeon has undergone a radical reversal of values, such that the specific attainments fostered by the Christian attitude—"the growth of the human personality and . . . the development of consciousness"—"are now gravely threatened in our antichristian age, not only by the sociopolitical delusional systems, but above all by the rationalistic hybris which is tearing our consciousness from its transcendent roots and holding before it immanent goals" (1968b, p. 221). In the secularism of modernity, Christianity has completed the development that was latent in its beginning: an enantiodromia from accentuation of the spiritual to its reverse, an accentuation of the material; from devotion to the Lord of Heaven and His good son to worship of the lord of this world, His disobedient son. The danger is that the psychological achievements won during the earlier stages of the Christian aeon will be lost in this reversal, and destruction and collapse will be the only achievements of the modern age. To avoid this, Jung felt a new symbol was needed that could contain the opposites inherent in Christian tradition and reconcile them.

If the Christian aeon has completed itself in this massive historical play of opposites, is this also the end of Christianity? To some extent, Jung believed this to be the case. Christianity as it has been known in its traditional forms is rapidly coming to an end. But this demise does not mean that the modern person's religious instinct is dead or that the religious need for wholeness is diminished. A new form of religious thought and practice will appear, and it was Jung's clear opinion and personal objective that this would be a transformed version of Christianity, rather than an entirely new form of religion or an importation from another culture. In his writings on Christianity and Western culture, Jung fragmentarily spelled out his understanding of the general trends this transformed version of Christianity would follow as it evolved out of its earlier historical expression.

The new symbolic of a transformed Christianity would recognize the completion of the Three in the Four. Its major value would shift from spiritual perfection to human wholeness. Its theology and symbolism would be integrative of polarities rather than divisive. Its thought and practice would integrate the unconscious shadow elements of the earlier Christian tradition. The final chapter of *Aion*, "The Structure and Dynamics of the Self," one of Jung's most opaque pieces of writing, should be read as a preliminary sketch of his vision of a transformed Christian dominant. It is his equivalent of a theological doctrine of God, a quaternitarian doctrine in place of the traditional Christian Trinitarian one.

The first part of this chapter is simply descriptive. Many images can indicate the self's presence and its activation in dreams: geometrical forms like the square and the circle; four related objects or persons; numbers like four, eight, and twelve; wheels and circumambulatory movements; houses, cities, geographies; human figures like princes and priests who transcend "the ego personality of the dreamer"; paradoxical or antinomian images (1968b, pp. 224–26). These dream images, moreover, are correlated to the attitude of consciousness towards the unconscious, between which there exists an indeterminancy principle: observation of the one by the other influences, but does not determine, its manifestations. This principle makes observation of the unconscious highly ambiguous. To mitigate the ego's distortions, Jung looks to the myths, images, and stories of the Gnostics and alchemists, who, he felt, allowed the unconscious to express itself in more or less pure form, undistorted by judgments of consciousness.

In sections 2 to 6 of this chapter, Jung analyzes and describes various Gnostic schemas, which, he argues, represent the structure of the self. Gnosticism antedates Christianity somewhat, then moves parallel to its tradition, and eventually merges with alchemy. Between the images of Gnosticism and those of alchemy, it is possible to piece together a vision of the self which, though enormously complex, serves to overcome the defects of Christian doctrine: It does not exclude any aspect of the human psyche but rather includes the full range of its manifestion and all aspects of human wholeness, including the Christian shadow and the feminine. Jung presents the final result of this analysis in section 6, where he shows how four quaternities (see fig. 1) stacked one on top of the other complete the passage from the heights of spirit to the depths of nature, and how the extremes of "above" and "below" touch and merge into one another.

This stack of four quaternios also represents, in Jung's exposition, a historical process extending over the last two millennia, the Christian aeon. It begins with a state of high spiritual aspiration and descends to the materialistic attitude of modern science, "a deification of matter"

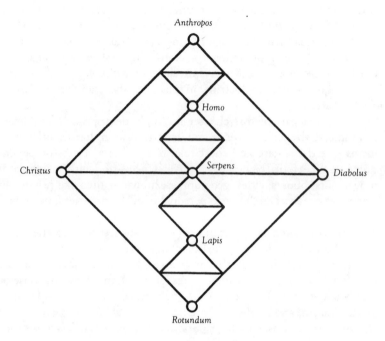

Figure 1*

(1968b, p. 257). This restatement of the earlier, and by now much repeated, view of the Christian aeon, namely that it represents an enantiodromic movement from one conscious attitude to its opposite, nevertheless also holds that this historical process resulted in greater human consciousness, even though in some respects it looks like a decline into darkness or a simple reversal of attitude. At bottom there is at work a process of transformation and integration (ibid., p. 259) that "consists in an unfolding of totality," and this equates to "becoming conscious" (ibid.). The "thing" that is undergoing this historical process of evolution toward greater conscious apprehension is the self, the "god

---

*Figure 1 is from *The Collected Works of C. G. Jung*, trans. R. F. C. Hull, Bollingen Series 20, Vol. 9, Part 2: AION: *Researches into the Phenomenology of the Self*, p. 247. Copyright © 1959, 1968 by Princeton University Press. Figure reprinted with permission of Princeton University Press.

image," whose "secret of existence . . . may well consist in a continually repeated process of rejuvenation" analogous to the

> carbon-nitrogen cycle in the sun, when a carbon nucleus captures four protons (two of which immediately become neutrons) and releases them at the end of the cycle in the form of an alpha particle. The carbon nucleus itself comes out of the reaction unchanged . . . . (Ibid., p. 260)

Jung justifies this analogy with physical science on the grounds that psychology and nuclear physics are converging in their views. Psyche and matter cannot be totally different, he argues, since both "exist in one and the same world, and each partakes of the other . . . " (1968b, p. 261). The psyche's structures and dynamics, as portrayed in the figures and patterns of myth and in the ideas and images of traditional cultures, also appear in the thought forms of modern science. Ultimately there must also be a correspondence between these psychic thought forms and the structures of nature as uncovered by experimental methods.

Aion closes on this note of imminent agreement between Jung's psychological findings regarding the psyche and the views of science, particularly of nuclear physics, regarding nature and matter. He briefly mentions his concept of synchronicity (1968b, p. 258), which, he argues, represents the "missing fourth" of modern science, the completion of its triad of dimensions of space, time, and causality. This notion will be developed more completely in his 1952 paper, "On Synchronicity."

The emergent synthesis of science and psychological awareness, when cast in a language whose symbolic focal point is the self, represents, in Jung's view, the way to resolve the impasse between Christian tradition and modernity and to move into the next stage of Christianity's development. This stage of the evolving Christian tradition would embrace the opposites that have torn Christian consciousness between light and dark, spiritual and physical, and masculine and feminine polarities (1968b, pp. 266–67). This vision of a transformed Christian tradition for the new aeon maintains continuity with Western cultural and religious history, in that the tradition contains prefigurations of it in its major doctrines and in its heretical offshoots. In a sense, Aion is an explication of prefigurations of the self in the testimony of the earlier Christian tradition (the new "old testament"), much as early Christian thinkers sought and found prefigurations of Christ in the Hebrew Bible.

I have been arguing that Aion forms a piece of Jung's psychotherapeutic design on Christianity. It represents his major two-fold therapeutic interpretation of Christian tradition. On the one hand, there is the reductive/reconstructionist movement, showing how Christian doctrine is rooted in dynamic relations to its wider cultural milieu and to cultural history; how it became a "dominant" of collective consciousness by repressing competing tendencies and creating a shadow (the heretical movements); and how Christian history and doctrine are rooted in psychological structures and dynamics. On the other hand, there is the synthetic/teleological interpretive movement, indicating how Christianity's central symbols and historical developments have played a meaningful role in the individuation of Western consciousness; how Christianity has laid the foundation for the next stage of religious and cultural development in the West; and how Christian tradition may itself be transformed and evolve new structures and patterns that will make it a viable religion in a new age of Western consciousness.

In brief, *Aion* is Jung's most complete, sustained psychological reconstruction and interpretation of Christian history. It concludes short of giving specific prescriptive advice for the future, but it does indicate general trends for future development. Clearly this work falls squarely within Jung's over-all therapeutic design for Christianity and for Western culture.

ANSWER TO JOB: JUNG'S INTERPRETATION OF CHRISTIANITY THROUGH THE COUNTERTRANSFERENCE

The publication of *Aion* (1951) was followed a year later by *Answer to Job*. In his Prefatory Note to this work (1969c, pp. 357–58), Jung tells the reader that it is an outgrowth of his critical comments in *Aion* on the doctrine of evil as *privatio boni*. Barbara Hannah (pp. 302ff) agrees that *Answer to Job* is fundamentally a statement about the problem of evil in Western Christendom.

That evil is a basic theme in this work is beyond dispute. *Answer to Job* clearly repeats Jung's often stated opposition to the doctrine of God as *Summum Bonum* and to Christianity's division between good and evil and its denial of the reality of evil. In the Book of Job, Jung found "a picture of God's tragic contradictoriness" (1969c, p. 216), with evil and good mixed together, which Job confronted and which Jung would also, in his own way, confront.

Answer to Job is, however, a good deal more than a treatise on evil. It is Jung's most intensely emotional and personal psychotherapeutic confrontation with biblical Christian tradition. Of all his published works, this one most clearly reveals his highly charged emotional relationship to Christianity, which I refer to as countertransference because it occurs within the context of his therapeutic designs on Christianity. While *Answer to Job* is both a recapitulation and an extension of Jung's earlier interpretation of biblical Christian tradition, it is, more significantly, passionate, engaged interpretation and intense dialogue, in which Jung plays the roles at once of the emotionally involved psychotherapist and of the angry son who brutally confronts the Father with His shortcomings. These are precisely the roles he played earlier (cf. Ch. 3, above) with his own father and with Sigmund Freud and psychoanalysis.

Answer to Job was written at a feverish pitch ("If there is anything like the spirit seizing one by the scruff of the neck, it was the way this book came into being" [Jung 1975, p. 20]). In it Jung leaves his usual reserved, scholarly manner to confront emotionally the foundational doctrine of God in the biblical tradition. This work is no less a psychological interpretation of Christian history than was *Aion*, but its tone is far more roiled with emotion and its parameters are more delineated by the biblical text than was the former work. It is a psycho*therapeutic*, rather than a psycho*logical*, interpretation of a biblical and post-biblical Christian drama, stretching over roughly three millennia. The author's personal motive is to transform what is being interpreted. So this work would fall into what Jung called the fourth phase of analysis, transformation.

At the outset, Jung confesses that he speaks neither as a theologian nor as a biblical scholar "but as a layman and physician" (1969c, p. 363). (This persona sets him apart from his father, who *was* a professional "custodian" [1961a, p. 217] of the ancient relics of tradition and a trained scholar of Near Eastern languages.) In his memoirs, Jung claims that the "problem of Job in all its ramifications had . . . been foreshadowed in a dream" (ibid., p. 217) about his father. The dream (ibid., pp. 217–19; cf. also Ch. 3, above, for a discussion of it) had Paul Jung making a brilliant interpretation of a passage from the Pentateuch; later father and son make their way to "the highest presence," where the father touches his head to the floor in honor and obeisance, but the son does not. This attitude of the rebellious son lends Jung the physician his particular emotional stance in *Answer to Job*.

Jung opens this inflammatory work with the usual apology: He is speaking here of religious images, symbols, and ideas, not of metaphysical or theological truths. In this regard, he has the right as a psychologist to give his professional opinion and interpretation of these materials, and he hopes that believers and theologians will not take offense. The image he wishes to focus on first is Yahweh,

> the picture of a God who knew no moderation in his emotions and suffered precisely from this lack of moderation. . . . Insight existed along with obtuseness, loving-kindness along with cruelty, creative power with destructiveness. Everything was there, and none of these qualities was an obstacle to the other. . . . A condition of this sort can only be described as *amoral*. (1969c, p. 365)

The Book of Job, which revolves around this image of God, unveils "the divine darkness" (ibid.), which still afflicts humanity in modern times.

Jung follows this diagnosis of Yahweh with a statement of his own attitude towards this figure, an attitude I have discussed as shamanic countertransference in Chapter 2:

> I shall not give a cool and carefully considered exegesis that tries to be fair to every detail, but a purely subjective reaction. In this way I hope to act as a voice for many who feel the same way as I do, and to give expression to the shattering emotion which the unvarnished spectacle of divine savagery and ruthlessness produces in us. . . . The Book of Job serves as a paradigm for a certain experience of God which has a special significance for us today. These experiences come upon man from inside as well as from outside, and it is useless to interpret them rationalistically and thus weaken them by apotropaic means. It is far better to admit the affect and submit to its violence than to try to escape it by all sorts of intellectual tricks or by emotional value-judgments. Although, *by giving in to the affect, one imitates all the bad qualities of the outrageous act that provoked it and thus makes oneself guilty of the same fault, that is precisely the point of the whole proceeding: the violence is meant to penetrate to a man's vitals, and he to succumb to its action. He must be affected by it, otherwise its full effect will not reach him. But he should know, or learn to know, what has affected him, for in this way he transforms the blindness of the violence on the one hand and of the affect on the other into knowledge.* For this reason I shall express my affect fearlessly and ruthlessly in what follows, and I shall answer injustice with injustice, that I may learn to know why and to what purpose Job was wounded, and what consequences have grown out of this for Yahweh as well as for man. (1969c, pp. 365–66; italics added)

This is the approach of the shamanic healer who allows himself to become infected with the illness of the patient. This type of healer takes the disease in, creates a medicine to cure it, and then returns the medicine to the patient by means of influence. In this instance, Jung was prepared to allow himself to be emotionally affected by the contradictoriness of the God-image at the heart of Biblical tradition, even to the point of imitating Yahweh's irrational behavior and rageful outbursts, for the purpose of transforming this inner violence into conscious knowledge. He would then communicate this acquired knowledge back to the tradition which houses and hallows this image of God, thereby offering it a higher level of consciousness. This is the transformational feedback loop of the transference/countertransference process as Jung described it in several of his writings.

Along with the God-image Yahweh, Jung takes into himself many other aspects of the biblical tradition. According to the therapeutic design, all of the patient's psychic material stimulates the therapist's unconscious so that what the therapist ends up experiencing and having to work with is an inseparable amalgam of his or her own unconscious contents and the psychic material of the patient. It is impossible ever to tell precisely where one process starts and the other leaves off. Reductively, one could interpret *Answer to Job* as Jung's attempt to come to terms with his own unmodified grandiose self ("Yahweh") under the guise of a hermeneutic of cultural and religious images. Or, this work can be, and indeed has been, read as a disguised attempt to deal with Freud. But these interpretations miss the point of the therapeutic design on the *patient*, Christianity. What Jung presents in *Answer to Job* is both an analysis of himself—of his father complex and his unresolved transferences to Paul Jung and Sigmund Freud—and a therapeutic analysis of the biblical Christian image of God through the countertransference. In the shamanic model of healing, both doctor and patient ultimately benefit from the healing process that transpires between them, and both are changed by it. This was Jung's wish.

After three introductory statements, Jung finally begins. Job is "a half-crushed human worm" (1969c, p. 367) who realizes it is the better part of valor to keep quiet before Yahweh's threats and not to mirror back to Him His brutality and injustice. Yet Job also believes in God's justice. And even though he is faced with this obvious contradiction, he does not doubt God's unity. This "is perhaps the greatest thing about Job" (ibid., p. 369), according to Jung: He can embrace the vision of God as "an *antinomy*—a totality of inner opposites" (ibid).

The Old Testament image of Yahweh, as Jung delineates it further, is heavily weighted with archaic and amoral features. The Bible emphasizes God's personality and his intense emotional relationships over any sort of steady commitment to principle. Yahweh is "jealous and irritable . . . prying mistrustfully into the faithless hearts of men and exploring their secret thoughts" (1969c, pp. 369–70). After making a covenant with his "chosen people," he breaks his own oath, according to Jung's reading of Psalm 89 (ibid., p. 370). Jung becomes exercised by this image of an all-powerful, angry, tyrannical Yahweh, and at one point he even imagines Him as a human being to whom he applies a dressing-down:

> For heaven's sake, man, pull yourself together and stop being such a senseless savage! It is really too grotesque to get into such a rage when it's partly your own fault that the plants won't flourish. You used to be quite reasonable and took good care of the garden you planted, instead of trampling it to pieces. (Ibid., p. 371)

Having presented this diagnostic picture of Yahweh, Jung turns to Job's ordeal. Here he develops the themes of Yahweh's unconsciousness and archaic brutality and the relative moral superiority of Job, representative of mankind. First Yahweh succumbs to Satan's trickery, and then He turns angrily on Job and overwhelms him with a display of brute force. To this Job submits, but he also sees Yahweh's contradictory nature and this vision of God's unreliable nature gives him the upper hand.

Jung next introduces Sophia, the *Sapientia Dei* (Wisdom of God), who is a coeternal with Him, a "hypostatized pneuma of feminine nature" (1969c, p. 386). This figure from Old Testament Wisdom Literature (Proverbs 8) is interpreted as a split-off and repressed aspect of the God-image of biblical tradition. She had been lost in the early Yahwistic period and returned to the manifest level of awareness only in the Wisdom period: God remembers "a feminine being who is no less agreeable to him than to man, a friend and playmate from the beginning of the world" (ibid., p. 391). The reason for this anamnesis is that "things simply could not go on as before, the 'just' God could not go on committing injustices, and the 'Omniscient' could not behave any longer like a clueless and thoughtless human being. Self-reflection becomes an imperative necessity, and for this Wisdom is needed" (ibid.).

To explain how Yahweh had arrived at this state of affairs, Jung turns to Genesis and proceeds now to offer a psychological interpretation of the whole biblical epic.

Job's discovery of Yahweh's dark unconsciousness occurs at a turning point in the history of the Bible's leading figure, God. God's story begins in pre-biblical times, when He and Sophia together created the world. By the time the biblical narrative begins, He is alone and is seen as creating the world and humanity in the patriarchal mode: first Adam, then Eve. No longer is there any sign of his feminine counterpart, Sophia. Satan, the wily serpent who disturbs the original paradisal harmony, may represent Adam's pre-biblical wife, Lilith. Like Yahweh who has two wives (Sophia and the "Chosen People"), Adam also has two (Lilith and Eve), and in both instances the awareness of the first wife is deleted from the biblical narrative. As Yahweh's chosen people, Israel is the wife who becomes subordinated to His will, and the more God forgets His original spouse, the more He becomes irritated with Israel's "faithlessness." Having lost His love of mankind with Sophia, Yahweh becomes increasingly interested in absolute control: He wants to *perfect* his wayward spouse rather than to love her.

In the Book of Job we witness Yahweh's obsession with faithfulness. Ironically, this leads Him into being faithless Himself. Through His consequent moral confrontation with a thoroughly faithful man who recognizes His faithlessness, Yahweh is forced into a transformation process. He recalls His own forgotten and repressed Wisdom, his "love of mankind," and Sophia's reappearance in the heavenly regions "betokens a new creation" (1969c, p. 397). This new act of creation will be God's incarnation in human flesh.

Jung's interpretation of the incarnation occupies the remaining 17 sections of *Answer to Job*. Let me summarize the argument. The birth of Christ represents the incarnation of the loving side of God and the splitting off of His destructive side, which remains unincarnated but is symbolically imaged in the figure of Satan (secs. 4–12). The Revelation to St. John vividly depicts the split between the conscious appropriation of the God of love in Christianity and its repressed image of a savage God of vengeance and destruction. John also predicts the enantiodromian development of the forthcoming Christian aeon and the preparation for the next stage of incarnation at the end of it (secs. 13–15). Standing at the end of the Christian aeon, the modern person discovers the very situation predicted by John. The religious task now is to prepare for the next development, which is the incarnation and integration of God's dark side. This will complete the biblical myth and the evolution of human consciousness that began millennia ago in pre-biblical times and was carried forward symbolically in the Old and New Testaments and in the Christian aeon (secs. 16–20).

In Jung's interpretation of this immense psychic development, there has been a gradual evolution in the Western psyche from a kind of archaic daimonianism to an integrated, ethical human consciousness. This has taken place through the dialectical process between God and man. This dialectic underlies the biblical tradition and accounts for the changing God-image within it, as well as for the development of ego-consciousness in Western culture. The key moments in this drama are: the creation myth, the confrontation between Job and Yahweh, God's incarnation in Christ, the subsequent Christian aeon as foreseen in The Revelation to St. John, and finally the psychological phenomenon of modernity and the contemporary task of incarnating the dark side of God. The first answer to Job, whose righteousness called God's right-eousness into question, was God's incarnation in Christ and His suffer-ing in the transformational process, as represented in the life, death, and resurrection of Jesus. The second answer to Job must be delivered by modernity, which will either succumb to destructiveness or manage to integrate this side of God into a structure of wholeness that includes the positive attainments of Christian tradition.

As Jung sees the Christian aeon, the second millennium has run in reverse to the first: It has been a descent from spirit to matter, with the result that science and technology have flowered as never before in human culture and history. Mythically speaking, "natural man" has learned "the divine arts and sciences from the fallen angels" (1969c, p. 460). This is "modern man." And this Luciferian creature of enlarged ego capacity and awesome power, who is precisely not the obedient son with whose words and image the aeon began, has been "chosen to become the vessel for the continuing incarnation" (ibid.).

Jung's message to Christian tradition in *Answer to Job* is that its transformation must result in a decisive inclusion of the "natural man" who values knowledge and experience above faith and belief. But Jung says this with affect, and, because he is reacting to Christianity from what I have called his shamanic countertransference, his thoughts and perceptions about Christianity are amalgamated with his own life and work. The resulting tone makes it understandable why some have come away with the impression that Jung wants Christianity to turn into analytical psychology or to emulate his own psychological processes. Is "be like me" the therapeutic message? Most therapists recognize the danger of imposing their own psychology on their patients, and in *Answer to Job* Jung runs this risk. To his credit, however, is his aware-ness that this is a very personal statement and one deeply implanted in his personal life and struggles.

Another argument, which is again both genuinely related to Christian tradition and to Jung's own psychology, arises from his interpretation of the new Catholic doctrine of the *Assumptio Mariae* as a "sign of the times," meaning that the anamnesis of Sophia has begun again in anticipation of the next stage of development in the biblical Christian tradition. When the feminine is recalled to the realm of diety, a *hieros gamos* (sacred marriage) is imminent, and soon we can expect the birth of a new religious symbol. The promulgation of this dogma by Pope Pius XII in 1950 followed centuries of preparation in the collective unconscious, as evidenced by multitudes of visions of the Virgin and by popular movements of adoration and veneration. This Papal Bull also coincided historically with the increasing pressure to include women more fully in the rites and the hierarchy of the Church as well as in Western culture generally. All of this is grounded in an archetypal dynamic that is represented by the image of a feminine figure approaching the innermost *sanctum sanctorum* of the Godhead, and this development will increasingly demand a transformation in Christian theological style and content. Jung encourages the Protestant churches to participate in this transformation, for it is preparing the way for the birth of a new, reconstituted religious attitude within biblical Christian tradition. As Jung reads the signs, the makings are coming together for a new phase in the biblical drama, and, like a therapist who recognizes a new development emerging in the patient, he is not very explicit about predicting what this new phase will look like.

Modernity is transitional for Christianity and for Western culture. As is true of all transitional periods, this one is full of doubt, chaos, and disorder. Its outcome, Jung asserts, "now depends on man: immense power of destruction is given into his hand, and the question is whether he can resist the will to use it, and can temper his will with the spirit of love and wisdom" (1969c, p. 459). For this spirit, he "needs the help of an 'advocate' in heaven" (ibid.), a representative of the loving and omniscient side of God. Unless modern persons can hold fast to the message of God's love and wisdom, which were communicated in God's first incarnation in Christ, they will be at great disadvantage in trying to resist the wish to destroy their civilization with the power now given into their hands by science and technology. Recognizing what Job saw, that God is *both* just and destructive, modern persons must learn that "God has a terrible double aspect: a sea of grace is met by a seething lake of fire. . . . That is the eternal, as distinct from the temporal, gospel" (ibid., p. 451). Like Job and John, the modern person can see the destructive side of God and realize that "God can be loved but must be feared" (ibid., p. 450). This attitude of caution will help mankind to face its immense potential for destructiveness and to place this beside its capacities for love and wisdom.

The mood of *Answer to Job* changes from being sharply critical and confrontative in the beginning to being hopeful and promising in the end. Images of union, the *hieros gamos*, and of new beginnings enter the interpretation. This indicates Jung's success at working through his psychic disturbance. In the end he arrives at a symbol of resolution, the *hieros gamos*, where the opposites unite. In *Answer to Job*, Jung works through his own conflicts, and as Christianity's therapist he offers it healing for its parallel conflicts.

ON SYNCHRONICITY: JUNG'S INTERPRETATION OF MODERN SCIENCE

"Synchronicity: An Acausal Connecting Principle" appeared in the same year as *Answer to Job*. Both were highly controversial. While the paper on synchronicity is not directly a piece of Jung's therapy of Christianity, it is a further elaboration of a possible religious attitude for the modern person that would not be entirely discontinuous from the biblical Christian tradition. What *Aion* and *Answer to Job* are to classical Western religious tradition, "Synchronicity" is to classical Western science: an appeal to include the "missing fourth."

In Western science, which is the product of the anti-Christian spirit of the second half of the Christian aeon, a myth of rationality has taken hold which has excluded perceptions of divine providence, of novel acts of creation in time, and of the significance of meaningful events that come grouped together and are causally unrelated. Jung's argument is that the rationalistic bias of science, while it has delivered powerful results, misses large portions of reality in its account of the cosmos. The principle of synchronicity—defined as the meaningful connection of causally unrelated events—must be included as a fourth dimension, along with space, time, and causality, to yield a full account of reality as science studies it. By including the principle of synchro-nicity as a fourth principle of science, modern man, whose intellectual commitment is to scientific rationality and empirical method, would have a way of including transcendence and divine activity within a world-view that also paid full recognition to the space-time-causality continuum.

Some of the philosophical and theological implications of Jung's concept of synchronicity have been worked out by M. L. von Franz in her books *Number and Time* and *Projection and Re-Collection in Jungian Psychology*. While this line of thinking may prove fruitful for Christian thought in a scientific age, or for scientific thought in a transformed Christian age, it is somewhat tangential to the main themes of the therapeutic Jung had been applying to Christianity over the prior 15 years. Nevertheless, it is an important piece of his therapeutic of Western scientific culture.

THE THERAPIST'S VISION OF CHRISTIANITY'S FUTURE WHOLENESS

With *Answer to Job*, Jung had all but completed the series of works on Christianity, which now stretched back to his Trinity paper of 1941. The fundamental theme throughout these works, played in many variations and at many levels of analysis, was that Christianity needs to go through a transformational process to integrate the "missing fourth" into its conscious attitude.

Jung summed up his vision of this union in his last great work, *Mysterium Coniunctionis* (1955), where he approached the question of healing Christianity's Amfortas wound through the conjunctive metaphors of alchemy.

He began working on this book in the mid-1940s. As recalled in the autobiography (1961a, p. 213), the impetus for it came from a dream (discussed in Ch. 3, above) in which his father was tending a zoological laboratory and his mother was managing a sleeping room for ghostly couples. According to his interpretation, this dream had to do with the "cure of Christian souls" and with his own unfinished business in carrying out this cultural and religious task: His father was tending Christian souls ("fish"), and his mother was hosting the *coniunctio*, two aspects of Jung's unconscious engaged in the task his ego-consciousness had not yet fulfilled.

Hannah (1976, p. 311) relates that *Mysterium Coniunctionis* was put aside while Jung was writing *Aion*, *Answer to Job*, and "On Synchronicity," and that the final chapter ("The Conjunction") was written only after this considerable interruption. The first five chapters were composed when Jung was at the very height of his therapeutic struggle with Christianity, while the book as a whole wraps around several other major works of this period.

Jung states in the Preface that *Mysterium Coniunctionis* is an attempt to summarize the essence of alchemy and its message for contemporary Western culture and Christian tradition. It is a wide-ranging commentary on many related subjects: the history of alchemical thought and Western science, contemporary culture, psychology and psychotherapy, unconscious processes in the collective unconscious, and traditional and contemporary Christianity. For our purposes, the commentary on Christianity is the central concern.

In general, what Jung says in *Mysterium Coniunctionis* about Christianity he has said before. The same critique of Christian tradition and doctrine and the same recommendations for change and transformation are put forward. In this work, however, the accent rests squarely on the integration of the "missing fourth" and on procedures for doing this. And while Jung is not explicit about what contemporary Christianity should do to effect the transformation, there are implications and suggestions that could be taken as programmatic.

One step toward therapeutic integration is to "take back" projections of unconscious shadow contents by recognizing that the "enemy" is oneself, that what one reacts to emotionally in an opponent represents an unclaimed piece of one's own psyche. Applied to contemporary Christianity, this means that a

> Christian of today . . . no longer ought to cling obstinately to a one-sided credo, but should face the fact that Christianity has been in a state of schism for four hundred years, with the result that every single Christian has a split in his psyche. Naturally the lesion cannot be treated or healed if everyone insists on his own standpoint. (1970c, p. 200)

Overcoming a chronic stalemate of this kind is possible only if individuals become "more conscious of what is unconscious to them and their age, above all of the inner opposite, namely those contents to which the prevailing views are in any way opposed" (ibid.). Christianity's record on reconciliation of opposites and on working through differences of attitude is not brilliant, however; in fact, it "seems as if Christianity had been from the outset the religion of chronic squabblers, and even now it does everything in its power never to let the squabbles rest. Remarkably enough it never stops preaching the gospel of neighborly love" (ibid.).

This step of psychological treatment, which calls for taking back shadow projections by identifying the "other" in oneself and by coming to terms with the opposite within rather than without, would obviously introduce a more ecumenical attitude within the splintered Christian tradition and more tolerance toward other religions. It would decrease isolation, reduce splitting, and improve communication. The abandonment of exclusivity and of claims to absolute knowledge also accompanies this integration of shadow.

As Jung describes this process in *Mysterium Coniunctionis*, it depends on a continual process of getting to know the counterposition in the unconscious: "The confrontation of conscious (rational) data with those that are unconscious (irrational) necessarily results in a modification of standpoint" (1970c, p. 200). In this integrative movement, then, there is a gradual process of expanding consciousness of the inner presence of the "missing fourth," as this has been represented by the despised and rejected, and has been projected upon opponents within the Christian tradition and upon its enemies without.

While therapeutic advice and interpretations of this sort are scattered throughout *Mysterium Coniunctionis*, the large point of the work is made most strongly in the last chapter, "The Conjunction," which, Barbara Hannah agrees, represents "the essence of the book" (1976, p. 311). Here Jung interprets developments in Christian doctrine that began in the earliest period and extend to the present and into the future, using alchemical symbolism of conjunction. The close interweaving in this discussion of alchemical symbolism and Christian doctrinal evolution has its rationale in Jung's psychotherapeutic aim. In this final work, he is offering Christianity a synthetic interpretation that shows how past developments of its consciousness and present symbolic expressions of the collective unconscious are directed toward a future goal of wholeness.

In brief, Jung's observation is that at the core of the entire alchemical tradition lay the symbol and the idea òf *coniunctio* (1970c, p. 457). What alchemy as a "science" meant by this was the uniting of various physical substances to produce a new, or "higher," substance. In its philosophy, however, these physical substances represented various spiritual or psychological qualities and contents. Jung's argument is that alchemical imagery and thought, because it reflected the rejected unconscious of Christian tradition, anticipated developments that would take centuries to appear at the level of Christian consciousness. The idea of conjunction, rather than of conflict between opposites, was the compensation from the unconscious for the dominant attitude of Christian consciousness. Not until the middle of the twentieth century, however, did this dynamic and its symbols finally reach conscious awareness as a problem and a vital concern within Christianity. This concern for integration moved to center stage with the dogmatic affirmation of the *Assumptio Mariae* in 1950 by Pope Pius XII.

Jung argues that alchemy had anticipated, indeed had prepared the ground for, this step toward a *coniunctio* between masculine and feminine in Christian doctrine. To explicate the meaning of this recent development in Christian symbolism, he turns to the work of the alchemist Gerard Dorn. Dorn described a succession of three conjunctions. The first separates "soul" from "body" and unites "soul" with "spirit." This operation Dorn called "*unio mentalis*." Jung says this stage of the work was achieved by Christian discipline and its denial of the flesh. The second conjunction reunites the product of "*unio mentalis*" with the "body." This stage indicates a movement toward integration of what has been abandoned and rejected earlier. This second stage is augured by the Papal Bull of 1950:

> The alchemists . . . pictured the *unio mentalis* as Father and Son and their union as the dove (the "spiration" common to both), but the world of the body they represented by the feminine or passive principle, namely Mary. Thus, for more than a thousand years, they prepared the ground for the dogma of the Assumption. It is true that the far-reaching implications of a marriage of the fatherly spiritual principle with the principle of matter, or material corporeality, are not to be seen from the dogma at first glance. Nevertheless, it does bridge over a gulf that seems unfathomable: the apparently irremediable separation of spirit from nature and the body. (1970c, p. 466)

In affirming doctrinally the symbol of Mary's bodily assumption into heaven, Christianity, Jung felt, was taking a step toward overcoming the split it had (necessarily) created in its earlier history between spirit and matter/body. Extended to the concerns and values of modernity, this doctrine would affirm the theological virtue of pursuing scientific knowledge of the material world. It would similarly lend theological dignity to active participation in politics, economics, and other worldly interests. On a personal level, it would overcome Christians' repression of sexuality and sensuality by elevating the value of bodily existence. This second union is not regressive to the *status quo ante bellum*, before Christianity had made its first separation from the body; rather, it is integrative, a shift of the repressed and denigrated aspects *up* into the consolidated ethical/spiritual position already achieved by Christian tradition. This is equivalent in psychotherapeutic treatment to the conscious integration of the shadow/anima aspects of the unconscious (1970c, p. 494).

Dorn's third conjunction joined the product of the second union to the *unus mundus*, the inherent unity of the world. Jung interprets this step to mean the union of an ego-consciousness that has integrated shadow and anima or animus aspects with the transcendent self. In this stage of development, "the whole of the conscious man is surrendered to the self, to the new centre of the personality which replaces the former ego" (1970c, p. 494). This stage can be realized, however, only after the self has been constellated in symbolic form. What the alchemists labored to extract from matter, the *imago Dei* or *anima mundi* that was "imprinted on the world" (ibid.), was precisely this symbolic expression of the self. All of the names for the treasure sought by the alchemists corresponded to the concept of psychic wholeness in modern psychology (ibid., p. 503).

In developmental terms, the first two conjunctions have to do with the consolidation and broadest possible integration of ego-consciousness. The first step, a separation and a conjunction, brings about a secured ego standpoint on which the integration of unconscious shadow and animus or anima aspects can take place in the second conjunction. This second step results in a stable and relatively inclusive state of ego-consciousness that is quite broadly representative of psychic wholeness. This is a difficult and remarkable achievement on the part of an individual, requiring much taxing and often repetitious effort to stabilize (1970c, p. 533). The third conjunction depends on this stability, for here this ego is subsumed to the self, "the ground and origin of the individual personality past, present, and future" (ibid., p. 534). This "ground and origin," in alchemy the *unus mundus*, is in modern psychological terms "the basic psychic structure common to all souls" (ibid., p. 535). So this third conjunction takes place between a unique, individual ego-consciousness and a universal substratum of the personality. In this conjunction, a connection is experienced in consciousness between time and eternity, between personal and universal elements of the psyche, between historical and trans-historical dimensions of existence (ibid.). Ultimately this amounts to "a synthesis of the conscious with the unconscious" (ibid., p. 539). Jung compares the experience of this third conjunction with "the ineffable mystery of the *unio mystica*, or *tao*, or the content of *samadhi*, or the experience of *satori* in Zen . . . " (ibid., p. 540).

Applying this developmental schema to the Christian tradition, Jung finds that Christianity achieved the first conjunction, *unio mentalis*. Christianity was successful in separating soul from body and in establishing a strong ego-standpoint against the instincts and the flesh: "Christ is . . . a dividing 'sword' which sunders the spiritual man from the physical" (1970c, p. 541). But this repression of the body also de-souled the physical world and consigned it to corruption and sin, to non-being. A psychological dissociation took effect, which, while necessary developmentally, now calls for healing. To this wound came a response from the alchemists, who searched for "the medicine that would heal all the sufferings of the body and the disunion of the soul" (ibid., p. 542) and would even promise immortality for the body (ibid.). To this end, the alchemists sought to prepare a quintessence of the material world ("body") that would be worthy of union with the Christian *unio mentalis*. What was left over of the body after this union would be "a dross that had to be abandoned to its fate" (ibid., p. 543).

While alchemy failed to enter modernity as a tradition of inquiry and thought, its concern with healing the body and its high evaluation of nature and the material world are reflected in modern science and medicine. The attitudes of the modern person are almost wholly governed by the concerns and assumptions of a materialistic, scientific *Weltanschauung*, which represents, as Jung pointed out in *Aion*, the end point of the Christian aeon: an enantiodromia from a spiritual to a materialistic orientation. Christianity, whose *unio mentalis* severed soul from body, has not yet achieved the second conjunction, the re-union of soul and spirit with body, perhaps because it has not formed an "essence" of physical nature worthy of union. As a consequence, an unresolvable conflict has raged between science and Christianity over the past several centuries. The parting of ways between Christian doctrine and modern science is a consequence of Christianity's much earlier denigration of nature and the physical body and of its later failure to complete the second conjunction by affirming the values on which modern science and medicine are based. This second conjunction would mean healing the split between science and Christian doctrine through a transformational integration of the opposites—spirit and matter—underlying this conflict. This is what alchemy attempted to represent in its conjunctive symbolism.

As Jung read the signs of the times, this second conjunction was in preparation within the collective unconscious, its symbolic prefiguration being the *Assumptio Mariae*. He considered the promulgation of this doctrine "to be the most important religious event since the Reformation" (1969c, p. 464), for it signified that there was a movement within the collective psyche of Christendom aimed toward a "second mixture." In this new doctrine, the masculine, spiritual Trinity would be joined by a feminine, physical figure. Father and mother would be reunited.

The modern affirmation by the Catholic magisterium of the belief in the bodily assumption of the Virgin also obliges Protestant theologians to reevaluate their theological methods and commitments. The modern emphasis on the doctrine of Mary's bodily assumption represents an emergent new *Zeitgeist,* and it is the essence of Protestantism, Jung points out, to react and to change according to the spirit of the age (1970c, p. 466). The Protestant theologian, therefore, "in accordance with his obligations to the *Zeitgeist* . . . should bend to the great task of reinterpreting all the Christian tradition" in the light of "the entry of the Mother of God into the heavenly bridal-chamber" (ibid., p. 467). Since this doctrine is so obviously symbolic, rather than literal, it requires that all of Christian doctrine be completely recast in an explicitly symbolic mode and affirmed as such. On this method hinges the revolution in Christian theology: It must be symbolical and psychological. Human nature, moreover, must be placed at the center of the theological enterprise. Theology must be grounded in human experience and in an empirical anthropology if the second conjunction is to be realized by Christianity.

CONCLUDING POSTSCRIPT

While the symbols emerging from the collective unconscious indicate that the times are ripening for a major transformation in the Christian dominant, this does not mean that it will necessarily come about through conscious awareness:

> The dogmatization of the *Assumptio Mariae* points to the *hieros gamos* in the pleroma, and this in turn implies . . . the future birth of the divine child, who, in accordance with the divine trend towards incarnation, will choose as his birthplace the empirical man. The metaphysical process is known to the psychology of the unconscious as the individuation process. In so far as this process, as a rule, runs its course unconsciously as it has from time immemorial, it means no more than that the acorn becomes an oak, a calf a cow, and the child an adult. But if the individuation process is made conscious, consciousness must confront the unconscious and a balance between the opposites must be found. As this is not possible through logic, one is dependent on *symbols* which make the irrational union of opposites possible. (1969c, pp. 467–68)

As indicated by the doctrine of the *Assumptio Mariae*, the second conjunction appears to be under way in Christianity. But it will not be completed until a child, who represents the fruit of a union of opposites, is born. This child, who first appeared in the Revelation to St. John and was hidden away in the womb of time, "belongs to another, future world. . . . Only in the last days will the vision of the sun-woman be fulfilled," when God is incarnated in a wholly creaturely (not in another semi-divine, virgin-born) human being (1969c, pp. 458). In this figure will be embodied the universal aspiration for human wholeness.

On this note of attentively looking to the unconscious and to the times for a new religious event that will heal the split within the Christian psyche, Jung concludes his therapy of the Christian tradition.

Chapter 5   **ON THE PATIENT'S PROSPECTS**

Jung regarded our times as the turbulent trough between two vast religious and cultural eras. Modernity, he felt, was a transitional space between two great epochs that stretched out over four millennia. And from his vantage point, he saw the religious and cultural scene of his time as both the receptacle of the wreckage of a passing aeon and the perceptibly swelling surface of a new.

The dominant religious tradition of the past era, which for nearly 20 centuries had been evolving through stages of growth and change side by side with developments in Western culture, had now flattened out at the nadir after a long period of decline. Christianity's influence on modern thought was negligible. Its symbols no longer commanded the imagination of gifted individuals or of the culture. Its doctrines failed to provide meaning for contemporary human experience. Much of its theology was unintelligible to a modern mind that was committed to empirical investigation and scientific knowledge rather than to faith and belief. Its rituals and images no longer effectively expressed the psyche or touched the heart. Its emphasis on spirituality had lost effect on a culture that was convinced by an exclusively materialistic and mechanistic account of existence and dedicated to hedonistic self-indulgence. Its capacity to fulfill the religious yearnings of modern men and women was enfeebled by the gulf between its devitalized symbols and secular attitudes.

Under these conditions, Christianity would soon become extinct as a living religious tradition unless a radical transformation occurred that would lead to a new stage of its existence. It is clear that Jung hoped a transformed Christianity would enter the new age, and his important late writings on Christian themes are a labor in the service of this future. I have called his effort in this regard "therapeutic" because Jung was above all a therapist, but also because these writings fall into line, both in detail and in overall strategy for change, with his psychotherapeutic methods and aims.

Jung's motives for engaging in this therapeutic of the Christian tradition were to some extent personal ones, as I have indicated, but they also included a deep and abiding concern on his part for the welfare of Christianity and Western culture. Beyond these, however, was his concern for the survival of human race itself. Without access to vital religious symbols that solidly support a religious attitude and a sense of ego-transcendent reality, humans run the risk, he felt, of terrifying pathological inflation-depression cycles. At times the ego, identifying with the self, becomes godlike and grandiose, and in this inflation it overrides all ethical and rational constraints. At other times, when the ego loses connection with the self, it falls into despair and becomes the victim of the nihilism engendered by the absence of a psychological center and a symbolic life. Either way, for modern technological society this pathology is particularly lethal because of the awesome power of modern tools and weapons. Mankind can now destroy itself either in an act of hubris under the illusion of invulnerability or in a suicidal act of nihilistic non-caring. Even worse, should the dark side of God incarnate itself in modern man, as Jung predicted it would, and find itself unmet by the full strength of a Christian (or Christian-like) spiritual standpoint, the annihilation of the race would be not only thinkable, it would be probable. The seeming inevitability of this outcome haunted Jung's last years. In the turbulence of the transition from one epoch to another, the entire human enterprise might shatter.

When Jung had his dream in 1938 of searching for the Holy Grail and thereupon committed himself to the healing of the foundering religious and cultural traditions of the West, he had no way of predicting the massiveness of his future outpouring of books, articles, and letters, nor the impact his words might have. Nor could he then have anticipated the development in Christian doctrine that he was to call "the most important religious event since the Reformation," the definition of the Assumptio Mariae as dogma by Pope Pius XII in 1950. But Jung's resolve was clearly at the ready in 1938 to bring all of his therapeutic know-how to bear on Christianity and Western culture, with the aim of helping to facilitate its transformation into its next stage of development.

As I have tried to demonstrate in these pages, Jung's writings on Christianity are organized around a complex therapeutic design for Christian tradition and Western culture. Coming to the end of this discussion, however, one is left with many questions. This is not un-common at the end of therapy, but it is even more so when the doctor dies before the treatment is completed.

In this final chapter I want to focus primarily on one set of related questions: To what extent can it be said that contemporary Christian thought and practice reflect the process of transformation envisioned and encouraged by Jung? And, to what extent is this not the case, and perhaps never will be, or in principle even ever can be, the case?

POSITIVE SIGNS OF HEALTH
ON THE CONTEMPORARY SCENE

Since the doctor died before the patient's transformation took place, his therapy could be regarded as laying the groundwork for that transformation. It was an attempt to prepare the patient emotionally and intellectually for a future stage of development. The effects of this therapy, and the future of the patient, will not of course be known for many years to come. Were Jung present today, though, he could tell us whether he thought the developments in Christian thought and prac-tice since his last view of the patient in 1961 have been in line with his understanding of its needed transformation. Is the patient progressing? relapsing? standing still? Knowing what we do about Jung's vision for a transformed Christian tradition, we can venture some estimates of what he would say about the patient's progress to date.

Were Jung to analyze the scene today, he would observe many changes in the Christian churches and in Christian theological and doctrinal style since he last viewed them closely in the 1950s. Pope John XXIII's *aggiornamento* ("updating") began the task of bringing the ancient Latin tradition into the modern world. Since the time of Vati-can II's groundbreaking revisions in tone, language, and style of theo-logical discourse and worship, many of the old stalemated conflicts among various Christian confessions, between tradition and modernity, and between religion and science have opened into dialogue.

In both Catholic and Protestant theological circles over the past several decades, there has been much greater interest in developing a new kind of relation between scientific and theological perspectives. To some extent at least, Jung's imperative that science be included within the *religious* world view of Western man has begun to be carried out.

Theologians like Tillich, Lonergan, Cobb, and Tracy have begun to influence the tradition to move toward a "one world" perspective, as opposed to maintaining the old view of a world divided between spirit and matter. This development conforms to Jung's therapeutic program of healing the splits within the Christian attitude.

Jung would possibly read other recent developments in Christian theology as therapeutically positive indicators, too. "Death of God" theology, while perhaps a flash in the theological pan from the historical viewpoint, nevertheless did signal the dissolution of the "old king" dominant in Christianity. This flash is like a dream, an ephemeral sign that an aeon is passing. I surmise that Jung would place this trend in Christian theological thought beside the dogma of the *Assumptio Mariae* as another symbolic indicator of deep structural change being prepared for in the collective psyche of Christendom. Both of these doctrines are harbingers of future changes. As the old God-image of Christianity dies and decays, a new one is incubating.

The recent appearance of narrative theology, with its appeal to the imagination and to the heart, Jung would have possibly interpreted in two ways. Insofar as it amounts only to retelling old stories and myths, it does not represent much hope for structural transformation. It may be more nostalgic than therapeutic, reflecting a resistance to change and an effort to hold on to past images and structures that no longer can actually integrate current experience. On the other hand, narrative theology exists in closer proximity to the unconscious than does more abstract, conceptual theological thinking, and therefore this trend in theological discourse may function to open the Christian imagination to a *new* story that is emerging from the depths of mystery. And certainly, too, because narrative theology's language is symbolic and psychological, Jung would see it as conforming to the contours of his therapeutic design.

Jung also would have looked favorably upon the recent expansion of Christian ethics into such complex and mundane areas as life-prolonging technical medical treatment, human sexuality and sexual preference, ecology, politics, and economics. This lowered gaze of ethical reflection into the realm of everyday concerns about physical existence represents, like the theology/science dialogue, a conjunction of the Christian *unio mentalis* with the repressed "body," the earth, the material world. In this new marriage of Christian ethical consciousness with the world, complex technical questions and scientific knowledge are making an impact on it, and it is influencing them.

Christian consciousness is here integrating the world that has been explored so thoroughly by scientists for the past two centuries, concerning itself closely now with aspects of human existence it had formerly split off and devalued as "too much of this world." In its reversal of direction from upward spiritual striving to attentive engagement with the concerns of mundane existence, Christianity is offering mankind hope that the "earth" can be redeemed. Perhaps the ego-inflation of modernity can be punctured and its Luciferian energies be harnessed to the human enterprise in such a way as not to threaten the frail fabric of human existence on earth. In these confrontations between the Christian *unio mentalis* and the Promethean powers that humans now have to wreak physical havoc—by altering the genetic codes and the course of human evolution or by destroying the race in nuclear holocaust—the Christian dominant, with its incarnation of God's bright side, is meeting the incarnation of God's dark side. The symbolic integrated outcome of this confrontation of opposites would be a a new image of God.

Another sign of increasing psychological maturity within Christianity is the intensification of ecumenical discussion among the churches. While the ecumenical exchanges that have been conducted among many Christian denominations have not thus far led to a host of resolutions of differences in belief and practice, they have reduced the level and intensity of malignant shadow projections. An ecumenical spirit among Christian churches may well signal diminished splitting within the Christian psyche, especially if, concurrently, there is significant "taking back" of shadow projections. This requires the willingness and the psychological strength to examine the enemy, the trickster, the heretic within one's own breast rather than in the beliefs and practices of others. This kind of critical self-examination will lead, in turn, to greater humility and more receptivity to the different views and theological convictions of others without considering those differences to be invidious or heretical. Additionally, the dialogue that has been started between Christian and non-Christian religions may not only open up new theological horizons and offer hope for establishing bases of understanding and mutual respect, but they may also prevent projections (of "heathenism" or "godlessness") from becoming fixated to these different belief systems.

One of the more vivid signs of transformation under way in Christian tradition is the increasing impact of women. The ordination of women in many denominations and the more effective integration of a feminine perspective and female images into Christian thought and practice at all levels are clearly in line with Jung's therapeutic of Christianity. This emergence of the feminine in Christianity augers a possible new integration of the anima, of Sophia, of the feminine aspect of what has been a predominantly masculine God image. Jung would not, of course, unequivocally applaud feminist theology and its excessively one-sided critique of Christian tradition, but he would see it as the most vocal and extreme part of a compensatory movement that has been under way in the collective unconscious of Christendom since the late Middle Ages: the emergence of the Goddess as the bearer of the seed for the next stage in the evolution of Christianity.

The issues of women's election to leadership roles in the churches and the inclusion of feminine symbolism and language in theological discourse about God have stirred vigorous opposition from the traditionalists in every faction of the Christian world. The feminization of Christianity represents a radical challenge to traditional theology, much as Jung's thought does: Both raise basic questions about the central doctrine of Christianity, the doctrine of God. Insofar as the feminization movement is a challenge to integrate the repressed, and therefore to press toward the evolution of Christianity into a new stage of consciousness, it does not threaten to unleash a revolutionary overthrow that would put women on top and transform God into the female gender. Such a swing would be without purpose or dialectical outcome and would merely prepare for another counter-reversal later in history.

Finally, I believe Jung's therapist's eye would look with approval on the subtle shift in Christianity's ethos away from its traditional emphasis on spiritual perfectionism toward greater awareness and appreciation of human wholeness. The recent developments just discussed have helped to create this change in climate. Not mentioned, but perhaps equally important, has been the pastoral counseling movement within the churches, with its high valuation of psychological maturity and wholeness, its psychological understanding of the doctrine of atonement, and its commitment to healing human brokenness. Doctrinally, a significant rearrangement has occurred in the nature-grace equation, moving away from the Augustinian-Calvinist vision of nature's fallenness, mankind's depravity, original sin, and God's sheer transcendence to a more balanced view of mixed good and evil within the natural and spiritual orders. In contemporary Christianity, one finds a less strident emphasis on man's depravity ("there is no health in us") and a greater recognition of the potential strength that may be within the scope of natural human development. Grace, concomitantly, is seen as less utterly transcendent and more closely woven into the natural order.

It could be argued, therefore, that the transformation of Christianity from a religion of spiritual perfectionism to a religion of psychological wholeness is under way, and that this promises to fulfill much of what Jung had worked and hoped for in his therapy of the Christian tradition.

MEASURING UP TO THE NEW AGE

Jung would have agreed, I think, that the patient shows signs of therapeutic change for the better, but the question now becomes, is this enough? Is this really transformation? Perhaps the Christian tradition *is* in the midst of structural metamorphosis, evolving into a new form of religious thought and practice that will be able to move ahead into the coming millennia with great vitality and conviction. Perhaps its new stage of existence will reflect the aspirations of mankind for wholeness and for the reconciliation of the warring opposites. But is this really the case? Even if we weight these developments in Christianity as heavily as I have, which is clearly not all of the story because I have not cited the many contraindications of transformation that could equally well be adduced, such as the extraordinary upsurge of conservative fundamentalism and the "moral majority" (which Jung would see as a defensive regression to cultural and religious repression), are they enough? Do these trends signify the imminent transformation of Christianity into a quaternitarian religion of psychological wholeness and the effective reconciliation of opposites, or do they represent merely some transient adjustments to modernity, a rather minor evolution of protective coloring rather than a transformation of deep structure? These questions cannot be answered definitively at this time, but I will venture some speculations about how Jung might have responded to them.

In response to questions of this sort, Jung would, I believe, grow cautious. Christian churches, seminaries, and other institutions continue to exist, even to thrive, in some areas of the world, and the Christian tradition continues to draw some talented and spirited people into its ranks. The conservative reaction has led some people back to the fundamental values and spiritual riches of Christian faith. Christian theology and ethics, moreover, are expanding into new areas of discussion that would seem to represent a second *coniunctio*: The Christian achievement of *unio mentalis* is uniting with the repressed body, the world. Even so, Christianity may still be falling critically short of a deep-going transformation process, which Jung regarded as the only long-range solution for this ailing tradition. And to my mind, it is highly dubious that traditional Christianity ever will, or could if it wanted to, voluntarily die and be reborn into the next phase of evolution as envisioned by Jung.

What Jung foresaw as a possible future for Christianity in Western culture was an expression of religious consciousness that would in many ways be continuous with Christian tradition, but also be very different from it. The model for this kind of relation between new and old is found in the Judeo-Christian tradition itself, in the relation between Christianity and Judaism. Jung's concept of Christianity's transformation is, I believe, of this magnitude: Christianity and its authoritative source book, the New Testament, would become for the transformed version of the tradition what Judaism and the Old Testament became for Christianity, a prefiguration and forerunner of the new revelation.

What this offspring of Christian tradition would look like Jung did not describe in detail. He was not that sort of visionary, and he felt the unconscious would, in its own time and manner, lead the way. The needed symbol would come together when the time was right. For the present, it was clear to Jung that an incubation process was under way in the collective unconscious. But it is also quite evident from Jung's writings that he had strong feelings about what some of the essential ingredients of this imminent new evolution of religious tradition would be. Most of these are major stumbling blocks between the Christian tradition and Jung's vision of a future transformed Christian tradition.

The Doctrine of God

First of all, and fundamental to everything else, is the doctrine of God. In the transformed Christian tradition as foreseen by Jung, this would be expressed in a symbol that represented God as a quaternity and a *unio oppositorum*. As the Yahweh of Judaism was transformed into the Trinity of traditional Christianity, so the Christian Trinity of Father, Son, and Holy Ghost would become a quaternity in the next stage of religious evolution.

The square, four-foldedness of all kinds, and all quadratic images represent two pairs of opposites held in tension. These quaternities represent a psychological state of conscious wholeness, in which the tension of opposites is maintained and contained rather than denied and collapsed into a false sense of peace and harmony through splitting, repression, and projection. The two pairs of opposites most frequently cited by Jung in relation to Christianity are the masculine-feminine and the good-evil polarities. These are the two pairs of opposites that a quaternitarian theology would hold in conscious tension in its God image: God would include both the masculine-feminine and the good-evil polarities, and all of the attributes contained in these four principles, as well as the cosmic implications of each, would be grounded in the central theological doctrine of God. The image of God as quaternity in conjunction with the concept of human wholeness would function in this transformed religious tradition as the master symbol.

The theological and ethical ramifications of changing Christianity's doctrine of God in this way would be transformational. Perhaps the most obvious and dramatic, if not ultimately the most significant, would be the changes in imagery and in metaphor. God could no longer be called "Father" without also being named "Mother" or conceived of as "Son" without also being understood as "Daughter." God would be implicated in all human relationships, feminine as well as masculine, and all human relationships could be developed into analogies for the inner life of God. God would be not only in "heaven" but also in "earth," in matter as well as in spirit, and persons would honor God in nature and in the body as well as in structures that point them toward the Heavenly City. The one-world theology that would flow from this doctrine of God would lead to a definition of God as inclusive of all aspects of reality, mundane and transcendent. God would become synonymous with reality and include all dimensions of what we crudely discriminate as good and evil, spiritual and physical, constructive and destructive, strong and weak, entropic and negentropic, active and passive. In this theology, God would be excluded from nothing, and nothing would be excluded from God.

This kind of radical transformation in its doctrine of God would be more than just difficult for Christianity to accommodate. It seems quite impossible. The change is so fundamental that 2,000 years of theological doctrine and ethical reflection would have to be completely rewritten or discarded. The biblical testimony to the complete revelation of God in Christ would have to be relativized or more or less relegated to an earlier phase of development in the tradition and no longer be considered definitive for the present. It seems beyond the realm of possibility that a whole religious tradition would undergo this kind of radical transformation in its fundamental structures of belief and practice.

Following the Jewish–early Christian model, however, it is clear that a transformation of this magnitude and depth takes place only for a small minority within a tradition, for a few persons who are gripped by the new vision. The transformation does not come about through the tradition's leadership's suddenly undergoing a conversion and leading the way. And indeed the old tradition does not itself transform: It gives birth to a new generation, and then the old and the newly developing traditions continue to exist side by side, much like a quarreling set of parents and children. Indeed, the emergence of a new tradition and its separation from the old may itself have a revitalizing effect on the parent tradition. What Jung foresaw as the future evolution of the Christian tradition could perhaps most accurately be thought of as the child of Christianity and the grandchild of Judaism. It would be a third generation of the great Judeo-Christian religious tradition.

There is some evidence that this is indeed how Jung foresaw the coming transformation of Christianity. Individuals who were scattered throughout the realms of Christendom and even beyond its doctrinal influence would be inwardly gripped by visions that, when shared, would eventuate in a new set of religious images for the human community. In a conversation with the Jungian analyst Dr. Max Zeller, as reported by Dr. Zeller, this is, indeed, the picture Jung painted. Zeller related a dream of his to Jung, which ran as follows:

> A temple of vast dimensions was in the process of being built. As far as I could see—ahead, behind, right and left—there were incredible numbers of people building on gigantic pillars. I, too, was building on a pillar. The whole building process was in its very beginnings, but the foundation was already there, the rest of the building was starting to go up, and I and many others were working on it. (Zeller 1975, p. 75)

In response to this dream, Jung is reported to have said:

> " . . . that is the temple we all build on. We don't know the people because, believe me, they build in India and China and in Russia and all over the world. That is the new religion. You know how long it will take until it is built?" I said, "How should I know? Do you know?" He said, "I know." I asked how long it would take. He said, "About six hundred years." "Where do you know this from?" I asked. He said, "From dreams. From other people's dreams and from my own. This new religion will come together as far as we can see." (Ibid.)

From this report, it is unclear whether Jung foresaw this new religion as a transformed version of Christianity or as a completely new world religion embracing, or supplanting, all other religions. But insofar as Jung was deeply concerned with Western religious traditions and with Western culture, and indeed regarded himself as a Parsifal to the ailing Christian dominant and a bringer of the Holy Grail back to Christendom, he would have hoped that the new religion would represent, as I have suggested, a therapeutic transformation of Christianity, partially Christianity's "child" and partially quite different from it, its own unique religious tradition.

Authority

The issue of religious and theological authority is a second great stumbling block in the way of Christianity's transformation along the lines suggested by Jung. Whether the locus of authority for creating theological doctrine and for regulating religious practice has been placed in tradition, in Scripture, or in the community of believers, it has invariably, since earliest times in Judaism and Christianity, lain outside the individual's experience of the divine. Individuals have not been allowed to create their own new doctrines or religious images without reference to the master doctrines and images of the tradition. Not that Judaism or Christianity has ever totally discredited personal religious experience as revelatory of God and His will, but they have always reserved to themselves the final judgment on the theological value of such experiences. The individual's visions of God have had to square with an external authority.

What Jung envisioned is a radical alteration in the locus of religious authority. His views on the relation of individual to external collective or traditional authority were similar to those of the far left wing of the Protestant Reformation. For Jung, the source of religious authority rested completely in the individual's experience of the divine, in the individual's fully experienced and integrated vision of the self. Without this relation to the unconscious, Jung felt, there could be no authentic religious life for modern men and women. In historical terms, Jung carried the Protestant emphasis on the individual's relation to God to its furthest possible extreme. Theologically, he regarded this radical reliance on a personal experience of the divine as the "age of the Holy Ghost," in which the spirit of God comes to function as the *spiritus rector* of everyday life for the conscious individual. Here a person's own experience of the divine becomes a continuous sense of God's presence, which relates to everything from the most mundane activity to the most numinous vision of the Godhead. This sustained individual conscious-ness of God's guiding spirit, which in his psychology Jung named the transcendent function, becomes the source of all religious authority. The unconscious provides the necessary symbols for maintaining a sense of life's meaning, and the transcendent function provides the ethical guidance of a self-tuned conscience.

Such experiences of the self and of the *spiritus rector* can, of course, be shared among individuals in a community, but there would be no canon within this community, beyond the individual's own experiences, to confirm or disconfirm their validity. So in the transformed version of Christianity as foreseen by Jung, dreams and visions from the uncon-scious would become scriptural and bear the authority traditionally invested in canon and bishop.

Shifting the locus of authority in this way to individuals would have revolutionary implications for theological method, for ethics, for church polity, for personal piety, and for religious practice. In this transformed offspring of Christian tradition, there would be no nor-mative text, no normative witness or revelation, no central figure or symbol or confession ("Jesus is Lord") to which a united community of believers would subscribe, and certainly no centralized ecclesiastical power. Perhaps a model for it on the ecclesiastical level would be the Quaker meeting, with each member searching the spirit with an "in-ward light," with no clerical leadership, and with minimal community constraints on the attitudes and behavior of the individual. What all members of this community would have in common would be a com-mitment to personal integration and psychological wholeness, to leading a religious life by maintaining a conscious dialectic with the uncon-scious, and to acknowledging the unconscious as the source of healing, transforming, and guiding symbols. Otherwise, leading this religious life would be an individual effort. Persons might occasionally share their reflections and experiences with others, but each one would experience his or her own religious symbols and create a personal theology.

Emblematic Lives

A third great obstacle to Christianity's deep transformation along the lines suggested by Jung is its historic commitment to certain em-blematic lives (Christ, the apostles, the saints) who embody its ideal of spiritual perfection. Jung's recommendation of psychological wholeness as the new master image for a transformed Christianity would lift up emblematic lives that embodied the principle of maximum integration, of those who were able to maintain consciousness of the opposites within themselves and to hold them in tension rather than splitting the opposites and identifying with only some aspects of the self. Jung did not point to any such emblematic historical figures in his writings, and, if questioned about hagiographable figures, he might well have rejoined that he was too busy trying to live a life of wholeness himself to be bothered with looking around for others who might be similarly engaged.

Since Jung's death and the posthumous publication of his autobiography in 1961, some of his more enthusiastic followers have written and spoken about *his* life as emblematic of the ideal of wholeness. The biographical studies written by such disciples as van der Post, Hannah, and von Franz ring with hagiographical overtones. While these efforts may be suspect to the disinterested historian, it is certainly not unfair to scrutinize Jung's life to see how he himself embodied his central doctrine of psychological wholeness, since he claimed that all psychologies were personal confessions of their creators anyway. He also appeared to be deeply opposed to the pretension of creating abstract psychological systems that contained no reference to their authors. Moreover, Jung did indeed live the second half of his life consciously oriented by the concept of psychological wholeness, which, he pointed out, functioned for modern man, in which category he included himself, as the new God image. So one is safe to conclude that he led the kind of religious life he was proposing for other modern persons and that a close analysis of his life should reveal a structure, or a style, that embodies, at least to some significant degree, the doctrine of psychological wholeness.

Without going into any detail about the emblematic features of Jung's life, the contrast to traditional Christian lives is immediately striking. On the surface, Jung lived a wholly secular life: He had no formal, or even very casual, connections to traditional Christian religiosity or institutions. He followed Swiss custom by getting married and buried in the Protestant church of his canton, but otherwise he took no part in institutional religious life. Nor did his life especially exemplify any of the great Christian virtues such as humility, long-suffering, patience, generosity, forbearance, or charity. He was not a saint. In fact, many accounts of his behavior and attitudes indicate shortness of temper, irascibility, bluntness to the point of brutality, impiety and skepticism, and intolerance of differing opinions. He was not a faithful husband nor a very conscientious father.

What almost all reports of him indicate as well, however, is that Jung was a man fully himself. His many positive attributes, among which were his notable intuitive wisdom and self-knowledge, his capacity for concentrating full attention on another person, and his remarkable ability to relate immediately to people in all walks of life, fade when compared with this overriding quality: Here was a man who could be himself completely, blemishes and all. He had come to terms with tremendous inner tensions, and as a result his immediate, spontaneous presence left an indelible impression.

That Jung did not point to other emblematic lives, or for that matter to his own as emblematic, should perhaps be ascribed to his therapeutic technique. In therapy, the patient is healed and made whole by integrating whatever emerges from the unconscious, and the resulting wholeness is thus tailored to that specific life. It is not governed by an external ideal of what, or how, the patient should be. Similarly, among the practitioners of a Christianity transformed, the images of wholeness would perhaps be shown forth less by emblematic historical persons who represent the ideal of wholeness for everyone than by inner symbolic figures who appear in dreams and fantasy and represent the state of wholeness that is specific to that individual. Among large numbers of persons such images of wholeness would undoubtedly have some features in common, but their variety would be much greater and more specifically tailored than are symbols of the self in traditional religions. In a sense, each person would be responsible for discovering his or her own sacred universe.

With regard to traditional images of sanctity (the "saints"), Jung's iconoclasm was as radical as any Protestant reformer's ever was. Unlike the classic reformers, however, Jung did not evoke the originative figures of tradition—Jesus and the apostles—as emblematic figures for his transformed Christianity. So, again, the model of religious life we derive from Jung's writings carries certain Protestant principles—complete freedom from the controlling influence of traditional images of holiness; a radical sense of the individual's personal relation and access to God; a doctrine of conscience as the final arbiter in ethical matters—to such a point of extremity, admitting such a great amount of diversity in symbol, interpretation and religious practice, that it is hard to conceive of the Christian tradition being able to allow for it. But, once more, Jung would have placed his trust for the future in individuals, hoping that enough of them would become gripped by a psychological individuation process and would choose to pursue this path of religious life.

If enough individuals grew disenchanted with the traditional churches and abandoned them, preferring to attend to religious life privately as a part of their own individuation processes, perhaps relying on the help of a spiritual director or counselor, it is conceivable that some traditional structures of Christianity would evolve, or produce some new forms, to accommodate this amount of individual diversity, while still containing this movement within the boundaries of the larger tradition and community. This movement could, in turn, form a vanguard and ally itself with the trends and developments in Christianity mentioned above, which are also moving along lines compatible with the Jungian therapeutic, and encourage the development within Christianity of a kind of Hinduistic spirit of ecumenical tolerance for every conceivable image of God and for every possible expression of the self. Within this vast diversity, individuals would still retain the sense that they were part of a larger communal and cultural identity whose tradition extended back through Western Judeo-Christian religion and was moving ahead toward states of more complete consciousness. There would be a meeting ground for Jews and Christians in this new, third phase of the Judeo-Christian tradition.

Beyond what would certainly be an initially florid diversity of images and theological ideation, there could ultimately emerge an overarching philosophy or metaphysic that would embrace these many individual expressions of diety. Jung's concepts of wholeness, synchronicity, and quaternity might come to function in this way, giving the diverse images and experiences of the self some common names and understandings. In addition, a few emblematic lives would be sure to appear, to illustrate and embody the ideal of psychological wholeness.

As he indicated to Dr. Zeller, Jung felt that the new development he foresaw would take 600 years to complete. This would occupy a little more than the first fourth of the new aeon, the next Platonic Year called the Age of Aquarius. By the year 2600 A.D., the new religion should have received a full and mature expression of its basic structures and attitudes. This is hard to imagine, standing as we do just at the beginning of such a possibly massive new development in our history. From his writings on Christian themes, it is clear that Jung hoped a transformed version of Christianity would be a part of this larger movement, both for its own sake and for the sake of modern men and women for whom historical continuity is such a fragile treasure. To this end, he sought to act as therapist for the transformation of Christianity. Whether his therapeutic efforts will assist Christianity to die and be reborn remains to be seen. But certainly Jung's writings on Christianity can help orient a tradition that is drifting relentlessly ahead into the uncharted waters of a new age.

BIBLIOGRAPHY

Alexander, I. 1982. The Freud-Jung relationship: The other side of Oedipus and countertransference. *American Psychologist* 37:1009-18.

Andreas-Salomé, L. 1964. *The Freud journal of Lou Andreas-Salomé.* New York: Basic Books.

Bakan, D. 1958. *Sigmund Freud and the Jewish mystical tradition.* Princeton: D. Van Nostrand.

Bennet, E. A. 1982. *Meetings with Jung.* London: Anchor Press.

Brome, V. 1978. *Jung: Man and myth.* New York: Atheneum.

Brown, C. A. 1981. *Jung's hermeneutic of doctrine.* Chico, Calif.: Scholars Press.

Buber, M. 1957. *Eclipse of God.* New York: Harper and Brothers, Harper Torchbook Edition.

Burrell, D. 1974. *Exercises in theological understanding.* Notre Dame and London: Notre Dame University Press.

Clift, W. B. 1982. *Jung and Christianity: The challenge of reconciliation.* New York: Crossroad.

Cox, D. 1959. *Jung and Saint Paul.* New York: Association Press.

Cuddihy, J. M. 1974. *The ordeal of civility.* New York: Basic Books.

Edinger, E. F. 1979. Depth psychology as the new dispensation. *Quadrant* 12/2:4-25.

Ellenberger, H. 1970. *The discovery of the unconscious.* New York: Basic Books.

Fordham, M. 1958. Analytical psychology and religious experience. The Guild of Pastoral Psychology: Guild Lecture No. 46.

Franz, M. L. von. 1974. *Number and time.* Evanston: Northwestern University Press.

_____. 1980. *Projection and re-collection in Jungian psychology*. La Salle, Ill., and London: Open Court.

Freud, S. 1939. *Moses and monotheism*. In *Standard edition*, 23:7–137. London: Hogarth Press, 1964.

Gedo, J. E. 1983. *Portraits of the artist*. New York, London: The Guilford Press.

Gelpi, D. L. 1978. *Experiencing God*. New York: Paulist Press.

Gray, L. H., ed. 1964. *The mythology of all races*, vol. VII. New York: Cooper Square Publishers, Inc.

Hanna, C. G. 1967. *The face of the deep: The religious ideas of C. G. Jung*. Philadelphia: Westminster Press.

Hannah, B. 1976. *Jung: His life and work*. New York: G. P. Putnam's Sons.

Heisig, J. 1973. Jung and theology: A bibliographical essay. *Spring* 1973:204–55.

_____. 1979. *Imago Dei: A study of Jung's psychology of religion*. Lewisburg: Bucknell University Press.

Henderson, J. 1982. Reflections on the history and practice of Jungian analysis. In *Jungian analysis*, ed. M. Stein, pp. 3–26. La Salle, Ill., and London: Open Court.

Homans, P. 1979. *Jung in context: Modernity and the making of a psychology*. Chicago: University of Chicago Press.

Hostie, R. 1957. *Religion and the psychology of Jung*. New York: Sheed and Ward.

Jaffé, A. 1971. Introduction. In *Memories, dreams, reflections*, pp. v–xiv. New York: Vintage Books.

James, W. 1902. *The varieties of religious experience*. New York: Modern Library.

Jung, C. G. 1897. Some thoughts on psychology. In *Collected works*, Supp. A: 21–47. Princeton: Princeton University Press, 1983.

_____. 1902. On the psychology and pathology of so-called occult phenomena. In *Collected works*, 1:3–88. Princeton: Princeton University Press, 1970.

_____. 1903. On manic mood disorder. In *Collected works*, 1:109–36. Princeton: Princeton University Press, 1970.

_____. 1904. On hysterical misreading. In *Collected works*, 1:89–92. Princeton: Princeton University Press, 1970.

_____. 1905a. Cryptomnesia. In *Collected works*, 1:95–106. Princeton: Princeton University Press, 1970.

_____. 1905b. An analysis of the associations of an epileptic. In *Collected works*, 2:197-220. Princeton: Princeton University Press, 1973.

———. 1906. Association, dream, and hysterical symptom. In *Collected works*, 2:353–407. Princeton: Princeton University Press, 1973.

———. 1907. *The psychology of dementia praecox*. In *Collected works*, 3:1–151. New York: Pantheon Books, 1960.

———. 1909. The significance of the father in the destiny of the individual. In *Collected works*, 4:301–23. New York: Pantheon Books, 1961.

———. 1912a. *Wandlungen und Symbole der Libido*. Leipzig and Vienna: Franz Deuticke.

———. 1912b. New paths in psychology. In *Collected works*, 7:245–68. New York: Pantheon Books, 1966.

———. 1913a. The theory of psychoanalysis. In *Collected works*, 4:83–226. Princeton: Princeton University Press, 1961.

———. 1913b. A contribution to the study of psychological types. In *Collected works*, 6:499–509. Princeton: Princeton University Press, 1974.

———. 1913c. General aspects of psychoanalysis. In *Collected works*, 4:229–42. New York: Pantheon Books, 1961.

———. 1916a. The structure of the unconscious. In *Collected works*, 7:269–304. New York: Pantheon Books. 1966.

———. 1916b. The transcendent function. In *Collected works*, 8:67–91. Princeton: Princeton University Press, 1969.

———. 1921. *Psychological types*. In *Collected works*, vol. 6. Princeton: Princeton University Press, 1971.

———. 1929. Problems of modern psychotherapy. In *Collected works*, 16:53–75. Princeton: Princeton University Press, 1966.

———. 1941. The psychology of the child archetype. In *Collected works*, 9/1:151–81. Princeton: Princeton University Press, 1969.

———. 1942a. A psychological approach to the dogma of the Trinity. In *Collected works*, 11:107–200. Princeton: Princeton University Press, 1969.

———. 1942b. Transformation symbolism in the mass. In *Collected works*, 11:201–96. Princeton: Princeton University Press, 1969.

———. 1944. Introduction to the religious and psychological problems of alchemy. In *Collected works*, 12:1–37. Princeton: Princeton University Press, 1968.

———. 1946. The psychology of the transference. In *Collected works*, 16:163–323. Princeton: Princeton University Press, 1966.

———. 1948. *Symbolik des Geistes*. Zurich: Rascher Verlag.

———. 1950. Foreword to the fourth Swiss edition. In *Collected works*, 5:xxiii–xxvi. Princeton: Princeton University Press, 1970.

——. 1951. *Aion: Researches into the phenomenology of the self.* In *Collected works,* vol. 9, part 2. Princeton: Princeton University Press, 1968.

——. 1952. *Answer to Job.* In *Collected works,* 11:355–470. Princeton: Princeton University Press, 1969.

——. 1955. *Mysterium coniunctionis.* In *Collected works,* vol. 14. Princeton: Princeton University Press, 1970.

——. 1960. *The psychogenesis of mental disease.* In *Collected works,* vol. 3. New York: Pantheon Books, 1960.

——. 1961a. *Memories, dreams, reflections.* New York: Random House.

——. 1961b. *Freud and psychoanalysis.* In *Collected works,* vol. 4. Princeton: Princeton University Press, 1961.

——. 1964. *Civilization in transition.* In *Collected works,* vol. 10. New York: Pantheon Books, 1964.

——. 1966a. *Two essays on analytical psychology.* In *Collected works,* vol. 7. New York: Pantheon Books, 1966.

——. 1966b. *The practice of psychotherapy.* In *Collected works,* vol. 16. Princeton: Princeton University Press, 1966.

——. 1967. *Alchemical studies.* In *Collected works,* vol. 13. Princeton: Princeton University Press, 1967.

——. 1968a. *Psychology and alchemy.* In *Collected works,* vol. 12. Princeton: Princeton University Press, 1968.

——. 1968b. *Aion: Researches into the phenomenology of the self.* In *Collected works,* vol. 9, part 2. Princeton: Princeton University Press, 1968.

——. 1969a. *The structure and dynamics of the psyche.* In *Collected works,* vol. 8. Princeton: Princeton University Press, 1969.

——. 1969b. *The archetypes and the collective unconscious.* In *Collected works,* vol. 9, part 1. Princeton: Princeton University Press, 1969.

——. 1969c. *Psychology and religion: West and East.* In *Collected works,* vol. 11. Princeton: Princeton University Press, 1969.

——. 1970a. *Psychiatric studies.* In *Collected works,* vol. 1. Princeton: Princeton University Press, 1970.

——. 1970b. *Psychology and alchemy.* In *Collected works,* vol. 12. Princeton: Princeton University Press, 1970.

——. 1970c. *Mysterium coniunctionis.* In *Collected works,* vol. 14. Princeton: Princeton University Press, 1970.

——. 1973. *Letters,* vol. 1. Princeton: Princeton University Press.

——. 1974. *Psychological types.* In *Collected works,* vol. 6. Princeton: Princeton University Press, 1974.

——. 1975. *Letters,* vol. 2. Princeton: Princeton University Press.

Kelsey, M. 1968. *Dreams: The dark speech of God*. Garden City: Double-day.

McGuire, W., ed. 1974. *The Freud-Jung letters*. Princeton: Princeton University Press.

_____, and Hull, R. F. C., eds. 1977. *C. G. Jung speaking*. Princeton: Princeton University Press.

Meier, C. A. 1977. *Jung's analytical psychology and religion*. Carbondale and Edwardsville: Southern Illinois University Press.

Moreno, A. 1970. *Jung, gods, and modern man*. Notre Dame and London: University of Notre Dame Press.

Oeri, A. 1970. Some youthful memories of C. G. Jung. *Spring* 1970:182–89.

Rieff, P. 1966. *The triumph of the therapeutic*. New York: Harper and Row.

Robert, M. 1976. *From Oedipus to Moses: Freud's Jewish identity*. New York: Doubleday Anchor.

Sandner, D. F., and Beebe, J. 1982. Psychopathology and analysis. In *Jungian analysis*, M. Stein, ed., pp. 294-334. La Salle, Ill., and London: Open Court.

Sanford, J. 1970. *The kingdom within: A study of the inner meaning of Jesus' sayings*. Philadelphia and New York: J. B. Lippincott Co.

_____. 1981. *Evil: The shadow side of reality*. New York: Crossroad.

Schaer, H. 1950. *Religion and the cure of souls in Jung's psychology*. New York: Pantheon Books.

Stern, P. 1976. *C. G. Jung–The haunted prophet*. New York: G. Braziller.

Tracy, D. 1975. *Blessed rage for order*. New York: Seabury Press.

White, V. 1942. The frontiers of theology and psychology. The Guild of Pastoral Psychology: Guild Lecture No. 19.

_____. 1952. *God and the unconscious*. Cleveland: World Publishing Co.

_____. 1955. Jung on Job. *Blackfriars* 36:52-60.

_____. 1959. Review of C. G. Jung's *Psychology and religion: West and east*. *Journal of Analytical Psychology* IV/1: 73-78.

_____. 1960. *Soul and psyche: An enquiry into the relationship of psychology and religion*. London: Collins.

Winnicott, D. W. 1964. Review of *Memories, dreams, reflections*. *International Journal of Psychoanalysis* 45:450-55.

Zeller, M. 1975. The task of the analyst. *Psychological Perspectives* 6/1:74-78.

Zumstein-Preiswerk, S. 1975. *C. G. Jung's medium*. Munich: Kindler Verlag.

INDEX